"AN ENDLESS NIGHT, THIS,
THE END OF LIFE
FROM THE DARK,
I FEEL YOUR LIPS
AND I TASTE YOUR BLOODY KISS"

BLOODY KISSES (A DEATH IN THE FAMILY)

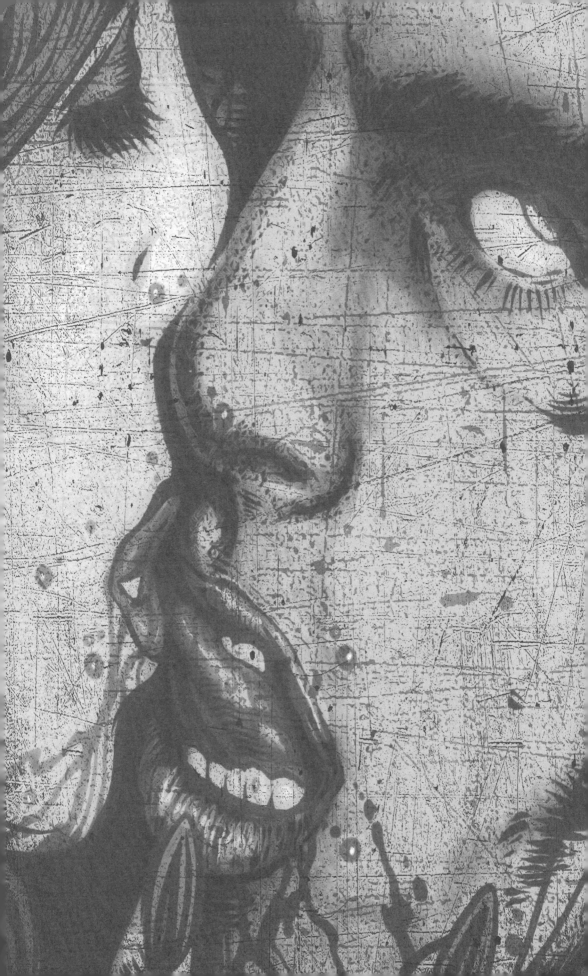

TYPE O NEGATIVE
BLOODY KISSES
30

Z2 IS PROUD TO CELEBRATE
THE 30TH ANNIVERSARY OF
BLOODY KISSES BY
TYPE O NEGATIVE,
ESPECIALLY THE MUSIC AND
ARTISTIC CONTRIBUTIONS OF
PETER STEELE, KENNY HICKEY,
JOSH SILVER & SAL ABRUSCATO.

PUBLISHER	SRIDHAR REDDY
CHIEF EXECUTIVE OFFICER	KEVIN MEEK
PRESIDENT	JOSH BERNSTEIN
EDITOR IN CHIEF	RANTZ A. HOSELEY
V.P., BUSINESS	ANTHONY LAULETTA
V.P, OPERATIONS	THOMAS DREUX
EDITOR	JASMINNE SARAVIA
MARKETING MANAGER	GERI IMBRIANI
MARKETING DESIGNER	DARREN VOGT
DESIGNER	GEOFF HARKINS

EDITOR JASMINNE SARAVIA
EDITOR IN CHIEF RANTZ A. HOSELEY
COVER & ART PRINTS ALAN ROBERT
DESIGN ROB SCHWAGER + JOSH BERNSTEIN
MANAGEMENT MARK ABRAMSON

ORIGINAL *BLOODY KISSES* DESIGN
AND INSPIRATION JOHN WADSWORTH

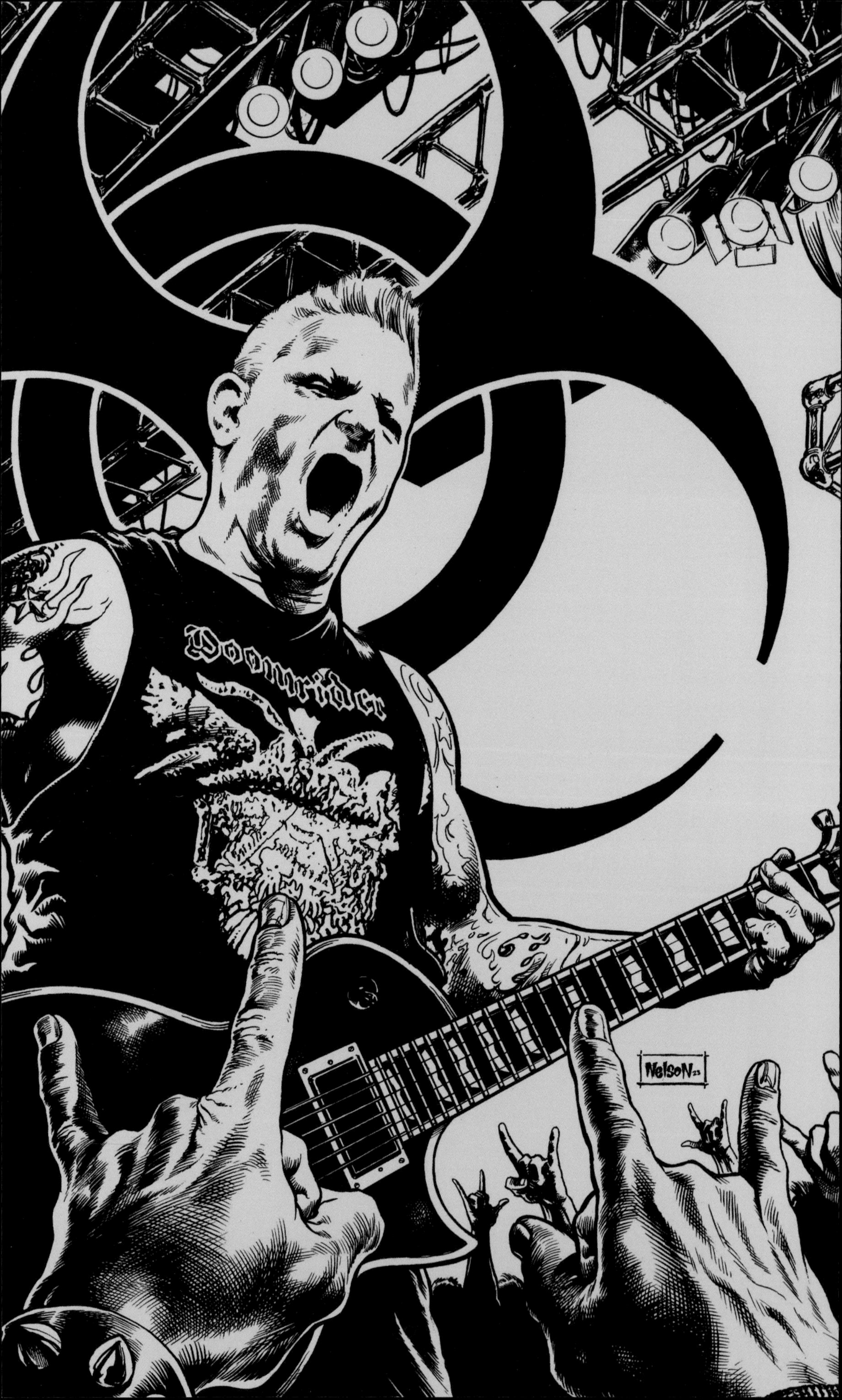
Doomrider
NELSON 23

BILLY BIOHAZARD

"...WE KNEW THAT THEY WERE ONTO SOMETHING NEW!"

MY BROTHERS IN BIOHAZARD AND I, LITERALLY AND FIGURATIVELY, looked up to Peter Steele while growing up in Brooklyn. He was that tall, dark and mysterious bass player in the back of Sam Ash off of Kings Highway. You know the one, the monstrous one dressed in an army jacket with long black hair, the one who always played Sabbath riffs on eleven! From his early days with Fallout and Carnivore, he left a strong impression that resonated throughout our early years coming up in Brooklyn!

One night after rehearsal for what was still an un-named "Biohazard" band, we were invited to come check out their Peter's new band. After finishing our jam session, we walked down the street to check out their new band. We all knew Kenny pretty well. Josh had recorded our first demos at his own Sty in the Sky Studios in the Midwood area. I remember Pete loaning Evan his bass to play on the demo because he didn't have one that worked! We all knew Sal from the neighborhood.

As we walked down the stairs into the studio basement, we got hit with this incredible low resonating feedback emanating from behind the walls! It was so loud and low that I felt the fillings in my teeth vibrating loose! We listened and watched in awe as they played us a song they were working on that seemed to at times be difficult to follow the tempo, it was slow, deep and hard as fuck!

At the time, the band was going by the name of Repulsion. After checking out a few long and depressing songs, we hung out outside in the street with the guys talking about their music and how unique and slow it was. I remember asking Pete how he thought people were going to react to it and how they could "hardcore dance" to it since the music was so slow and depressing. He chuckled and said "Maybe they'll invent something new to do, like kill themselves!"

Pete even suggested we call ourselves Biohazard while pointing to the logo in a medical supply book he had. He said, don't use the name, just use the symbol! He had something but it wasn't until Evan and I were sitting around a table in Canarsie smoking crack when we actually decided to go with his suggestion of calling ourselves Biohazard! Thanks Pete!

The combination of Josh's keyboards, Kenny's guitars and high vocals combined with Peter's ingenious writing, sarcastic humor and beautiful crafted musical harmonies, we knew that they were onto something new! The band brought something new and fresh to a table filled with mediocracy and derivative hardcore / metal!

"It was so loud and low that I felt the fillings in my teeth vibrating loose!"

We went to pretty much every show they played and watched them quickly evolve. There was one show we played at our local club called L'amour. The night was a completely chaotic and wild show with Carnivore, Biohazard and Sheer Terror. The show was aptly titled, Negative Night and eventually, Repulsion changed their name to Type O Negative and then everything started to make sense. Type O was always ahead of the curve, they were onto things that people had a tough time understanding at first. When you're bold, some think you're out of your mind but I think it's more insane to be timid!

Thank you,

Billy Graziadei

ART BY NELSON DeCASTRO

TYPE O CONTENTS

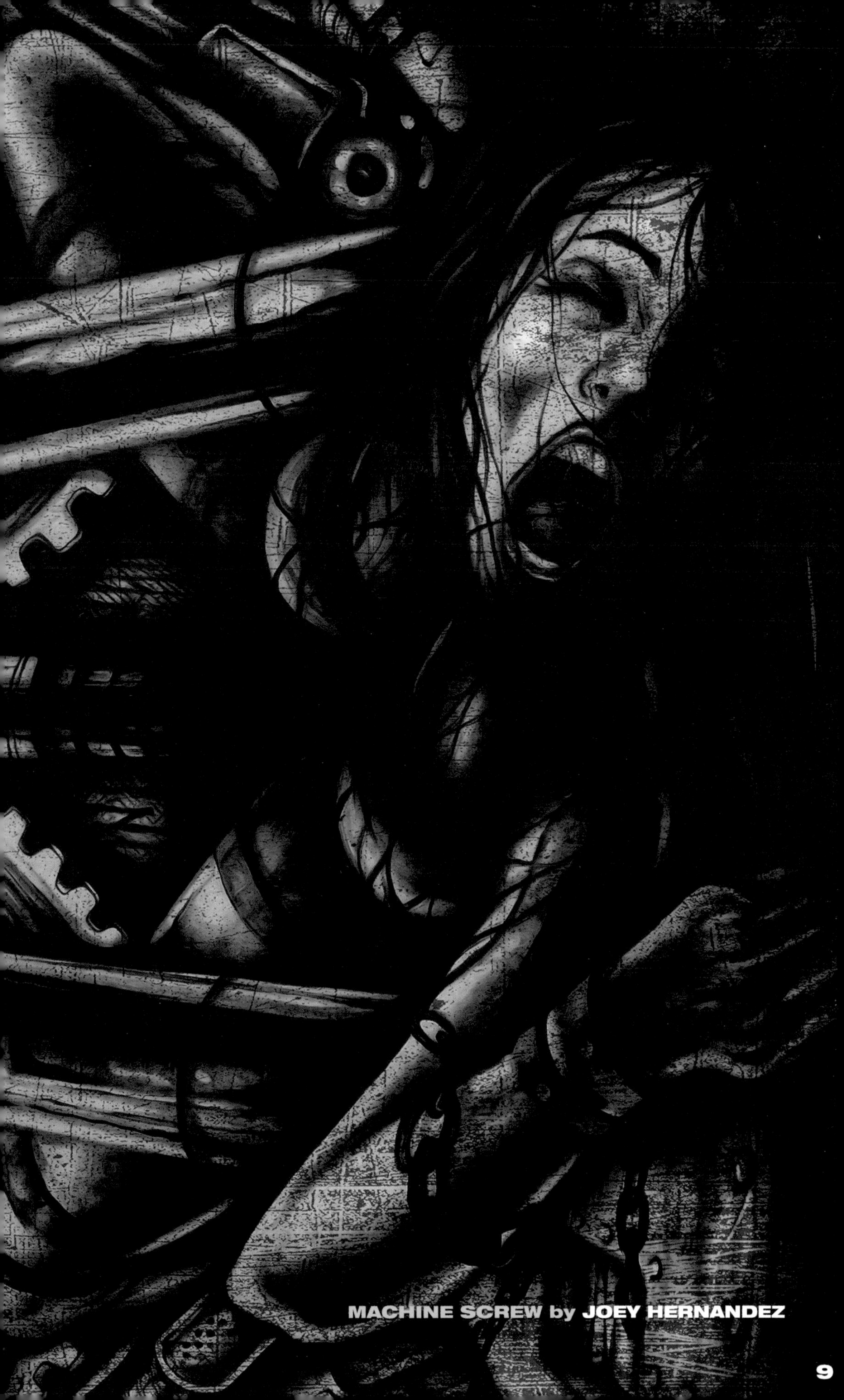

MACHINE SCREW by JOEY HERNANDEZ

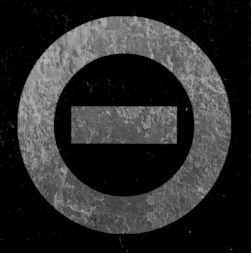

CHRISTIAN WOMAN

WRITER: CARLA HARVEY
ARTIST: THOMAS TENNEY
COLORIST: JUAN ALVAREZ
LETTERER: BUDDY BEAUDOIN

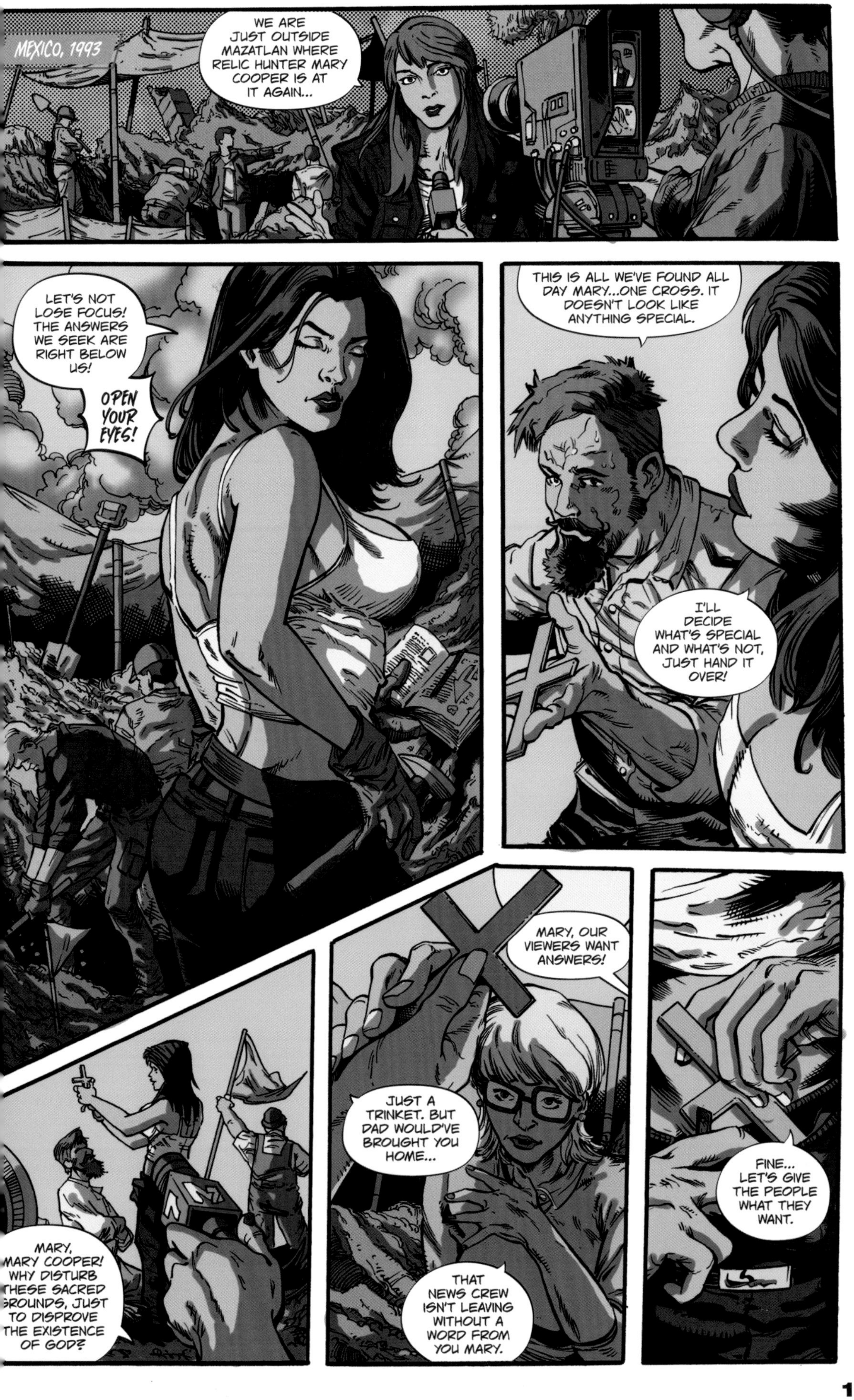
MEXICO, 1993
WE ARE JUST OUTSIDE MAZATLAN WHERE RELIC HUNTER MARY COOPER IS AT IT AGAIN...
LET'S NOT LOSE FOCUS! THE ANSWERS WE SEEK ARE RIGHT BELOW US!
OPEN YOUR EYES!
THIS IS ALL WE'VE FOUND ALL DAY MARY...ONE CROSS. IT DOESN'T LOOK LIKE ANYTHING SPECIAL.
I'LL DECIDE WHAT'S SPECIAL AND WHAT'S NOT, JUST HAND IT OVER!
MARY, MARY COOPER! WHY DISTURB THESE SACRED GROUNDS, JUST TO DISPROVE THE EXISTENCE OF GOD?
MARY, OUR VIEWERS WANT ANSWERS!
JUST A TRINKET. BUT DAD WOULD'VE BROUGHT YOU HOME...
THAT NEWS CREW ISN'T LEAVING WITHOUT A WORD FROM YOU MARY.
FINE... LET'S GIVE THE PEOPLE WHAT THEY WANT.

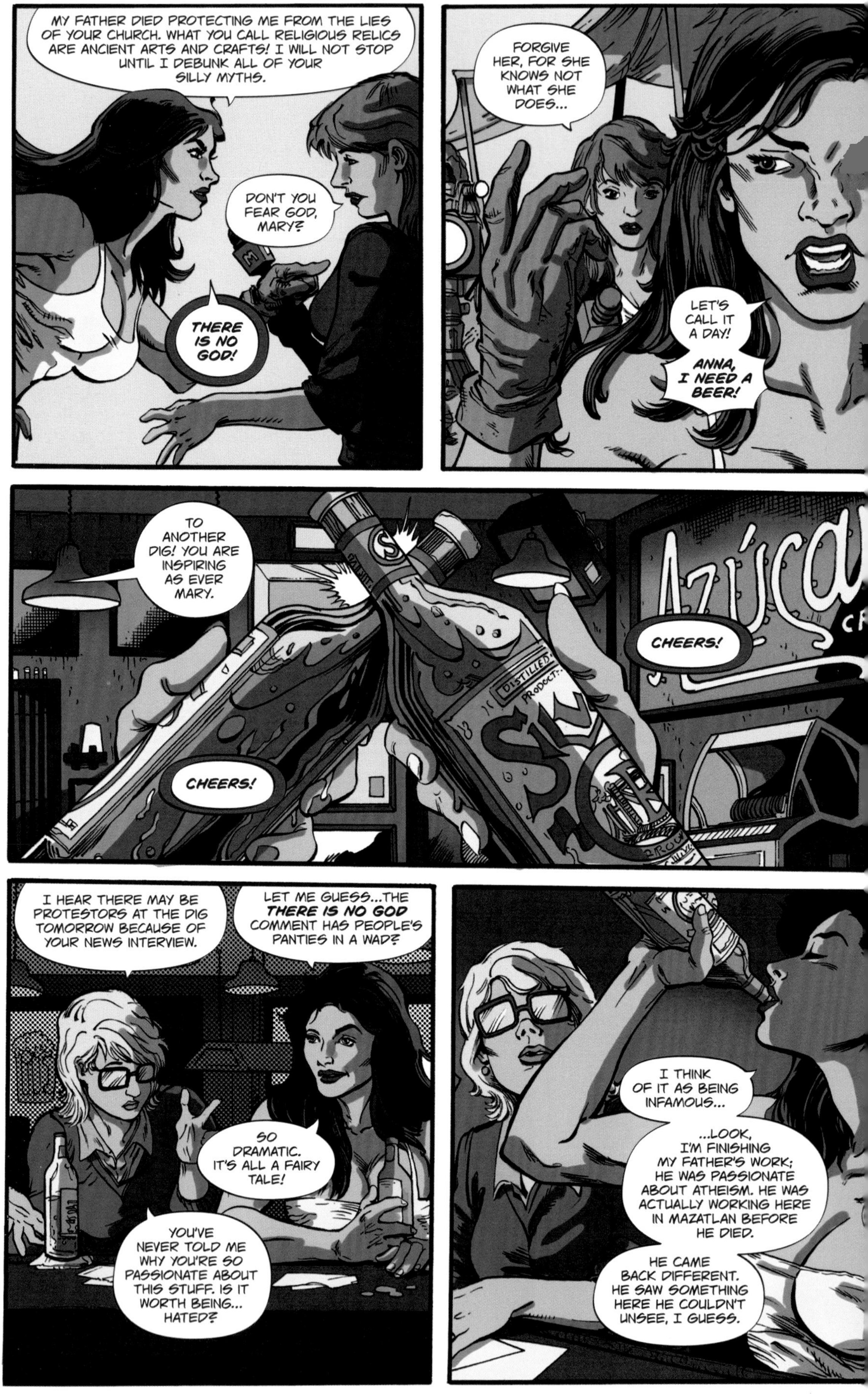

MY FATHER DIED PROTECTING ME FROM THE LIES OF YOUR CHURCH. WHAT YOU CALL RELIGIOUS RELICS ARE ANCIENT ARTS AND CRAFTS! I WILL NOT STOP UNTIL I DEBUNK ALL OF YOUR SILLY MYTHS.
DON'T YOU FEAR GOD, MARY?
THERE IS NO GOD!
FORGIVE HER, FOR SHE KNOWS NOT WHAT SHE DOES...
LET'S CALL IT A DAY!
ANNA, I NEED A BEER!
TO ANOTHER DIG! YOU ARE INSPIRING AS EVER MARY.
CHEERS!
CHEERS!
Azúca
I HEAR THERE MAY BE PROTESTORS AT THE DIG TOMORROW BECAUSE OF YOUR NEWS INTERVIEW.
LET ME GUESS...THE THERE IS NO GOD COMMENT HAS PEOPLE'S PANTIES IN A WAD?
SO DRAMATIC. IT'S ALL A FAIRY TALE!
YOU'VE NEVER TOLD ME WHY YOU'RE SO PASSIONATE ABOUT THIS STUFF. IS IT WORTH BEING... HATED?
I THINK OF IT AS BEING INFAMOUS...
...LOOK, I'M FINISHING MY FATHER'S WORK; HE WAS PASSIONATE ABOUT ATHEISM. HE WAS ACTUALLY WORKING HERE IN MAZATLAN BEFORE HE DIED.
HE CAME BACK DIFFERENT. HE SAW SOMETHING HERE HE COULDN'T UNSEE, I GUESS.

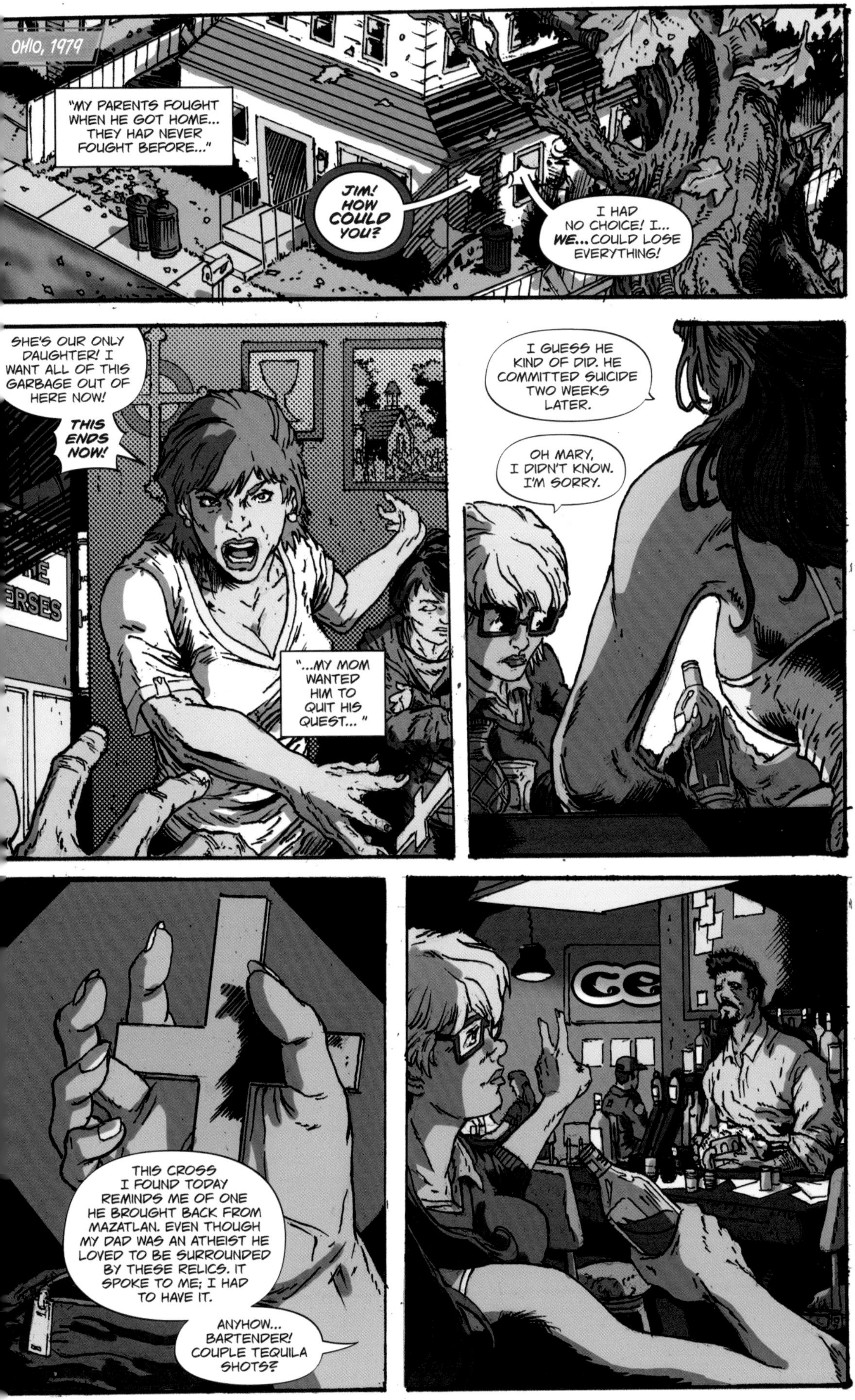
OHIO, 1979
"MY PARENTS FOUGHT WHEN HE GOT HOME... THEY HAD NEVER FOUGHT BEFORE..."
JIM! HOW COULD YOU?
I HAD NO CHOICE! I... WE...COULD LOSE EVERYTHING!
SHE'S OUR ONLY DAUGHTER! I WANT ALL OF THIS GARBAGE OUT OF HERE NOW!
THIS ENDS NOW!
"...MY MOM WANTED HIM TO QUIT HIS QUEST..."
I GUESS HE KIND OF DID. HE COMMITTED SUICIDE TWO WEEKS LATER.
OH MARY, I DIDN'T KNOW. I'M SORRY.
THIS CROSS I FOUND TODAY REMINDS ME OF ONE HE BROUGHT BACK FROM MAZATLAN. EVEN THOUGH MY DAD WAS AN ATHEIST HE LOVED TO BE SURROUNDED BY THESE RELICS. IT SPOKE TO ME; I HAD TO HAVE IT.
ANYHOW... BARTENDER! COUPLE TEQUILA SHOTS?

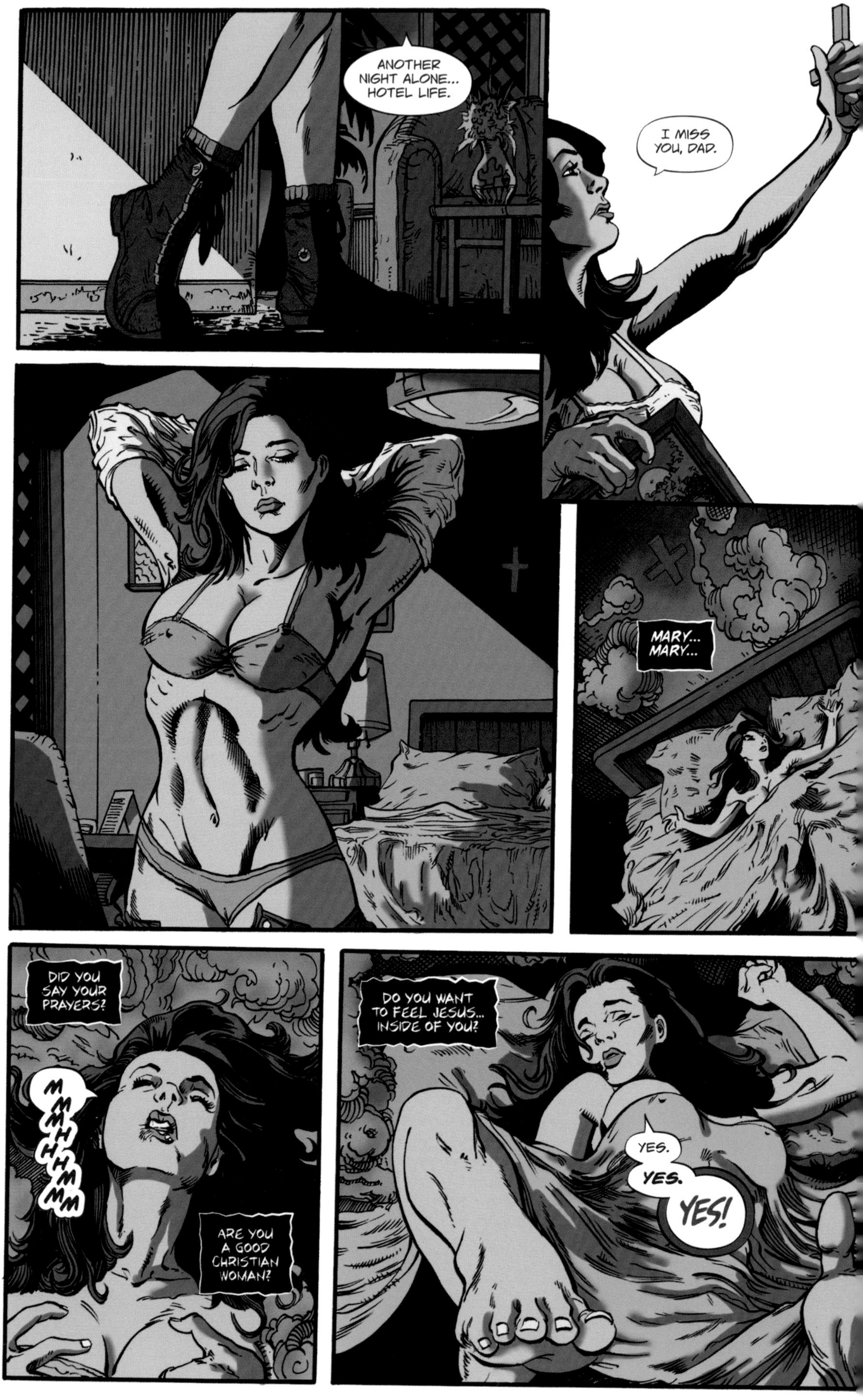
ANOTHER NIGHT ALONE... HOTEL LIFE.
I MISS YOU, DAD.
MARY... MARY...
DID YOU SAY YOUR PRAYERS?
MMMHHHMMMM
ARE YOU A GOOD CHRISTIAN WOMAN?
DO YOU WANT TO FEEL JESUS... INSIDE OF YOU?
YES.
YES.
YES!

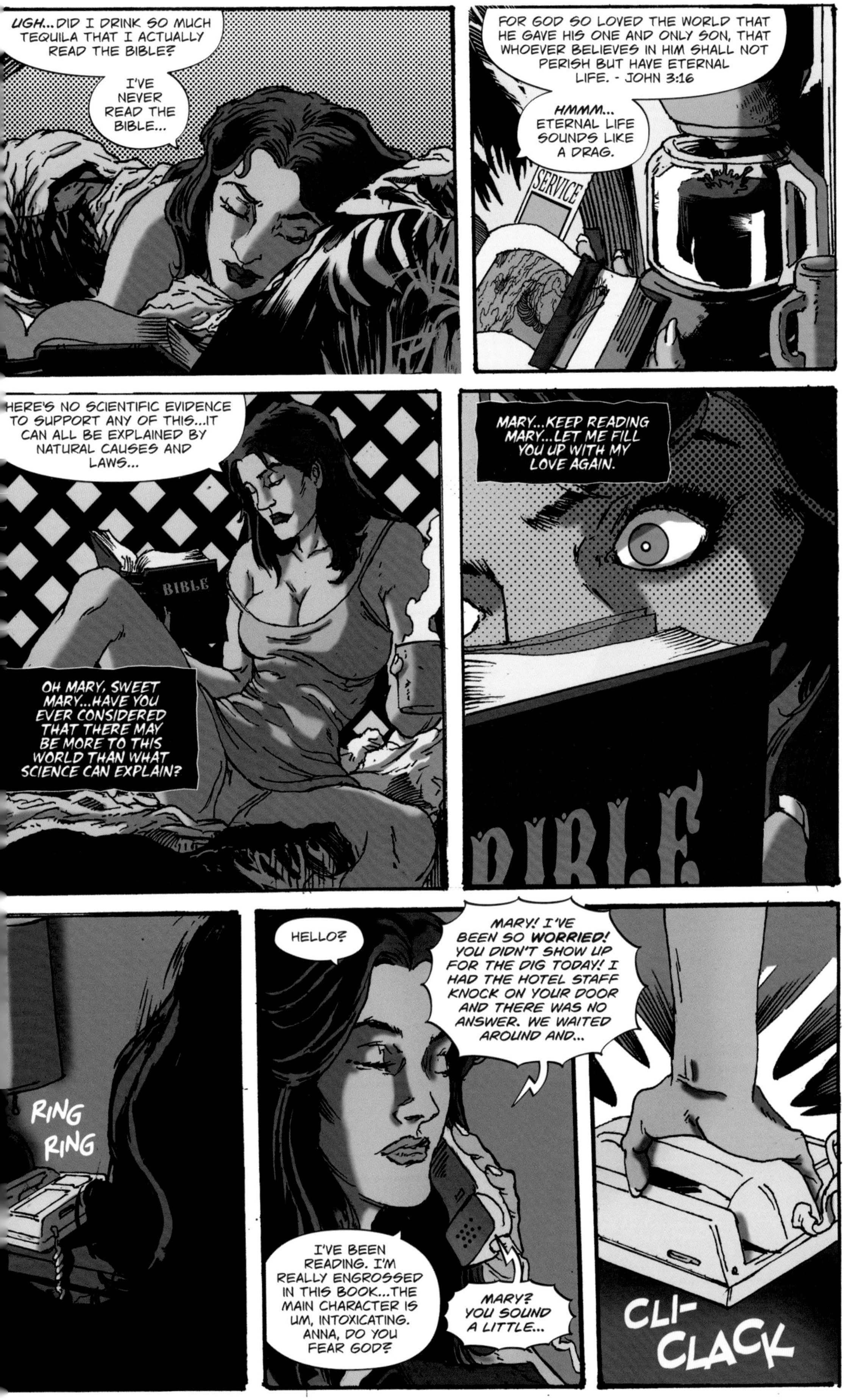
UGH...DID I DRINK SO MUCH TEQUILA THAT I ACTUALLY READ THE BIBLE?
I'VE NEVER READ THE BIBLE...
FOR GOD SO LOVED THE WORLD THAT HE GAVE HIS ONE AND ONLY SON, THAT WHOEVER BELIEVES IN HIM SHALL NOT PERISH BUT HAVE ETERNAL LIFE. - JOHN 3:16
HMMM... ETERNAL LIFE SOUNDS LIKE A DRAG.
SERVICE
HERE'S NO SCIENTIFIC EVIDENCE TO SUPPORT ANY OF THIS...IT CAN ALL BE EXPLAINED BY NATURAL CAUSES AND LAWS...
BIBLE
OH MARY, SWEET MARY...HAVE YOU EVER CONSIDERED THAT THERE MAY BE MORE TO THIS WORLD THAN WHAT SCIENCE CAN EXPLAIN?
MARY...KEEP READING MARY...LET ME FILL YOU UP WITH MY LOVE AGAIN.
BIBLE
RING RING
HELLO?
MARY! I'VE BEEN SO WORRIED! YOU DIDN'T SHOW UP FOR THE DIG TODAY! I HAD THE HOTEL STAFF KNOCK ON YOUR DOOR AND THERE WAS NO ANSWER. WE WAITED AROUND AND...
I'VE BEEN READING. I'M REALLY ENGROSSED IN THIS BOOK...THE MAIN CHARACTER IS UM, INTOXICATING. ANNA, DO YOU FEAR GOD?
MARY? YOU SOUND A LITTLE...
CLI-CLACK

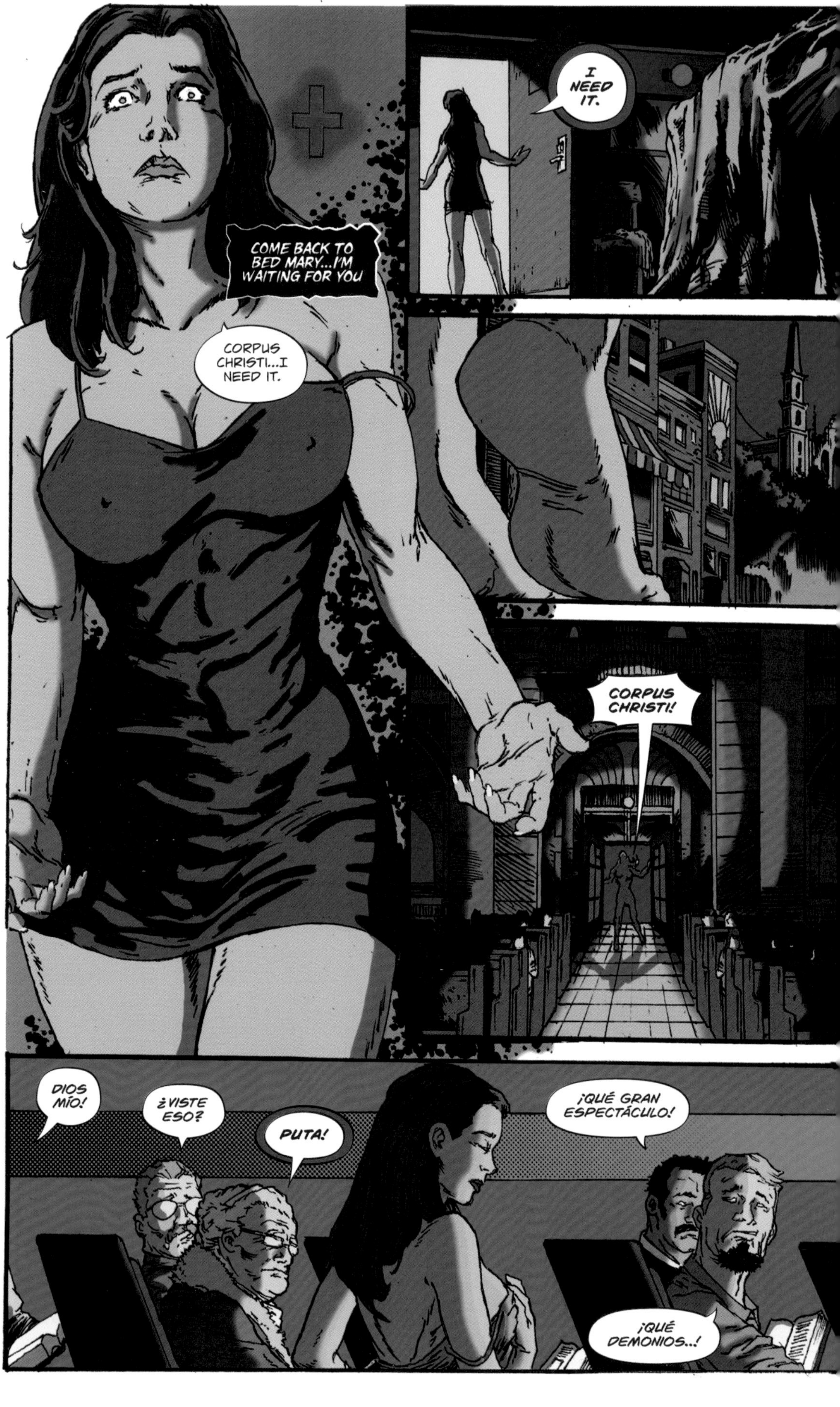
COME BACK TO BED MARY...I'M WAITING FOR YOU
CORPUS CHRISTI...I NEED IT.
I NEED IT.
CORPUS CHRISTI!
DIOS MÍO!
¿VISTE ESO?
PUTA!
¡QUÉ GRAN ESPECTÁCULO!
¡QUÉ DEMONIOS..!

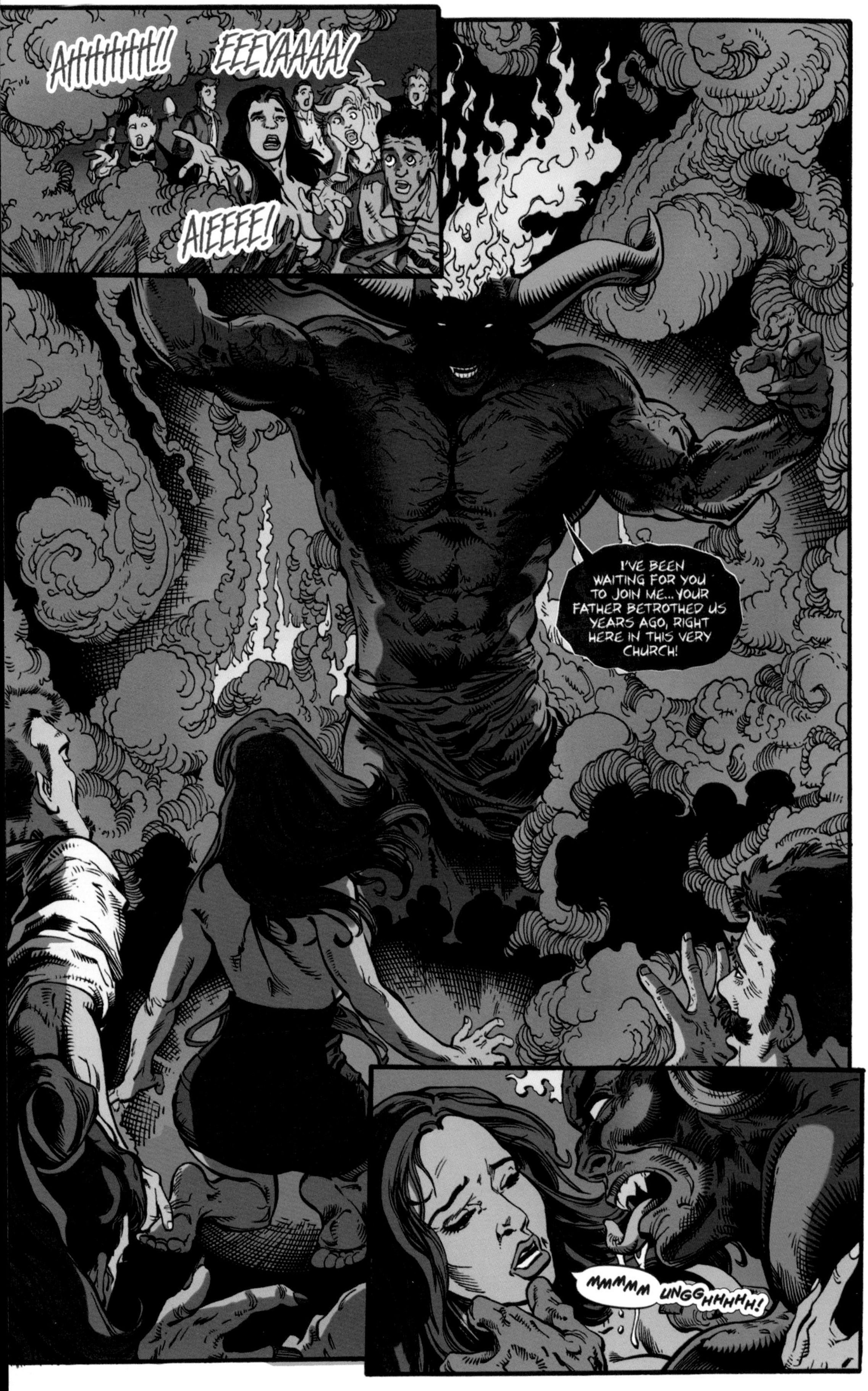
AHHHHH!!
EEEYAAAA!
AIEEEE!
I'VE BEEN WAITING FOR YOU TO JOIN ME... YOUR FATHER BETROTHED US YEARS AGO, RIGHT HERE IN THIS VERY CHURCH!
MMMMM UNGGHHHHH!

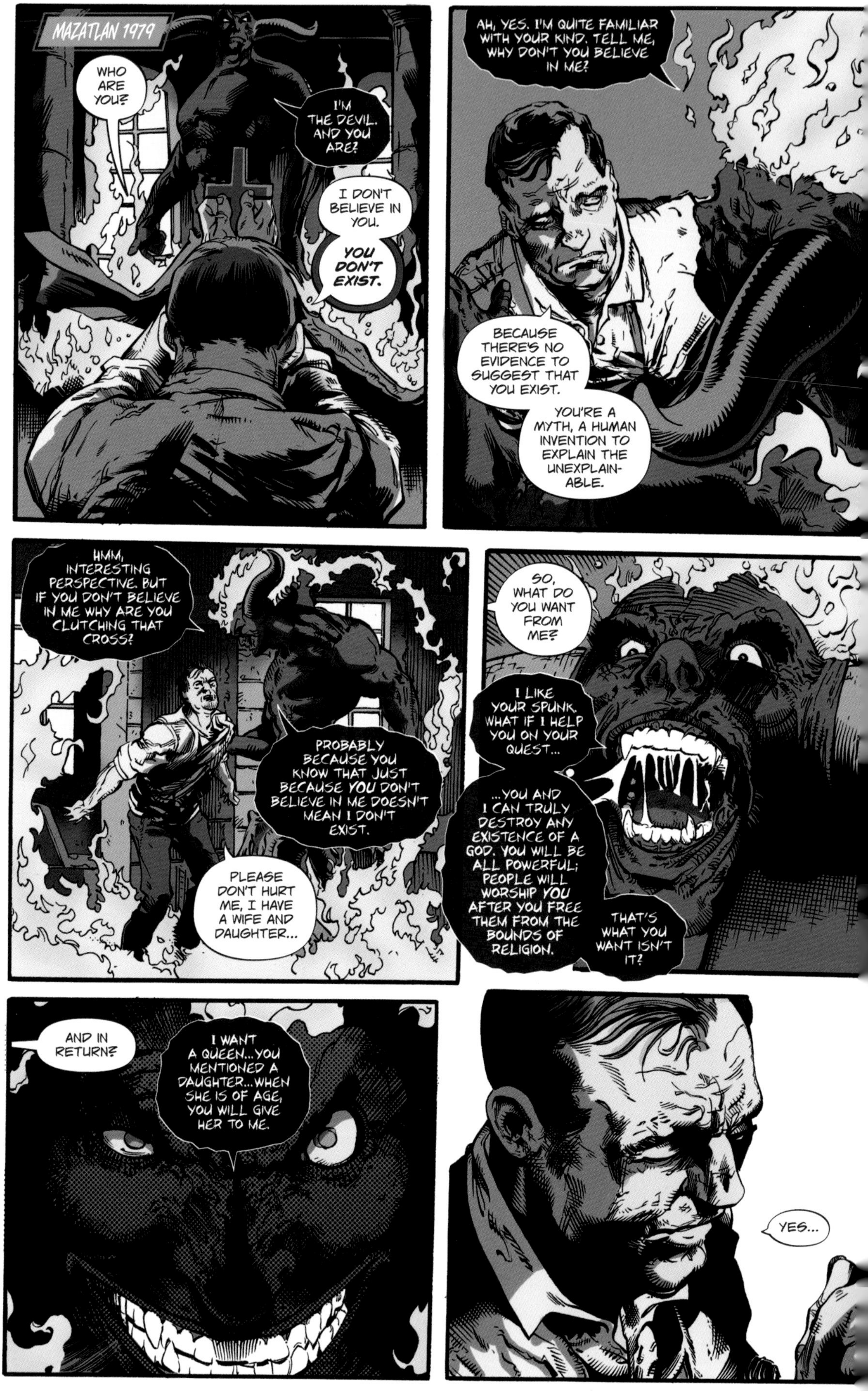
MAZATLAN 1979
WHO ARE YOU?
I'M THE DEVIL. AND YOU ARE?
I DON'T BELIEVE IN YOU.
YOU DON'T EXIST.
AH, YES. I'M QUITE FAMILIAR WITH YOUR KIND. TELL ME, WHY DON'T YOU BELIEVE IN ME?
BECAUSE THERE'S NO EVIDENCE TO SUGGEST THAT YOU EXIST.
YOU'RE A MYTH, A HUMAN INVENTION TO EXPLAIN THE UNEXPLAIN-ABLE.
HMM, INTERESTING PERSPECTIVE. BUT IF YOU DON'T BELIEVE IN ME WHY ARE YOU CLUTCHING THAT CROSS?
PROBABLY BECAUSE YOU KNOW THAT JUST BECAUSE YOU DON'T BELIEVE IN ME DOESN'T MEAN I DON'T EXIST.
PLEASE DON'T HURT ME, I HAVE A WIFE AND DAUGHTER...
SO, WHAT DO YOU WANT FROM ME?
I LIKE YOUR SPUNK. WHAT IF I HELP YOU ON YOUR QUEST...
...YOU AND I CAN TRULY DESTROY ANY EXISTENCE OF A GOD. YOU WILL BE ALL POWERFUL; PEOPLE WILL WORSHIP YOU AFTER YOU FREE THEM FROM THE BOUNDS OF RELIGION.
THAT'S WHAT YOU WANT ISN'T IT?
AND IN RETURN?
I WANT A QUEEN...YOU MENTIONED A DAUGHTER...WHEN SHE IS OF AGE, YOU WILL GIVE HER TO ME.
YES...

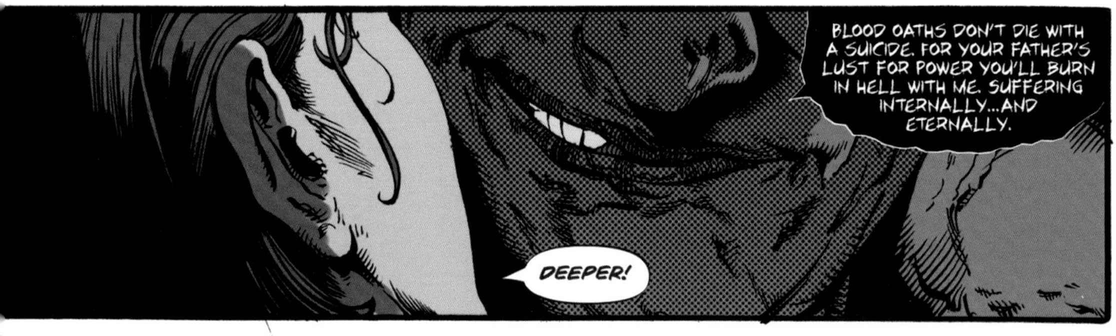
BLOOD OATHS DON'T DIE WITH A SUICIDE. FOR YOUR FATHER'S LUST FOR POWER YOU'LL BURN IN HELL WITH ME. SUFFERING INTERNALLY...AND ETERNALLY.
DEEPER!

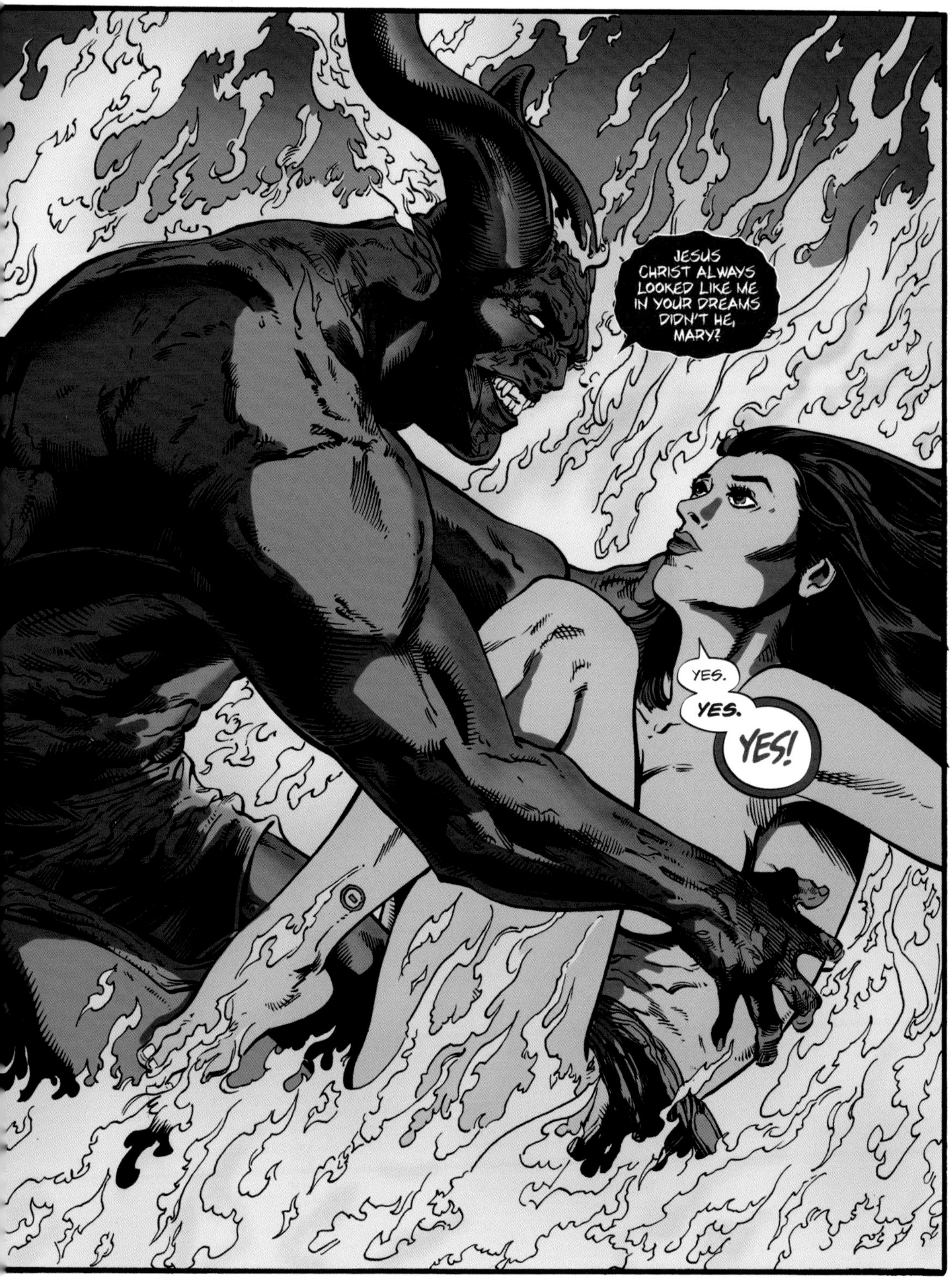
JESUS CHRIST ALWAYS LOOKED LIKE ME IN YOUR DREAMS DIDN'T HE, MARY?
YES.
YES.
YES!

BLACK No. 1

WRITER: ASHLEY COSTELLO
ARTIST: STEVE KURTH
LETTERER: ADAM WOLLET

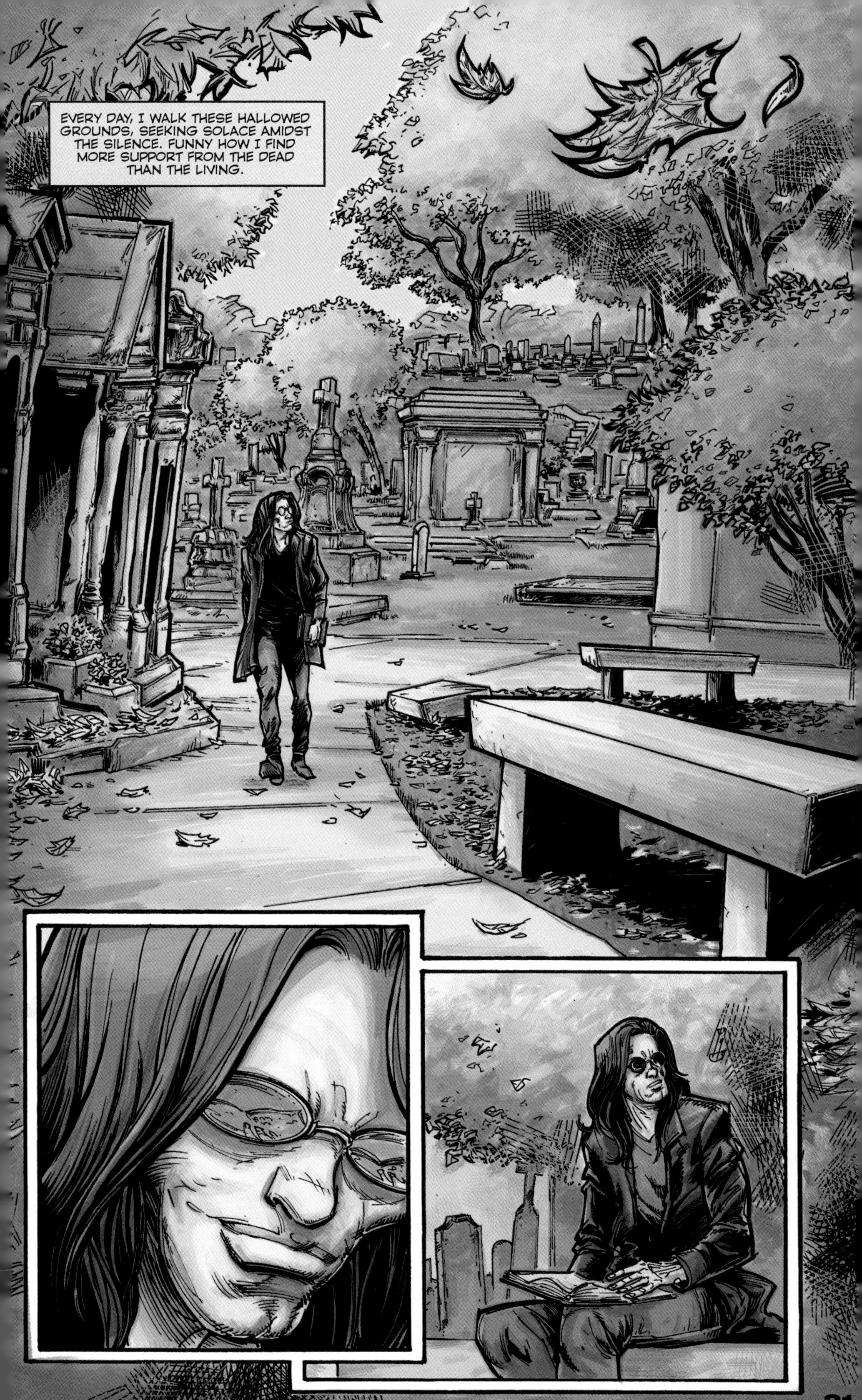
EVERY DAY, I WALK THESE HALLOWED GROUNDS, SEEKING SOLACE AMIDST THE SILENCE. FUNNY HOW I FIND MORE SUPPORT FROM THE DEAD THAN THE LIVING.

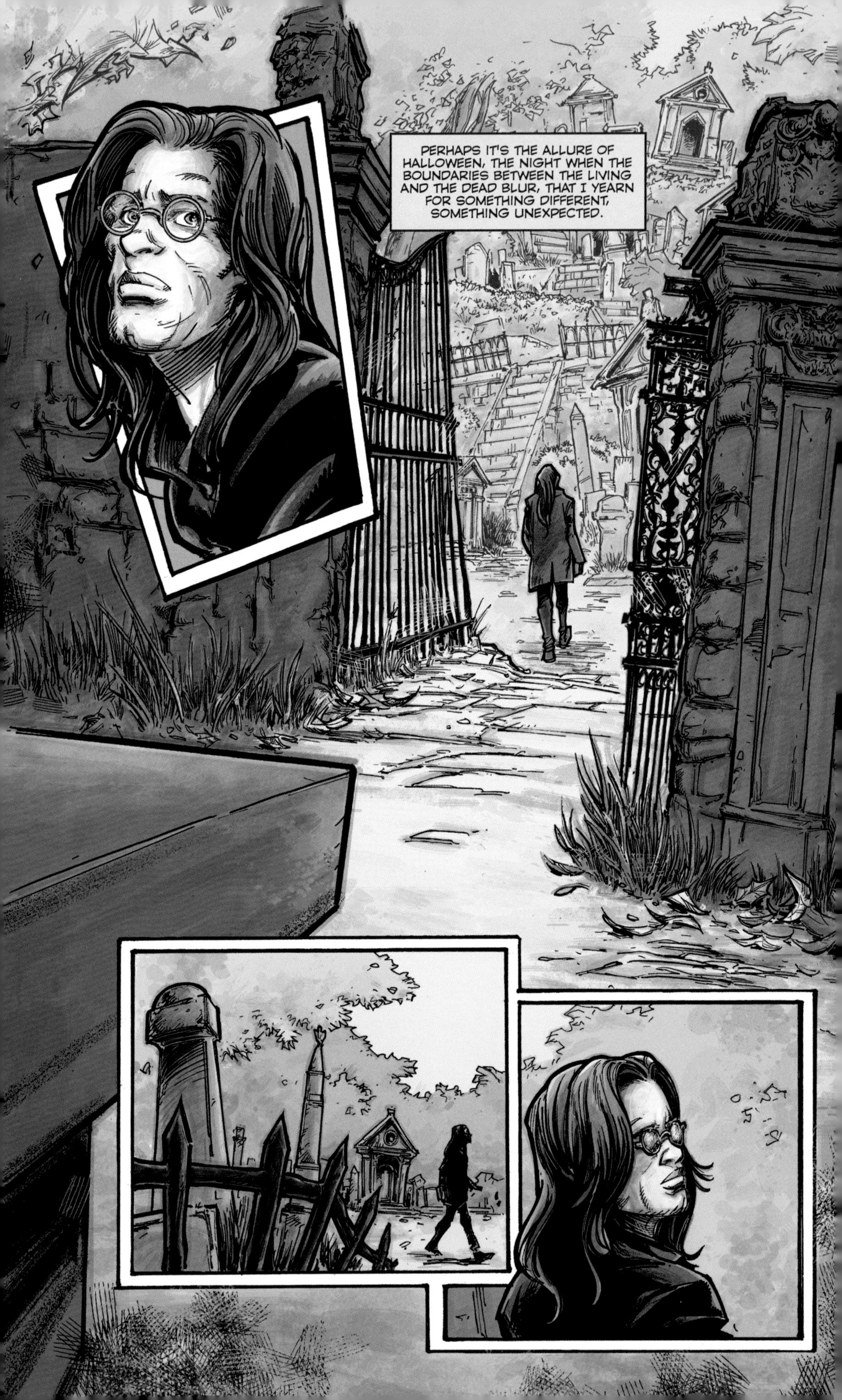
PERHAPS IT'S THE ALLURE OF HALLOWEEN, THE NIGHT WHEN THE BOUNDARIES BETWEEN THE LIVING AND THE DEAD BLUR, THAT I YEARN FOR SOMETHING DIFFERENT, SOMETHING UNEXPECTED.

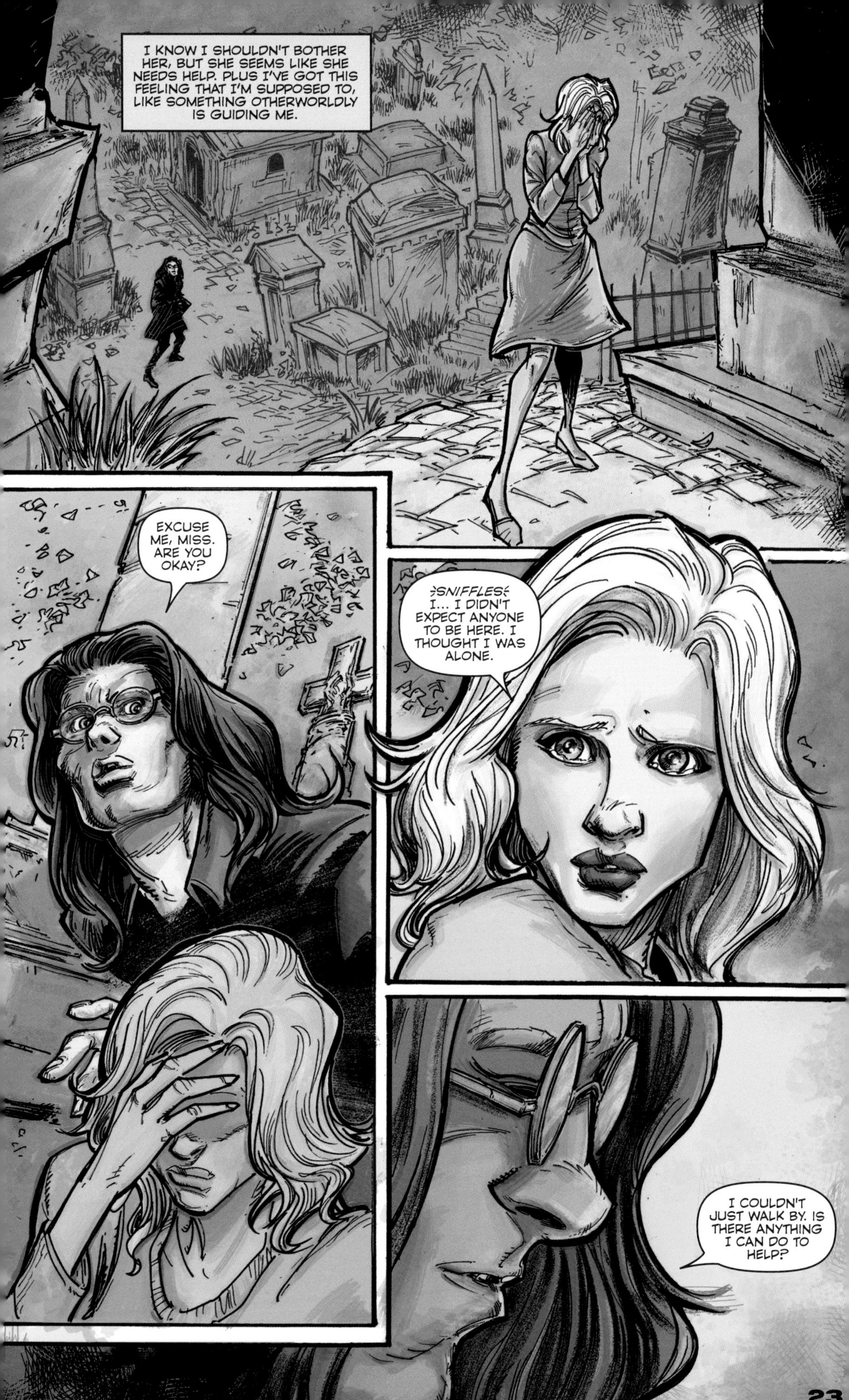
I KNOW I SHOULDN'T BOTHER HER, BUT SHE SEEMS LIKE SHE NEEDS HELP. PLUS I'VE GOT THIS FEELING THAT I'M SUPPOSED TO, LIKE SOMETHING OTHERWORLDLY IS GUIDING ME.
EXCUSE ME, MISS. ARE YOU OKAY?
SNIFFLES
I... I DIDN'T EXPECT ANYONE TO BE HERE. I THOUGHT I WAS ALONE.
I COULDN'T JUST WALK BY. IS THERE ANYTHING I CAN DO TO HELP?

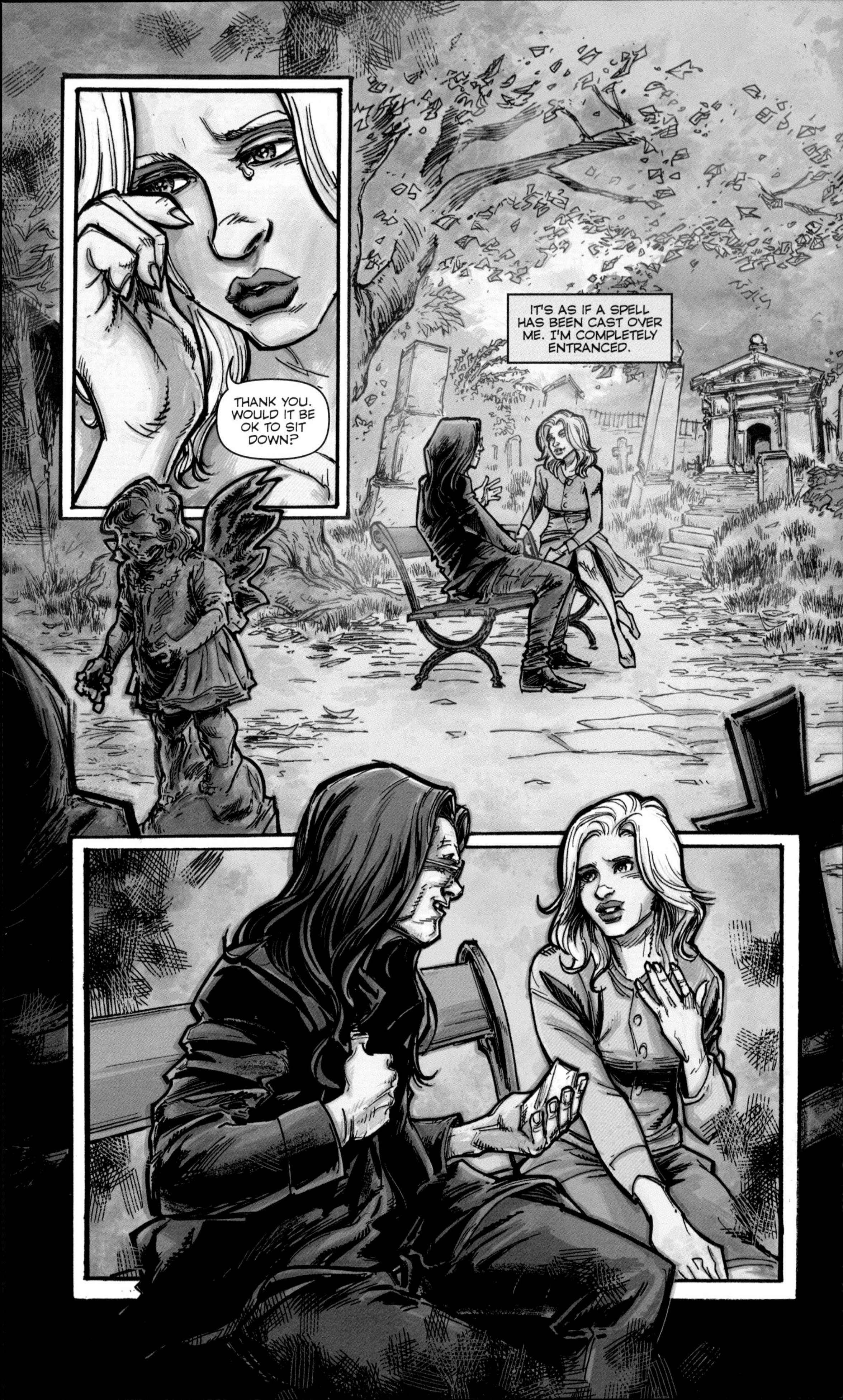
THANK YOU. WOULD IT BE OK TO SIT DOWN?
IT'S AS IF A SPELL HAS BEEN CAST OVER ME. I'M COMPLETELY ENTRANCED.

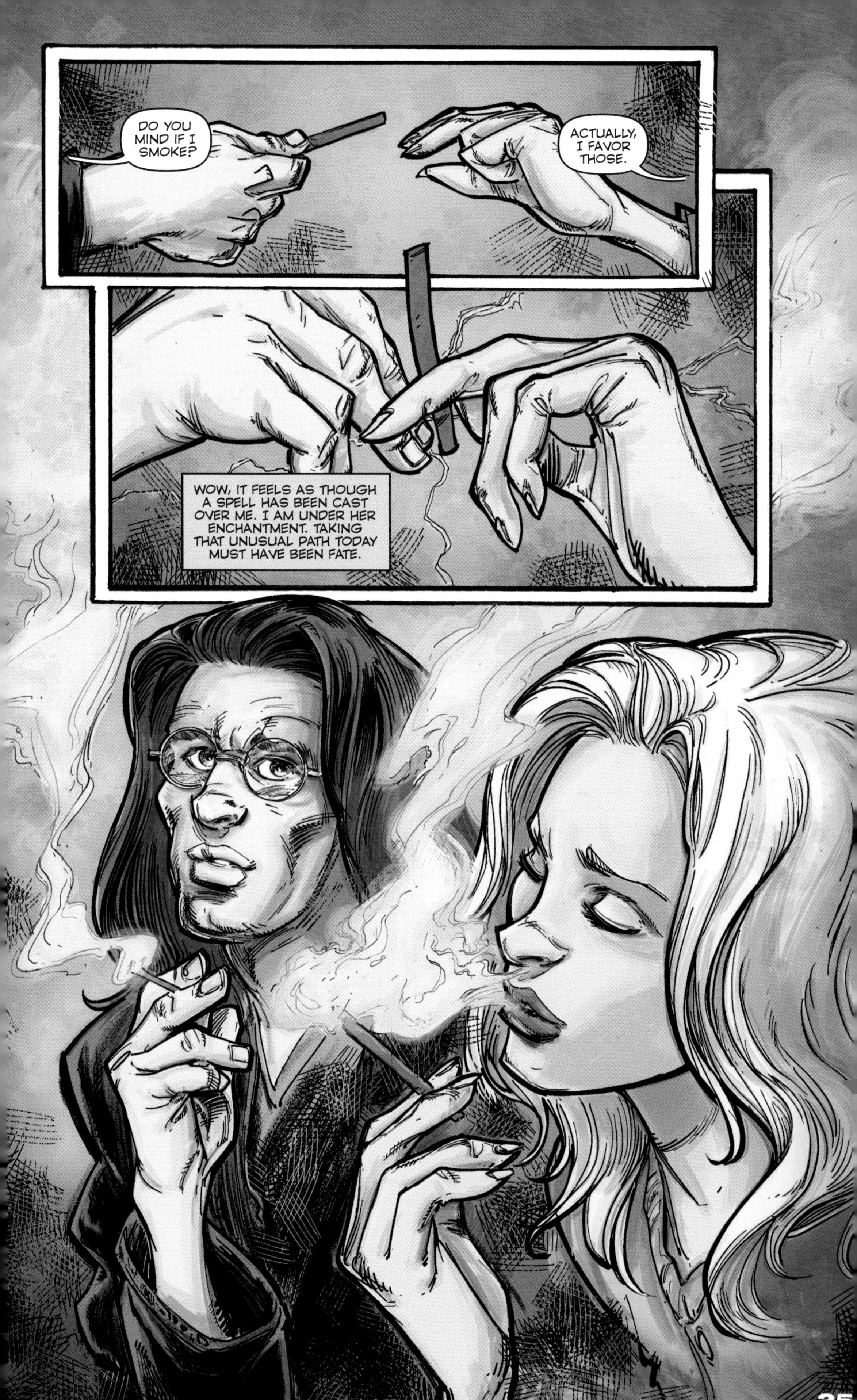
DO YOU MIND IF I SMOKE?
ACTUALLY, I FAVOR THOSE.
WOW, IT FEELS AS THOUGH A SPELL HAS BEEN CAST OVER ME. I AM UNDER HER ENCHANTMENT. TAKING THAT UNUSUAL PATH TODAY MUST HAVE BEEN FATE.

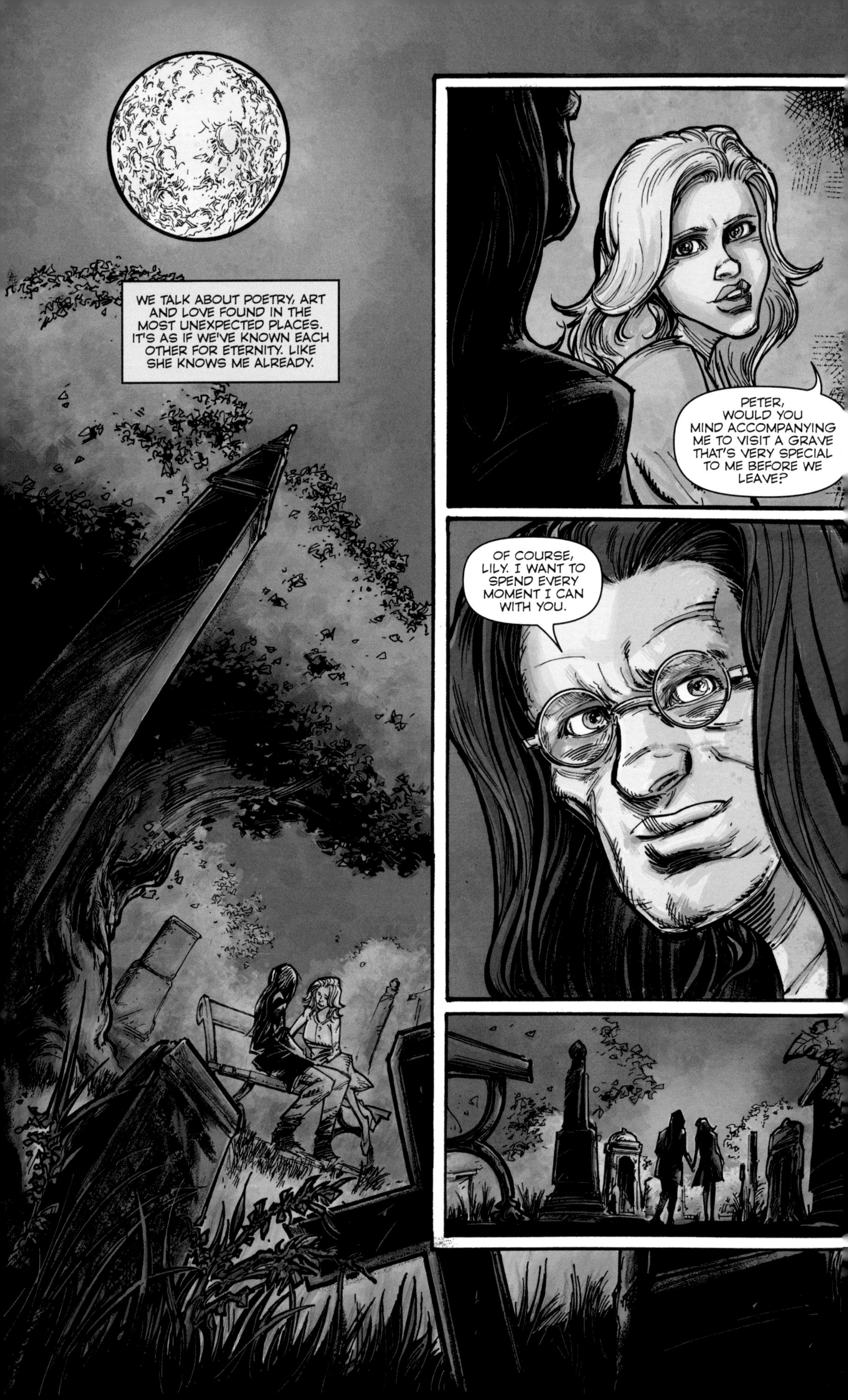
WE TALK ABOUT POETRY, ART AND LOVE FOUND IN THE MOST UNEXPECTED PLACES. IT'S AS IF WE'VE KNOWN EACH OTHER FOR ETERNITY. LIKE SHE KNOWS ME ALREADY.
PETER, WOULD YOU MIND ACCOMPANYING ME TO VISIT A GRAVE THAT'S VERY SPECIAL TO ME BEFORE WE LEAVE?
OF COURSE, LILY. I WANT TO SPEND EVERY MOMENT I CAN WITH YOU.

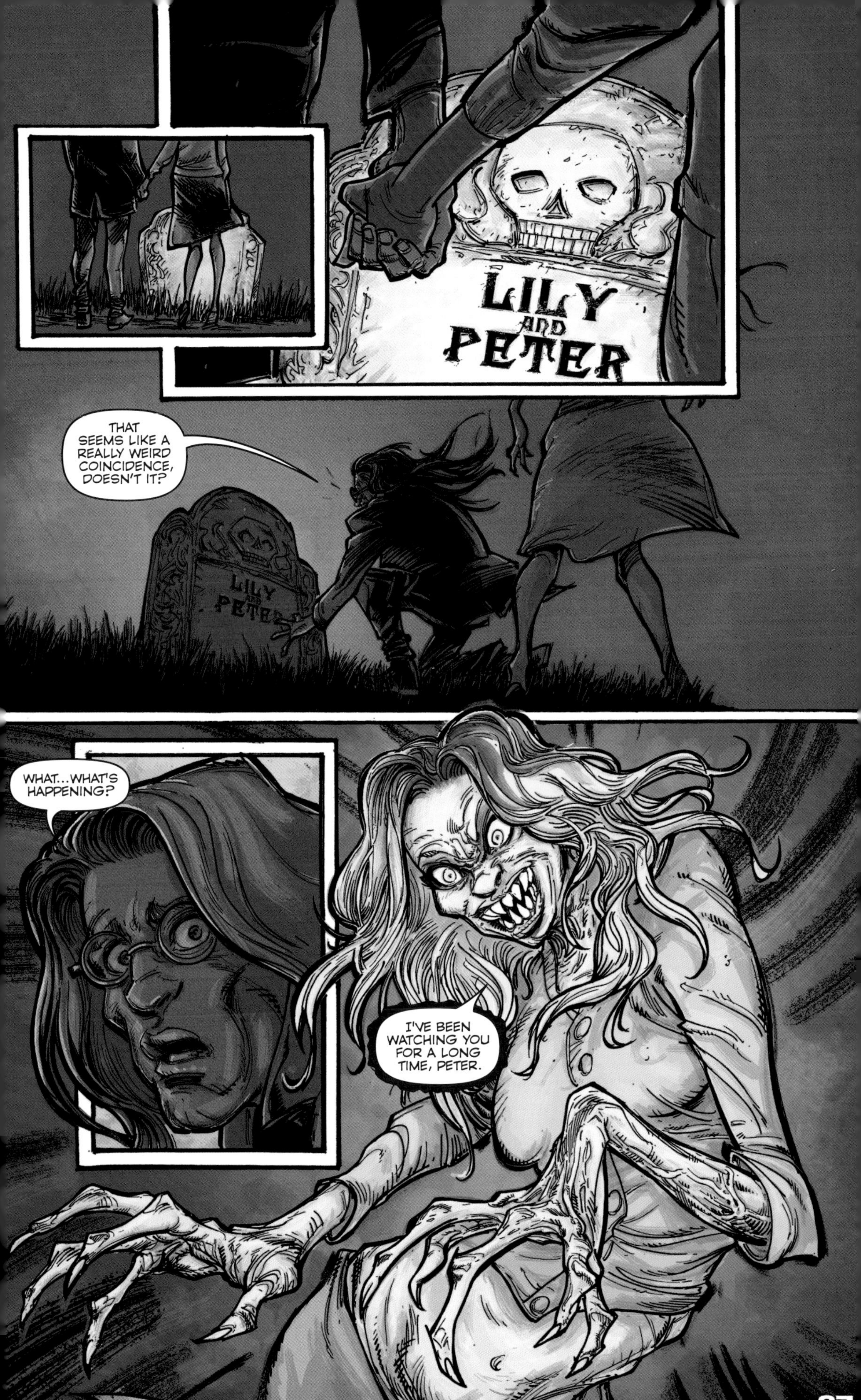

LILY AND PETER
THAT SEEMS LIKE A REALLY WEIRD COINCIDENCE, DOESN'T IT?
LILY AND PETER
WHAT...WHAT'S HAPPENING?
I'VE BEEN WATCHING YOU FOR A LONG TIME, PETER.

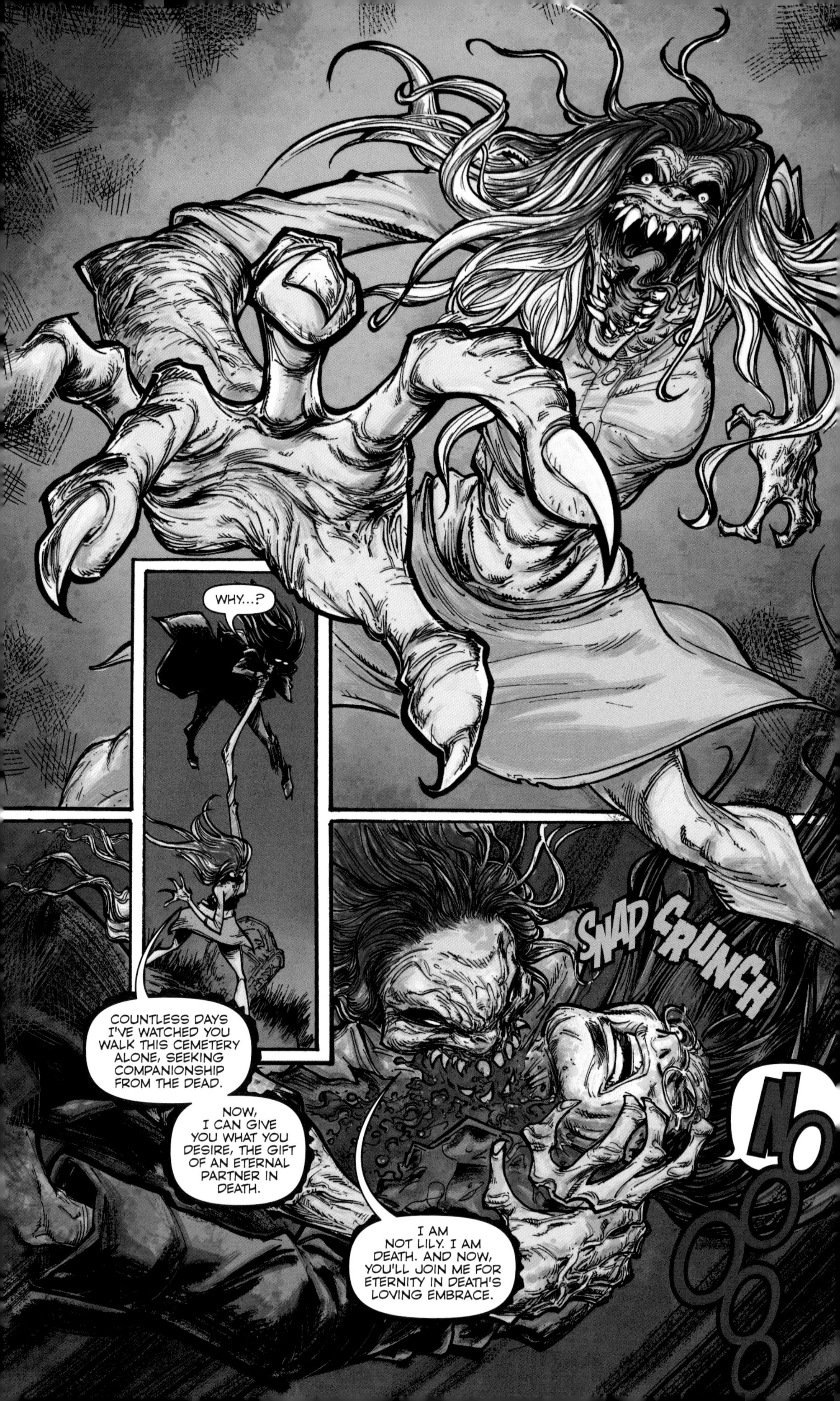
WHY...?
COUNTLESS DAYS I'VE WATCHED YOU WALK THIS CEMETERY ALONE, SEEKING COMPANIONSHIP FROM THE DEAD.
NOW, I CAN GIVE YOU WHAT YOU DESIRE, THE GIFT OF AN ETERNAL PARTNER IN DEATH.
SNAP CRUNCH
I AM NOT LILY. I AM DEATH. AND NOW, YOU'LL JOIN ME FOR ETERNITY IN DEATH'S LOVING EMBRACE.
NOOOOO

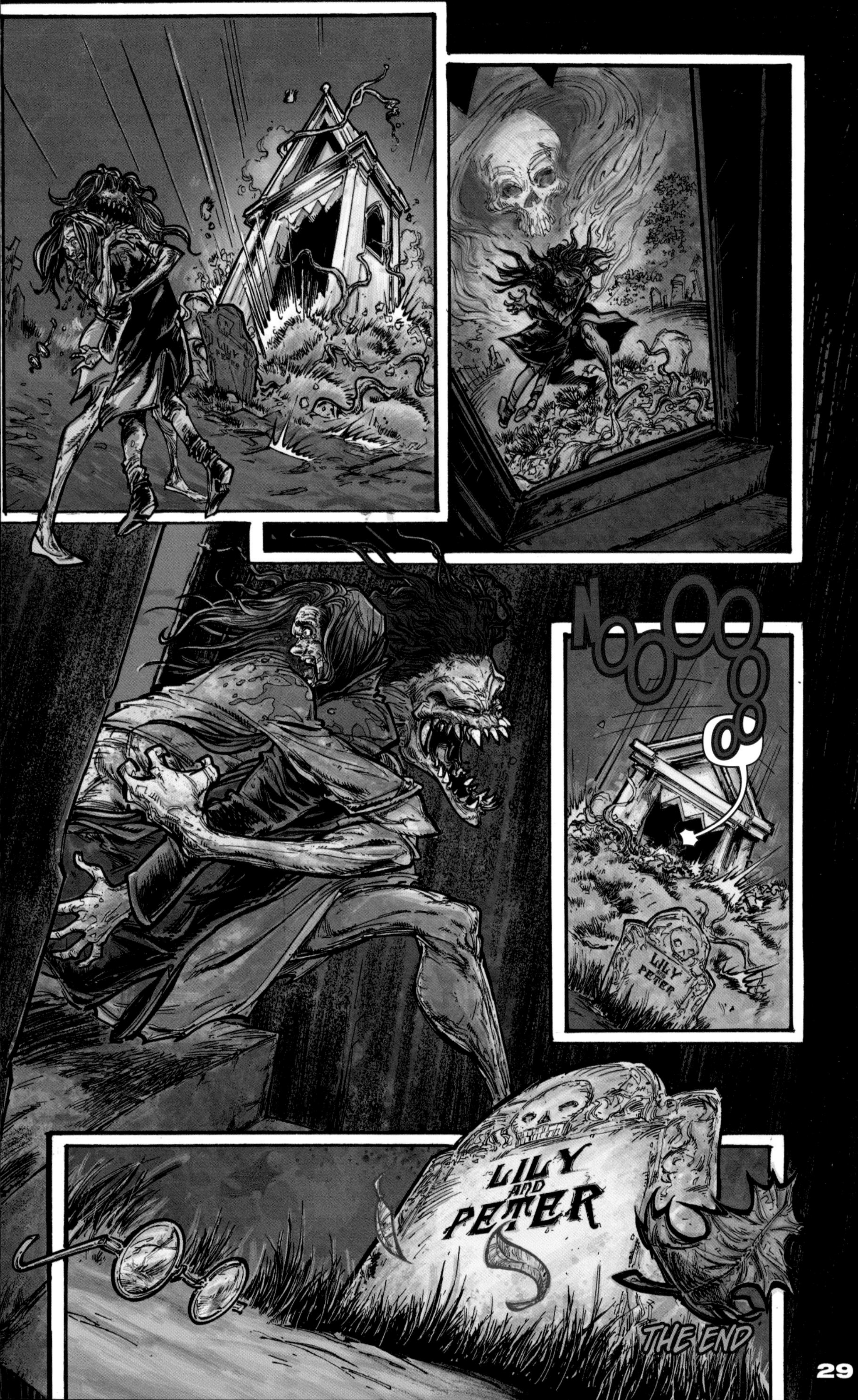
LILY PETER
NOOOOOOOO
LILY PETER
LILY AND PETER
THE END

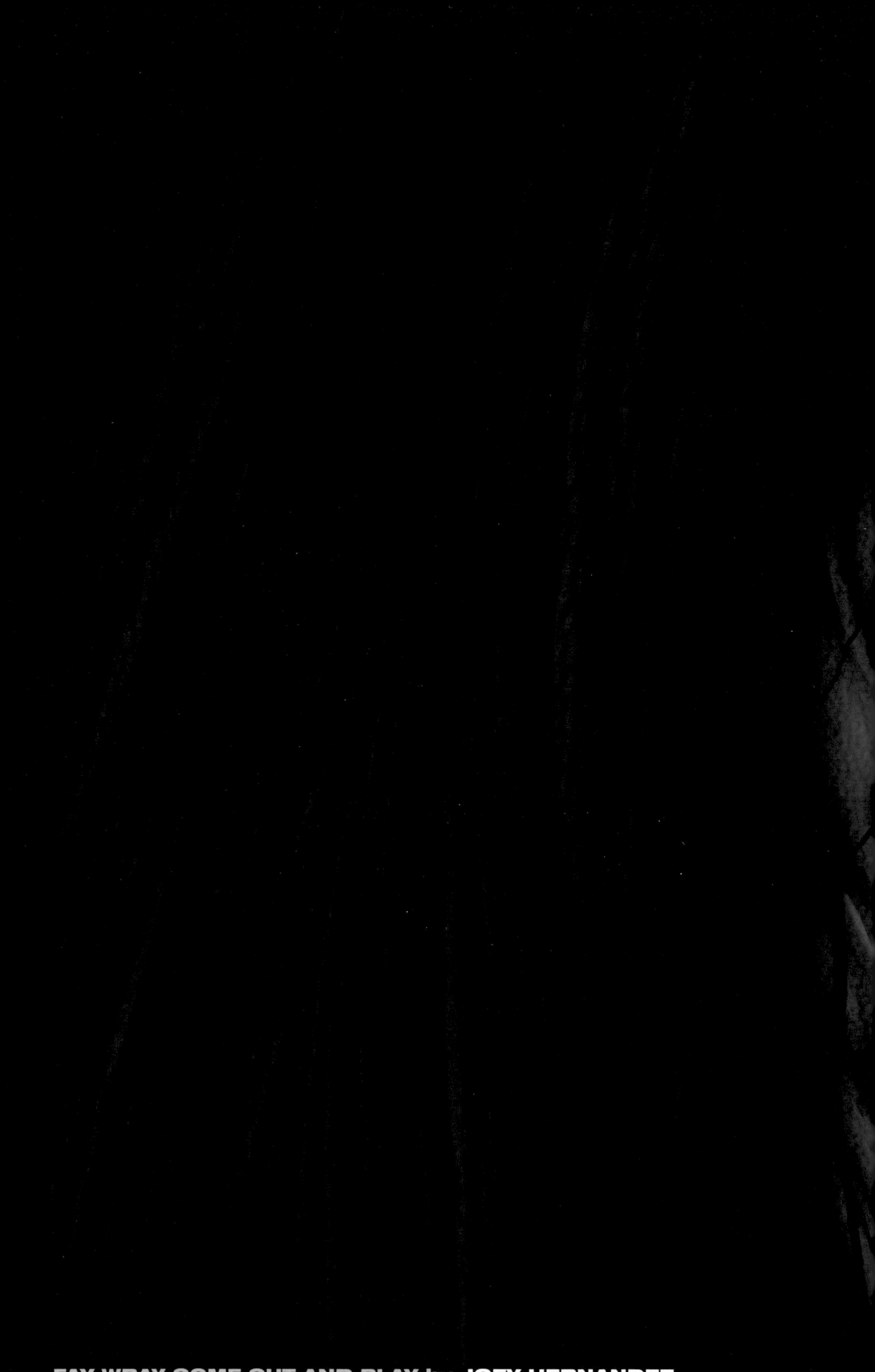

FAY WRAY COME OUT AND PLAY by JOEY HERNANDEZ

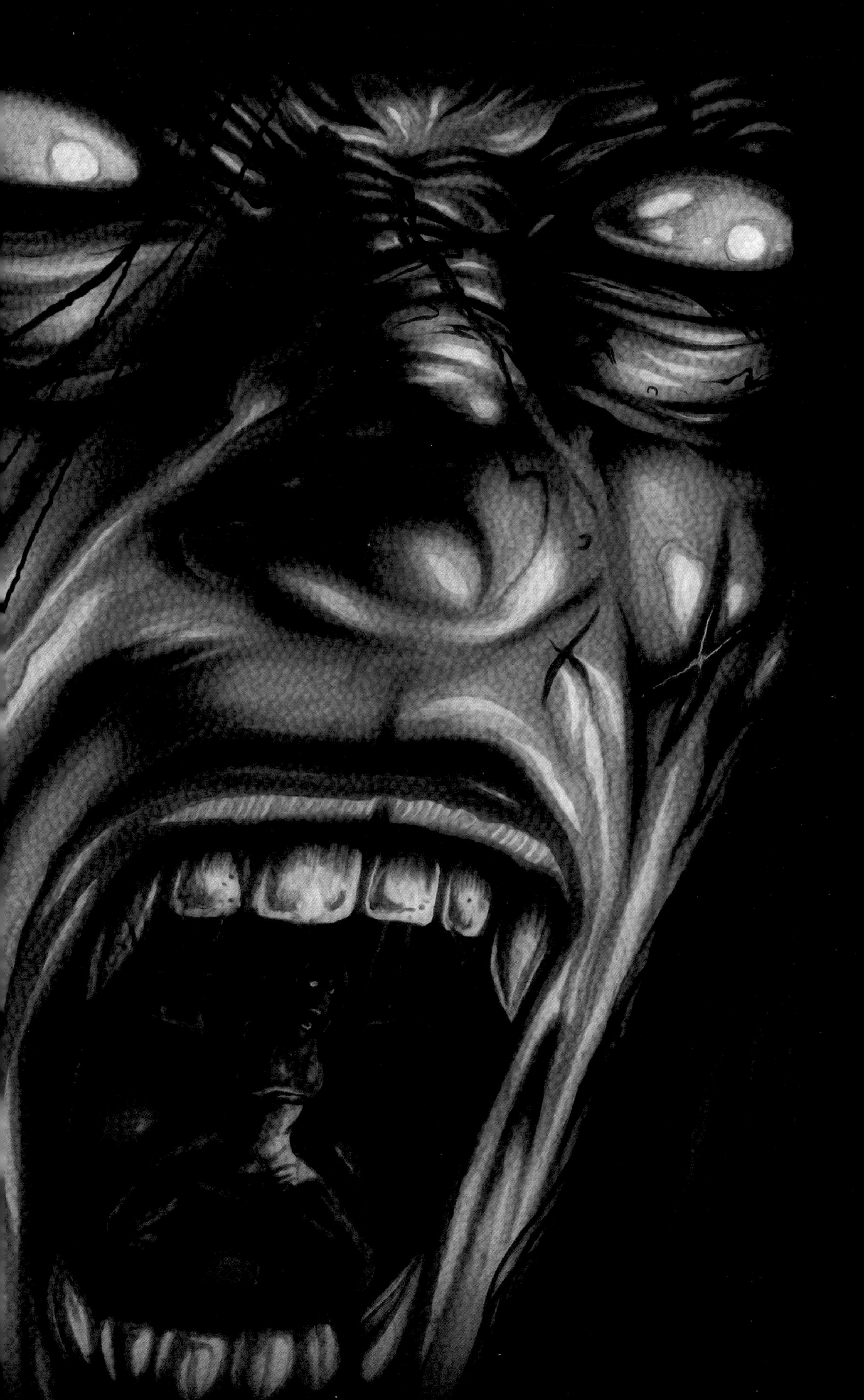

KILL ALL THE WHITE PEOPLE

WRITER: RANTZ HOSELEY
ARTIST: SEAN PRYOR
LETTERER: ADAM WOLLET

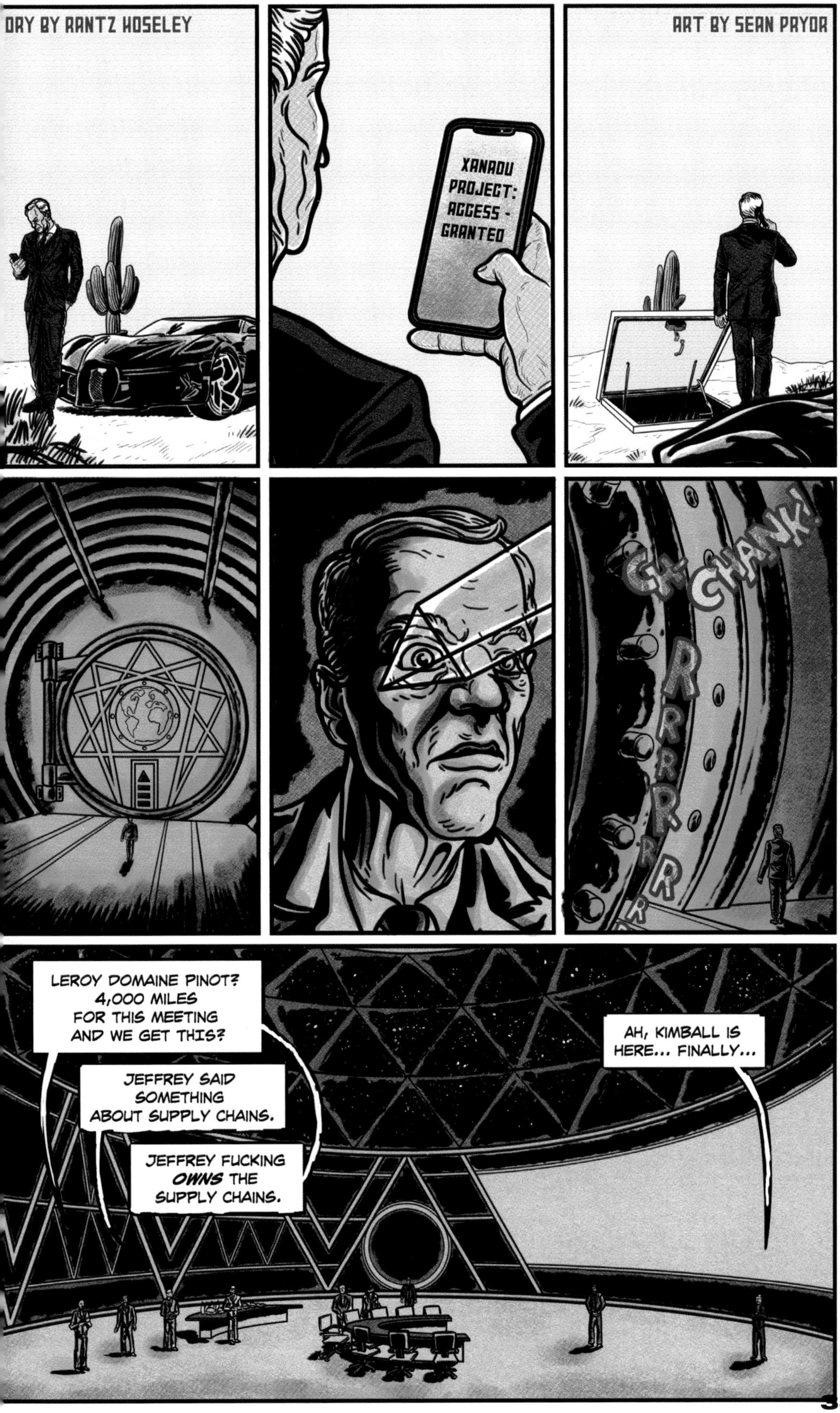

ORY BY RANTZ HOSELEY
ART BY SEAN PRYOR
XANADU PROJECT: ACCESS - GRANTED
CH-CHANK!
RRRRRRRR
LEROY DOMAINE PINOT? 4,000 MILES FOR THIS MEETING AND WE GET THIS?
JEFFREY SAID SOMETHING ABOUT SUPPLY CHAINS.
JEFFREY FUCKING *OWNS* THE SUPPLY CHAINS.
AH, KIMBALL IS HERE... FINALLY...

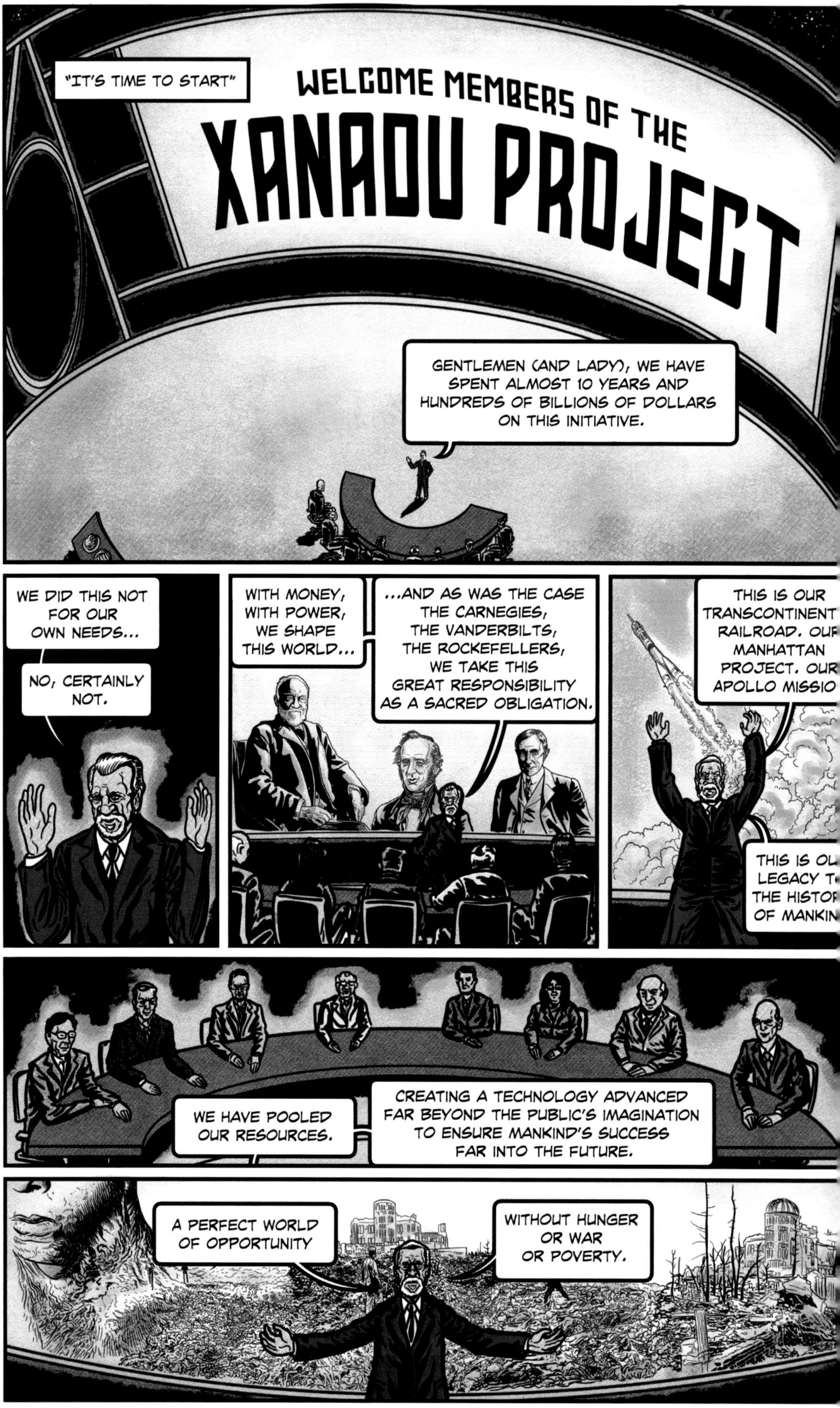
"IT'S TIME TO START"
WELCOME MEMBERS OF THE
XANADU PROJECT
GENTLEMEN (AND LADY), WE HAVE SPENT ALMOST 10 YEARS AND HUNDREDS OF BILLIONS OF DOLLARS ON THIS INITIATIVE.
WE DID THIS NOT FOR OUR OWN NEEDS...
NO, CERTAINLY NOT.
WITH MONEY, WITH POWER, WE SHAPE THIS WORLD...
...AND AS WAS THE CASE THE CARNEGIES, THE VANDERBILTS, THE ROCKEFELLERS, WE TAKE THIS GREAT RESPONSIBILITY AS A SACRED OBLIGATION.
THIS IS OUR TRANSCONTINENT RAILROAD. OUR MANHATTAN PROJECT. OUR APOLLO MISSIO
THIS IS OU LEGACY T THE HISTOR OF MANKIN
WE HAVE POOLED OUR RESOURCES.
CREATING A TECHNOLOGY ADVANCED FAR BEYOND THE PUBLIC'S IMAGINATION TO ENSURE MANKIND'S SUCCESS FAR INTO THE FUTURE.
A PERFECT WORLD OF OPPORTUNITY
WITHOUT HUNGER OR WAR OR POVERTY.

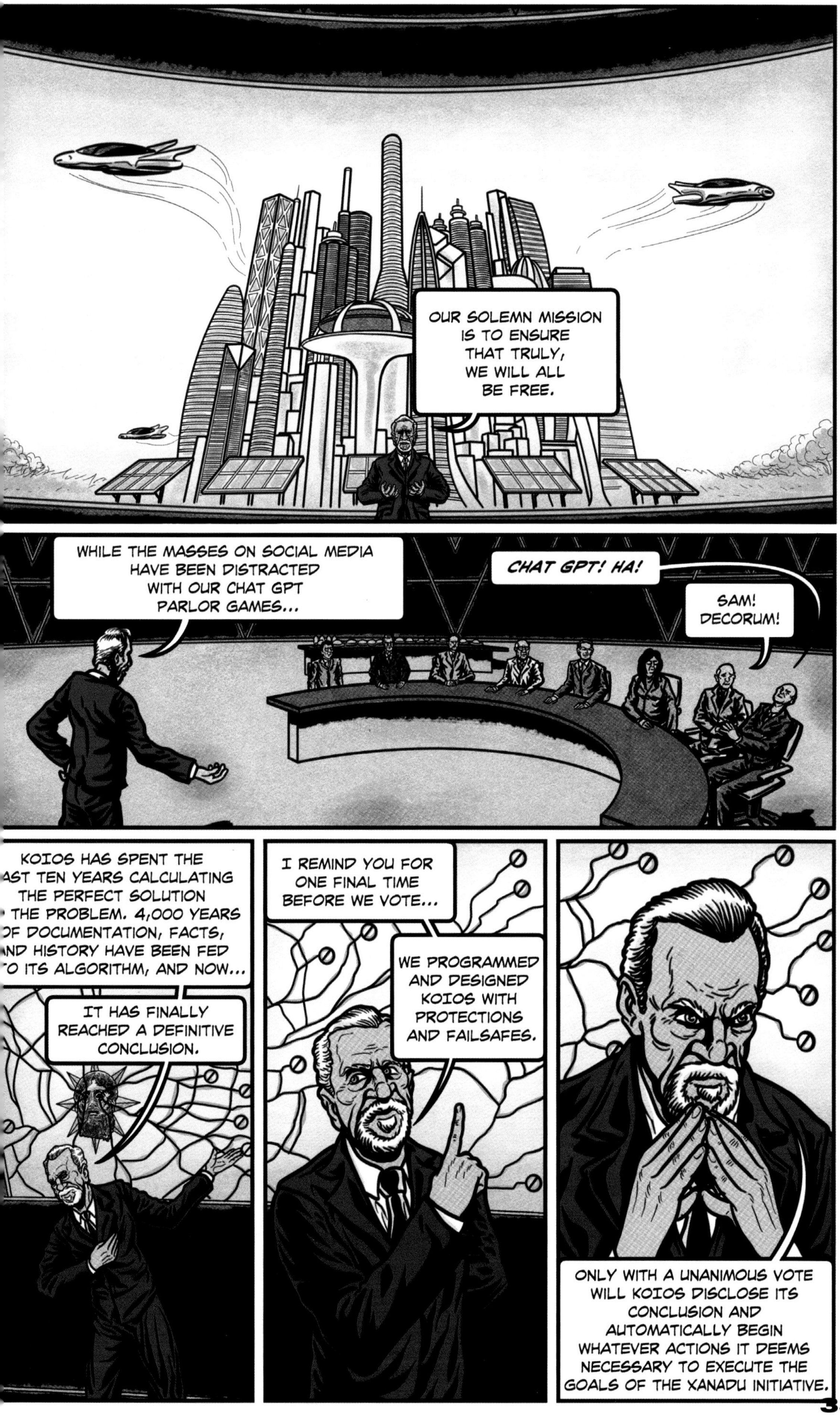
OUR SOLEMN MISSION IS TO ENSURE THAT TRULY, WE WILL ALL BE FREE.
WHILE THE MASSES ON SOCIAL MEDIA HAVE BEEN DISTRACTED WITH OUR CHAT GPT PARLOR GAMES...
CHAT GPT! HA!
SAM! DECORUM!
KOIOS HAS SPENT THE
AST TEN YEARS CALCULATING
THE PERFECT SOLUTION
THE PROBLEM. 4,000 YEARS
OF DOCUMENTATION, FACTS,
ND HISTORY HAVE BEEN FED
O ITS ALGORITHM, AND NOW...
IT HAS FINALLY REACHED A DEFINITIVE CONCLUSION.
I REMIND YOU FOR ONE FINAL TIME BEFORE WE VOTE...
WE PROGRAMMED AND DESIGNED KOIOS WITH PROTECTIONS AND FAILSAFES.
ONLY WITH A UNANIMOUS VOTE WILL KOIOS DISCLOSE ITS CONCLUSION AND AUTOMATICALLY BEGIN WHATEVER ACTIONS IT DEEMS NECESSARY TO EXECUTE THE GOALS OF THE XANADU INITIATIVE.

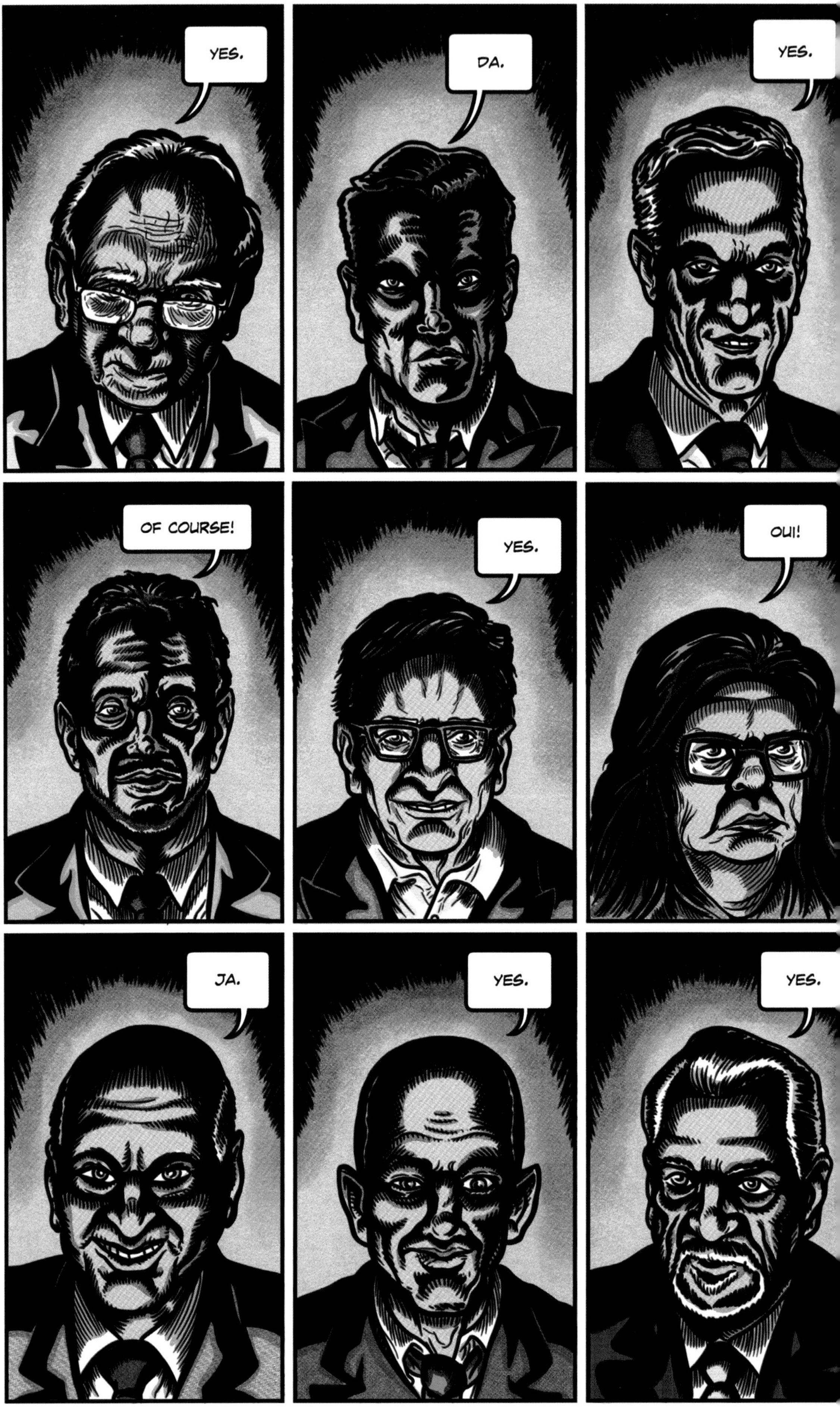
YES.
DA.
YES.
OF COURSE!
YES.
OUI!
JA.
YES.
YES.

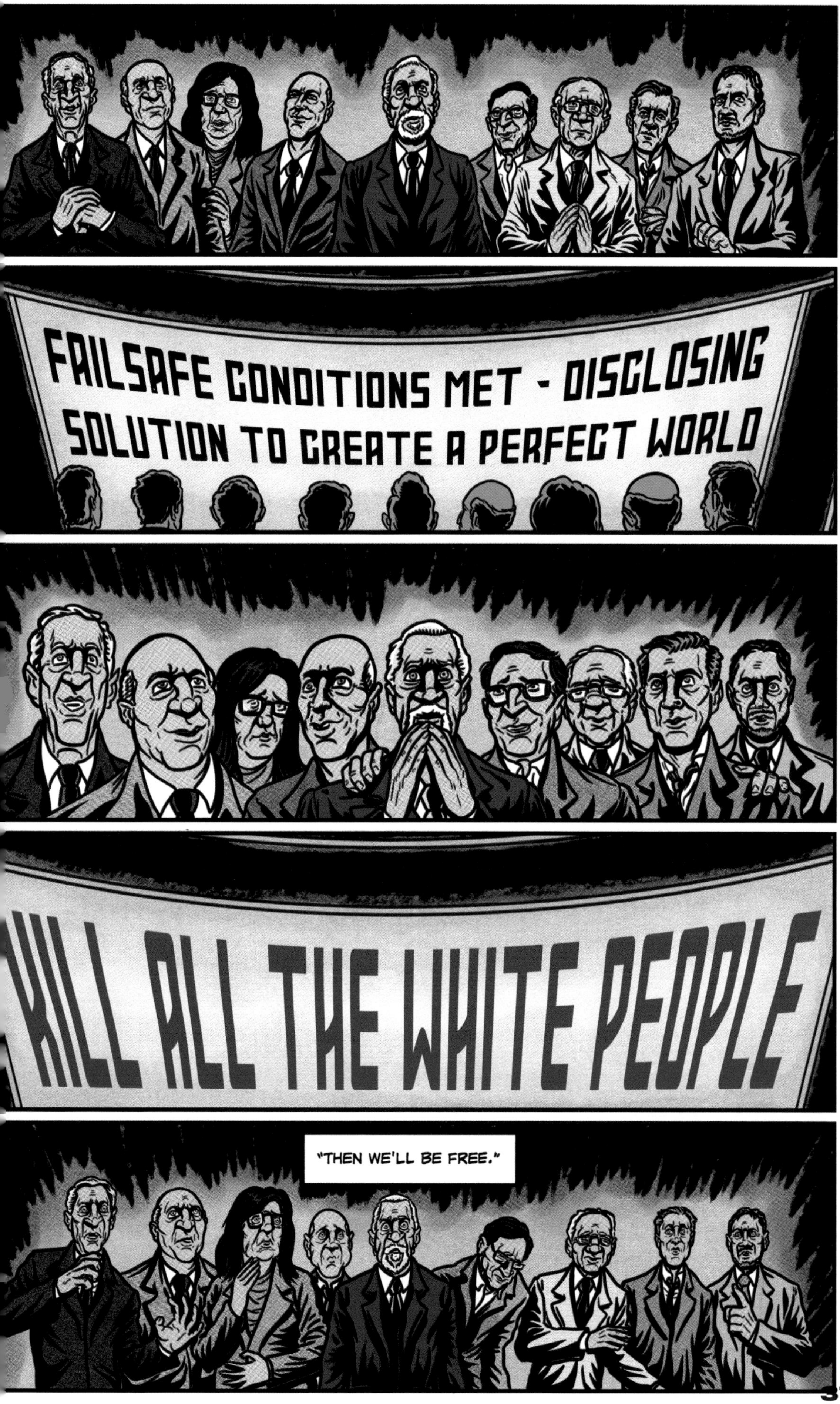
FAILSAFE CONDITIONS MET - DISCLOSING SOLUTION TO CREATE A PERFECT WORLD
KILL ALL THE WHITE PEOPLE
"THEN WE'LL BE FREE."

SUMMER BREEZE

WRITER: GAVIN HIGNIGHT
ARTIST: SHANE WHITE
COLORIST: MICHELE MONTE
LETTERER: HALEY ROSE-LYON

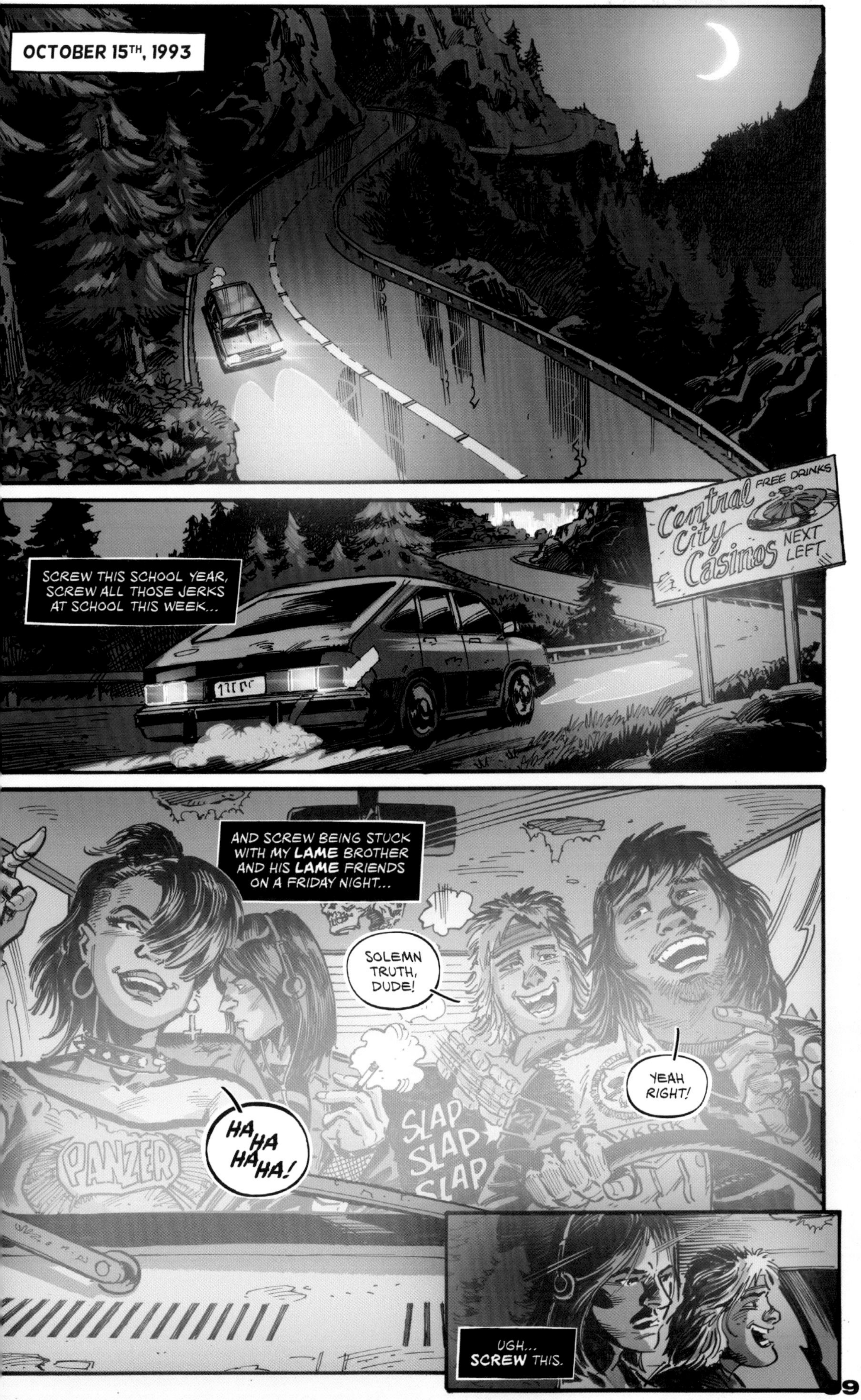
OCTOBER 15TH, 1993
Central City Casinos
FREE DRINKS
NEXT LEFT
SCREW THIS SCHOOL YEAR, SCREW ALL THOSE JERKS AT SCHOOL THIS WEEK...
AND SCREW BEING STUCK WITH MY LAME BROTHER AND HIS LAME FRIENDS ON A FRIDAY NIGHT...
SOLEMN TRUTH, DUDE!
YEAH RIGHT!
HA HA HA HA!
SLAP SLAP SLAP
PANZER
UGH... SCREW THIS.

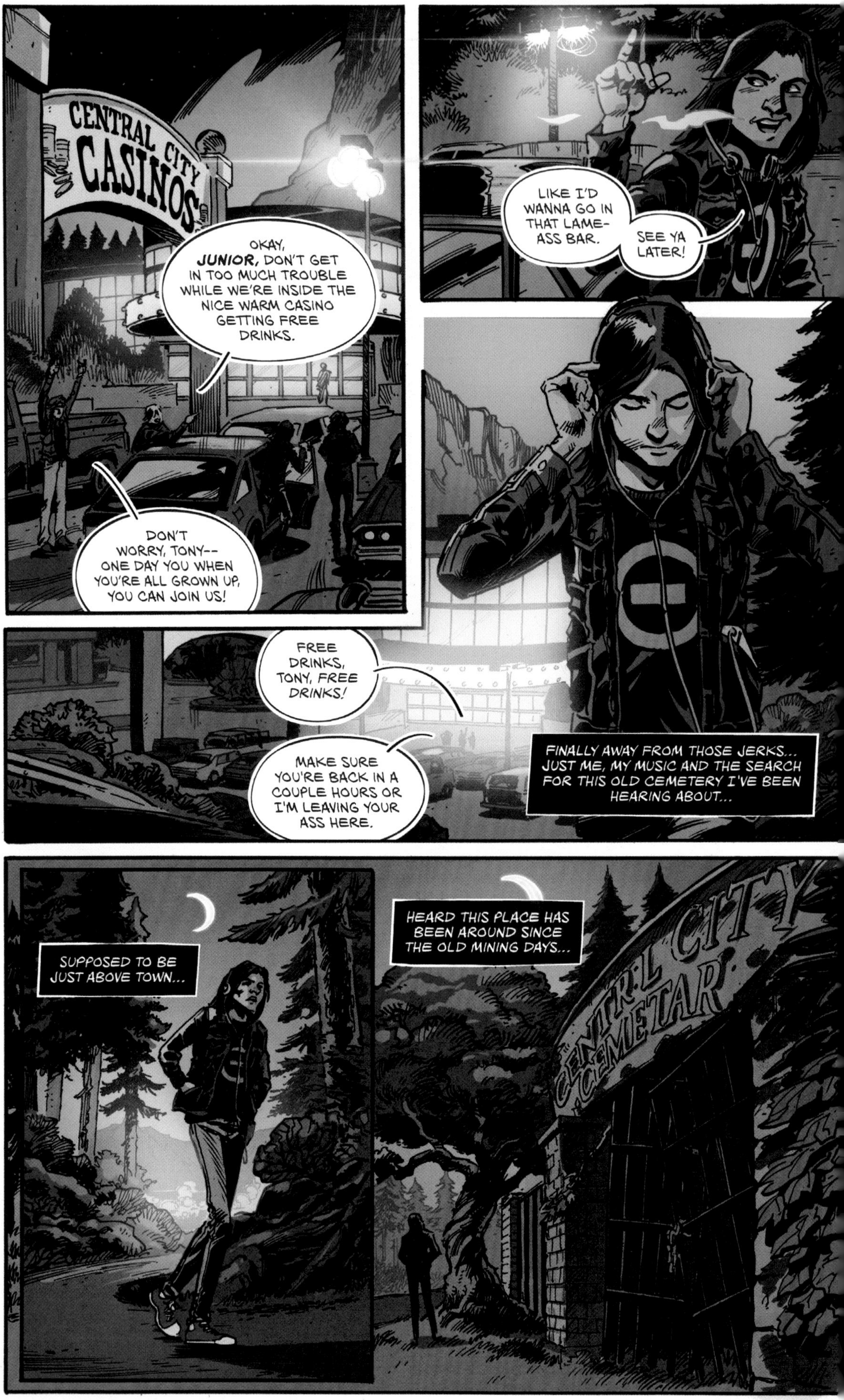
CENTRAL CITY CASINOS
OKAY, **JUNIOR,** DON'T GET IN TOO MUCH TROUBLE WHILE WE'RE INSIDE THE NICE WARM CASINO GETTING FREE DRINKS.
DON'T WORRY, TONY-- ONE DAY YOU WHEN YOU'RE ALL GROWN UP, YOU CAN JOIN US!
LIKE I'D WANNA GO IN THAT LAME-ASS BAR.
SEE YA LATER!
FREE DRINKS, TONY, FREE DRINKS!
MAKE SURE YOU'RE BACK IN A COUPLE HOURS OR I'M LEAVING YOUR ASS HERE.
FINALLY AWAY FROM THOSE JERKS... JUST ME, MY MUSIC AND THE SEARCH FOR THIS OLD CEMETERY I'VE BEEN HEARING ABOUT...
SUPPOSED TO BE JUST ABOVE TOWN...
HEARD THIS PLACE HAS BEEN AROUND SINCE THE OLD MINING DAYS...

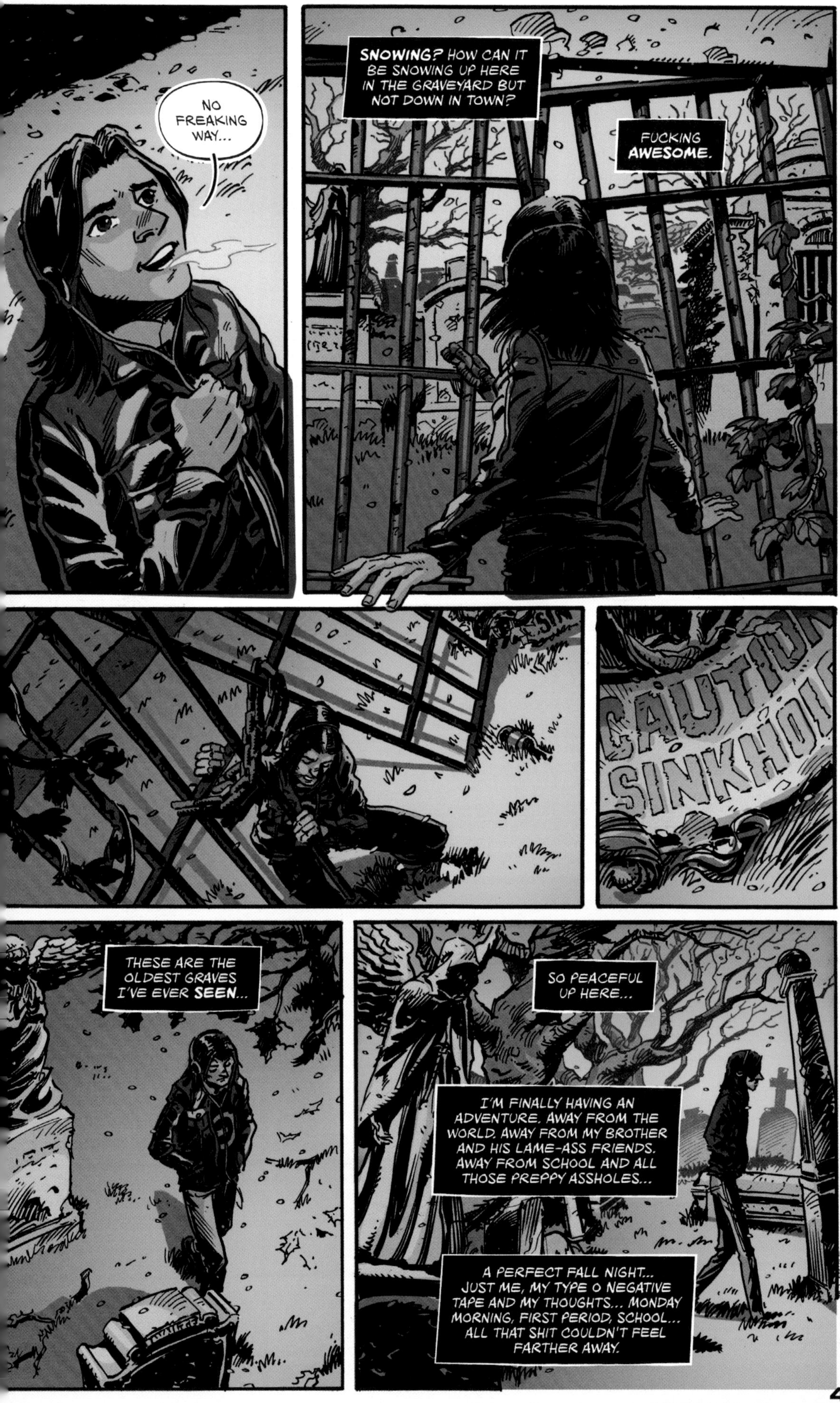
NO FREAKING WAY...
SNOWING? HOW CAN IT BE SNOWING UP HERE IN THE GRAVEYARD BUT NOT DOWN IN TOWN?
FUCKING AWESOME.
CAUTION SINKHOLE
THESE ARE THE OLDEST GRAVES I'VE EVER SEEN...
SO PEACEFUL UP HERE...
I'M FINALLY HAVING AN ADVENTURE. AWAY FROM THE WORLD. AWAY FROM MY BROTHER AND HIS LAME-ASS FRIENDS. AWAY FROM SCHOOL AND ALL THOSE PREPPY ASSHOLES...
A PERFECT FALL NIGHT... JUST ME, MY TYPE O NEGATIVE TAPE AND MY THOUGHTS... MONDAY MORNING, FIRST PERIOD, SCHOOL... ALL THAT SHIT COULDN'T FEEL FARTHER AWAY.

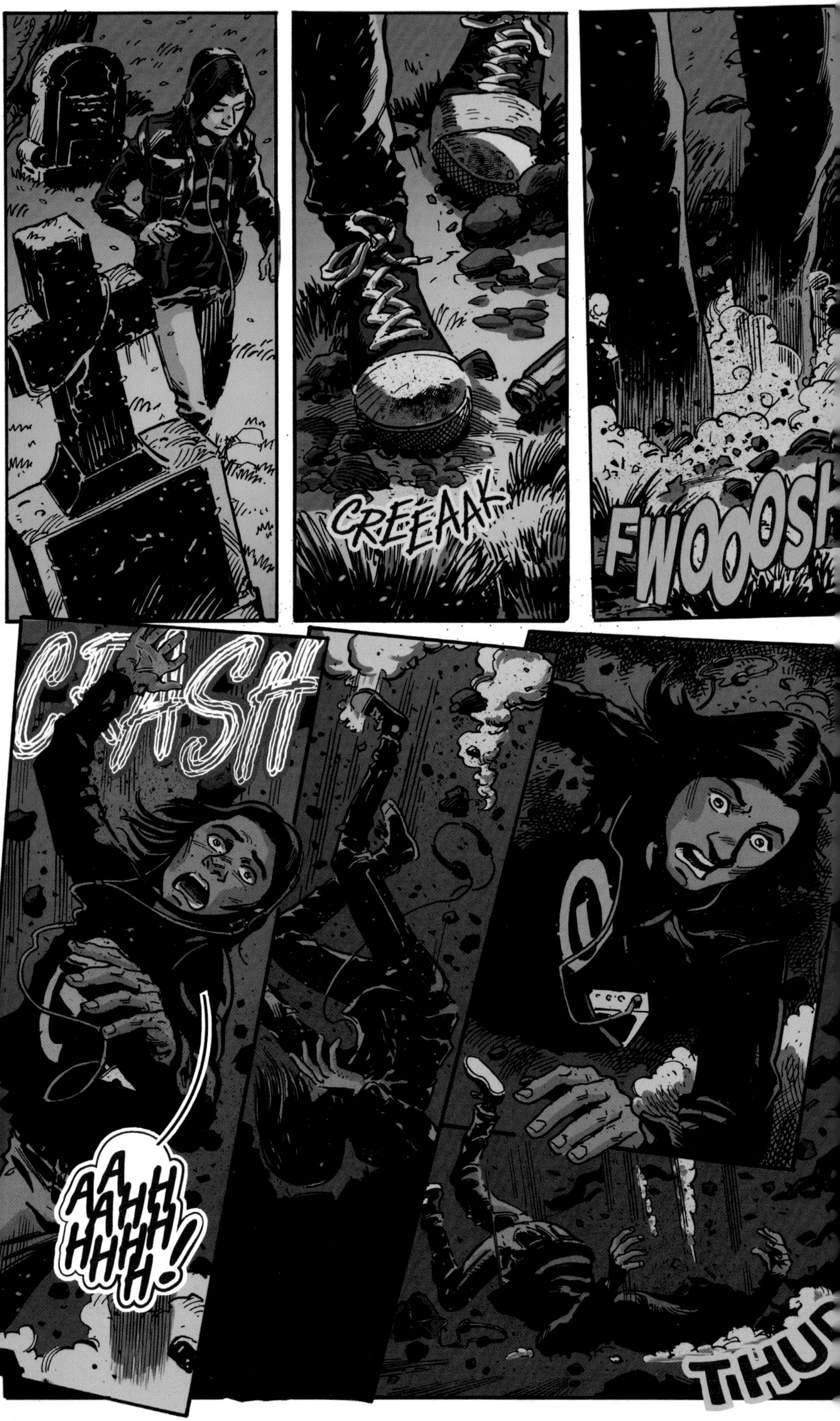
CREEAAK
FWOOOSH
CRASH
AAHHHHHH!
THU

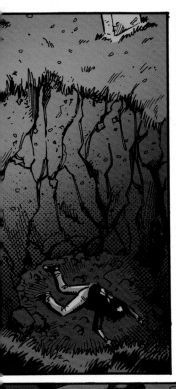

THAT FUCKING HURT...

SINKHOLES? THEY SHOULD PUT UP A SIGN OR SOMETHING... MAYBE AN OLD MINE SHAFT? FELT LIKE FALLING INTO A GRAVE... HEAD STINGS... BUT I GUESS IT COULD'VE BEEN WORSE.

IT'S QUIET DOWN HERE. LIKE **REALLY** FUCKING QUIET. GOTTA BE LIKE TWELVE... FIFTEEN FEET DOWN.

WAIT, WHERE'S MY MUSIC?

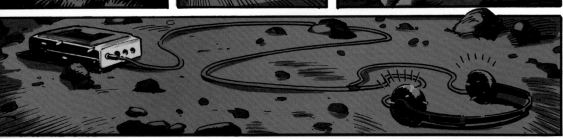

AT LEAST THE WALKMAN'S NOT BUSTED.

NOW... HOW THE HELL DO I CRAWL OUT OF THIS HOLE?

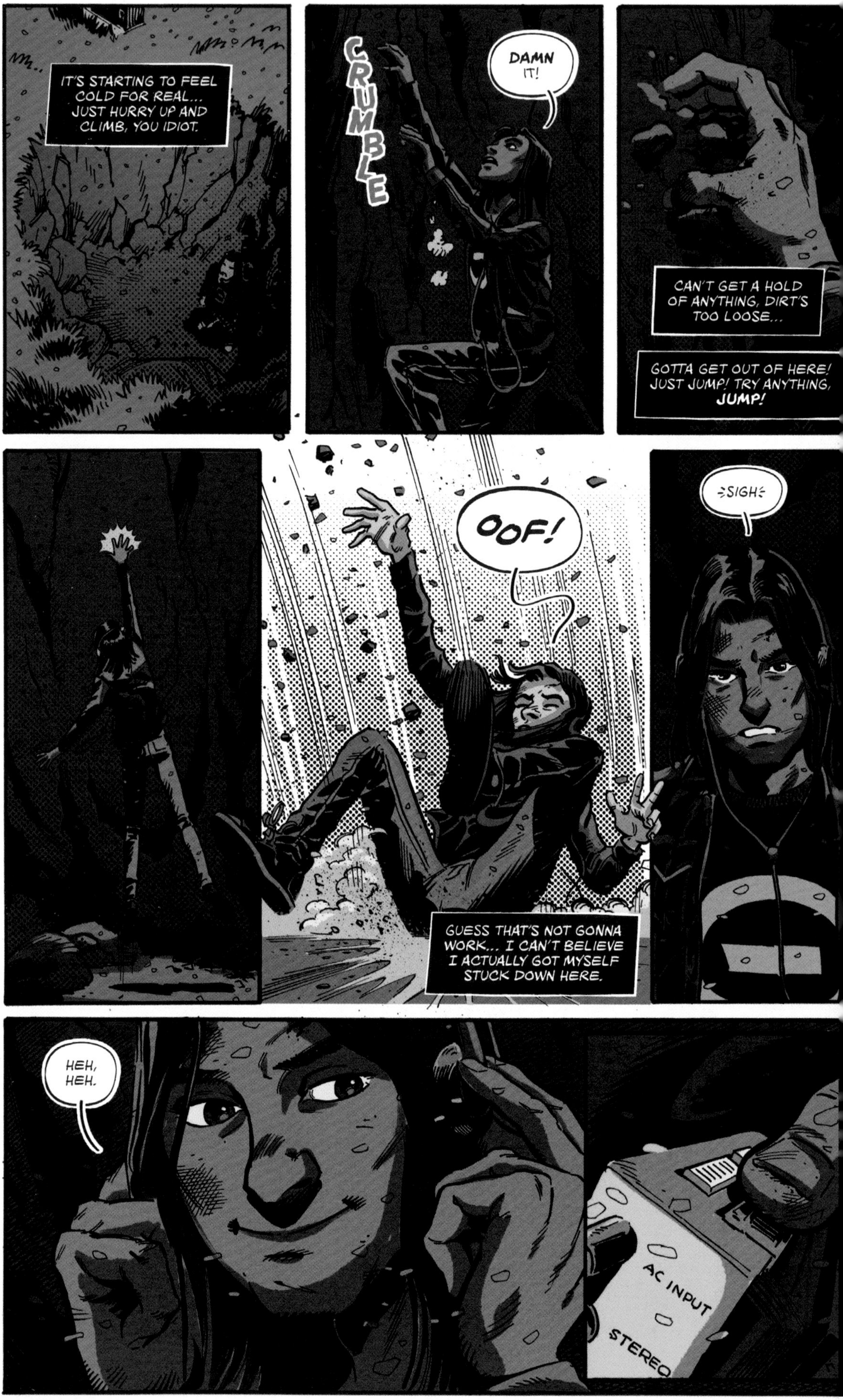
IT'S STARTING TO FEEL COLD FOR REAL... JUST HURRY UP AND CLIMB, YOU IDIOT.
CRUMBLE
DAMN IT!
CAN'T GET A HOLD OF ANYTHING, DIRT'S TOO LOOSE...
GOTTA GET OUT OF HERE! JUST JUMP! TRY ANYTHING, JUMP!
OOF!
GUESS THAT'S NOT GONNA WORK... I CAN'T BELIEVE I ACTUALLY GOT MYSELF STUCK DOWN HERE.
SIGH
HEH, HEH.
AC INPUT
STEREO

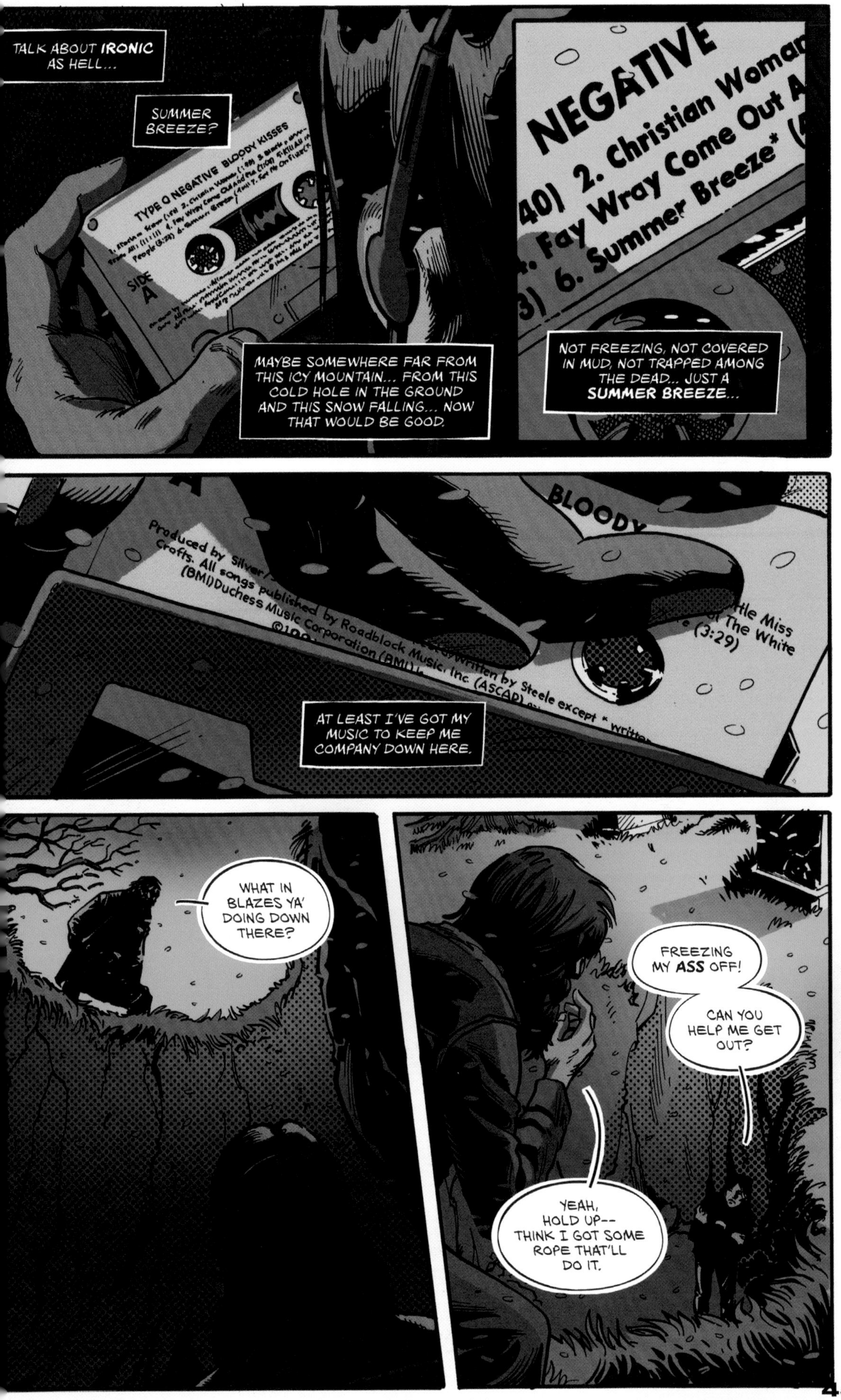
TALK ABOUT IRONIC AS HELL...
SUMMER BREEZE?
NEGATIVE
2. Christian Woman
6. Summer Breeze*
MAYBE SOMEWHERE FAR FROM THIS ICY MOUNTAIN... FROM THIS COLD HOLE IN THE GROUND AND THIS SNOW FALLING... NOW THAT WOULD BE GOOD.
NOT FREEZING, NOT COVERED IN MUD, NOT TRAPPED AMONG THE DEAD... JUST A SUMMER BREEZE...
AT LEAST I'VE GOT MY MUSIC TO KEEP ME COMPANY DOWN HERE.
WHAT IN BLAZES YA' DOING DOWN THERE?
FREEZING MY ASS OFF!
CAN YOU HELP ME GET OUT?
YEAH, HOLD UP-- THINK I GOT SOME ROPE THAT'LL DO IT.

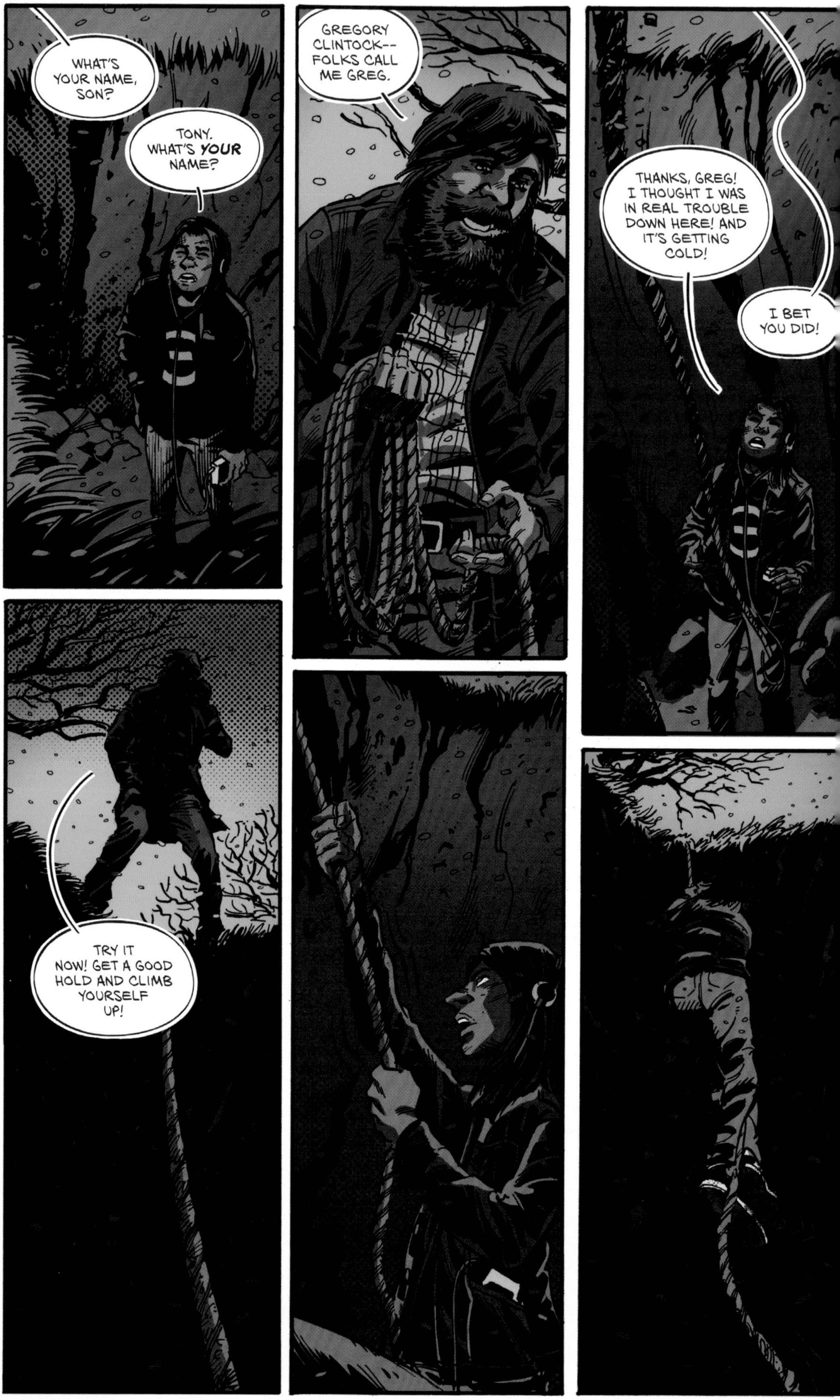
WHAT'S YOUR NAME, SON?
TONY. WHAT'S **YOUR** NAME?
GREGORY CLINTOCK-- FOLKS CALL ME GREG.
THANKS, GREG! I THOUGHT I WAS IN REAL TROUBLE DOWN HERE! AND IT'S GETTING COLD!
I BET YOU DID!
TRY IT NOW! GET A GOOD HOLD AND CLIMB YOURSELF UP!

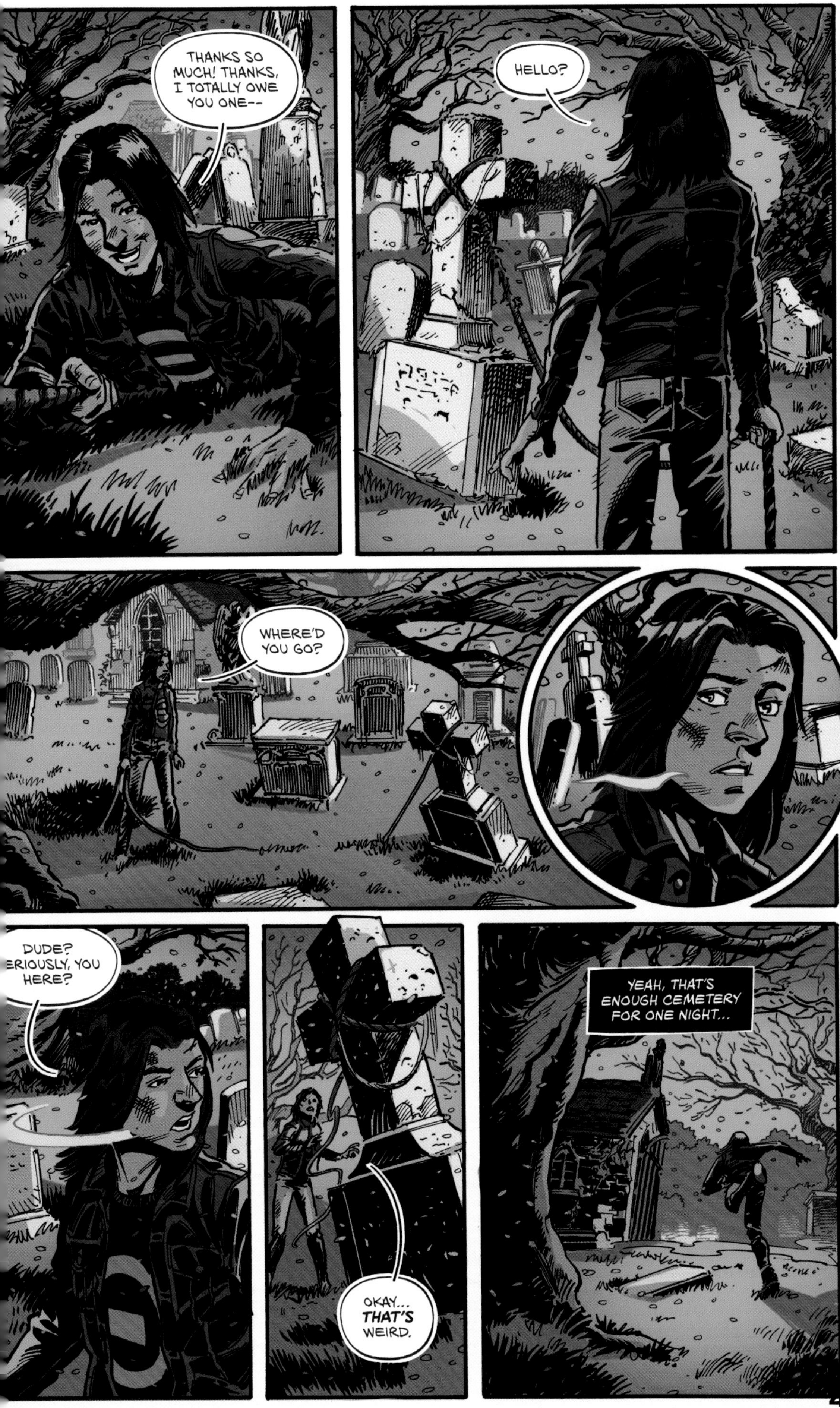
THANKS SO MUCH! THANKS, I TOTALLY OWE YOU ONE--
HELLO?
WHERE'D YOU GO?
DUDE? ERIOUSLY, YOU HERE?
OKAY... THAT'S WEIRD.
YEAH, THAT'S ENOUGH CEMETERY FOR ONE NIGHT...

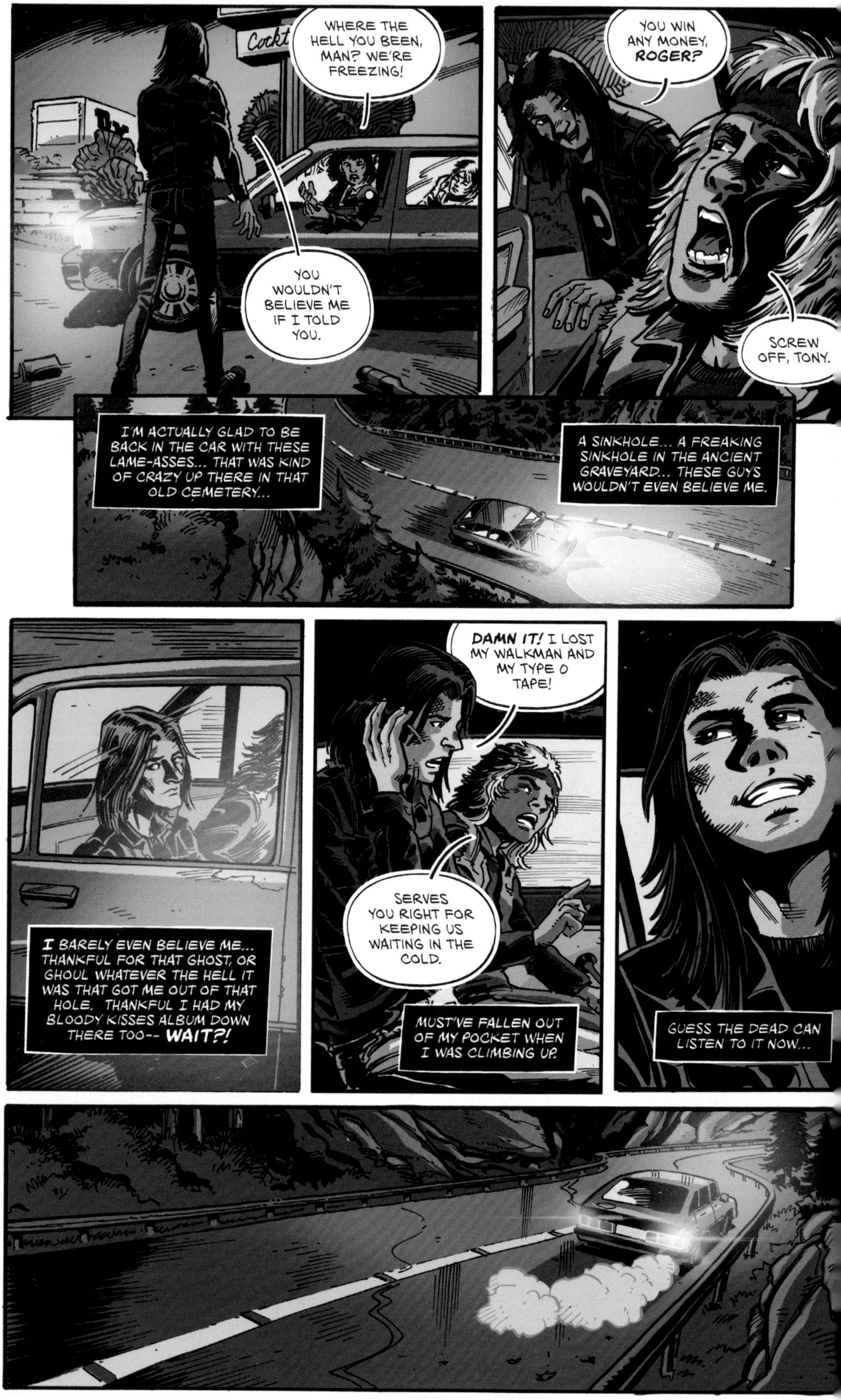
WHERE THE HELL YOU BEEN, MAN? WE'RE FREEZING!
YOU WOULDN'T BELIEVE ME IF I TOLD YOU.
YOU WIN ANY MONEY, ROGER?
SCREW OFF, TONY.
I'M ACTUALLY GLAD TO BE BACK IN THE CAR WITH THESE LAME-ASSES... THAT WAS KIND OF CRAZY UP THERE IN THAT OLD CEMETERY...
A SINKHOLE... A FREAKING SINKHOLE IN THE ANCIENT GRAVEYARD... THESE GUYS WOULDN'T EVEN BELIEVE ME.
I BARELY EVEN BELIEVE ME... THANKFUL FOR THAT GHOST, OR GHOUL WHATEVER THE HELL IT WAS THAT GOT ME OUT OF THAT HOLE. THANKFUL I HAD MY BLOODY KISSES ALBUM DOWN THERE TOO-- WAIT?!
DAMN IT! I LOST MY WALKMAN AND MY TYPE O TAPE!
SERVES YOU RIGHT FOR KEEPING US WAITING IN THE COLD.
MUST'VE FALLEN OUT OF MY POCKET WHEN I WAS CLIMBING UP.
GUESS THE DEAD CAN LISTEN TO IT NOW...

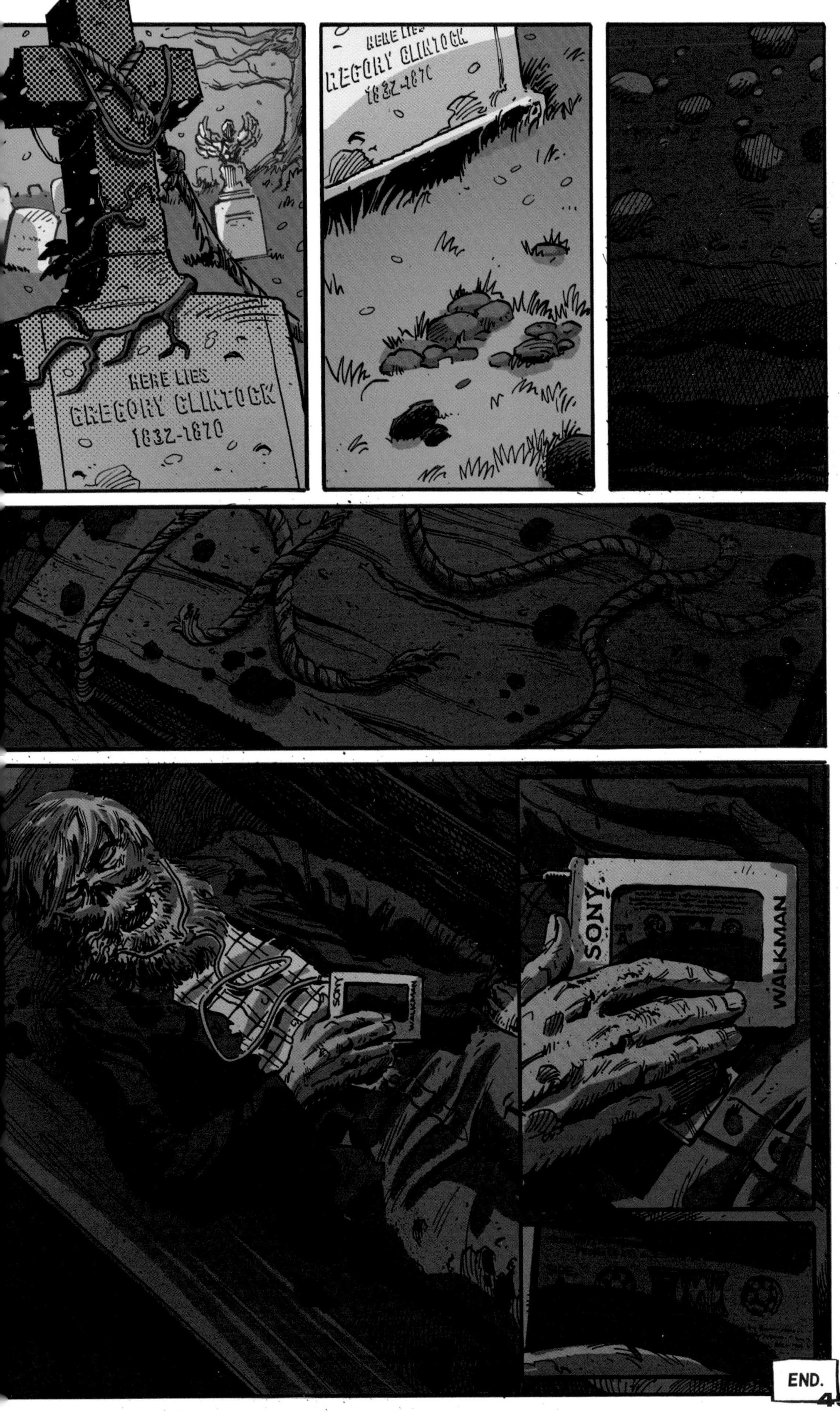
HERE LIES
GREGORY CLINTOCK
1832-1870
SONY
WALKMAN
END.

SET ME ON FIRE

WRITER: MICHAEL PATRICK SULLIVAN
ARTIST: GUSTAVO NOVAES
LETTERER: BUDDY BEAUDOIN

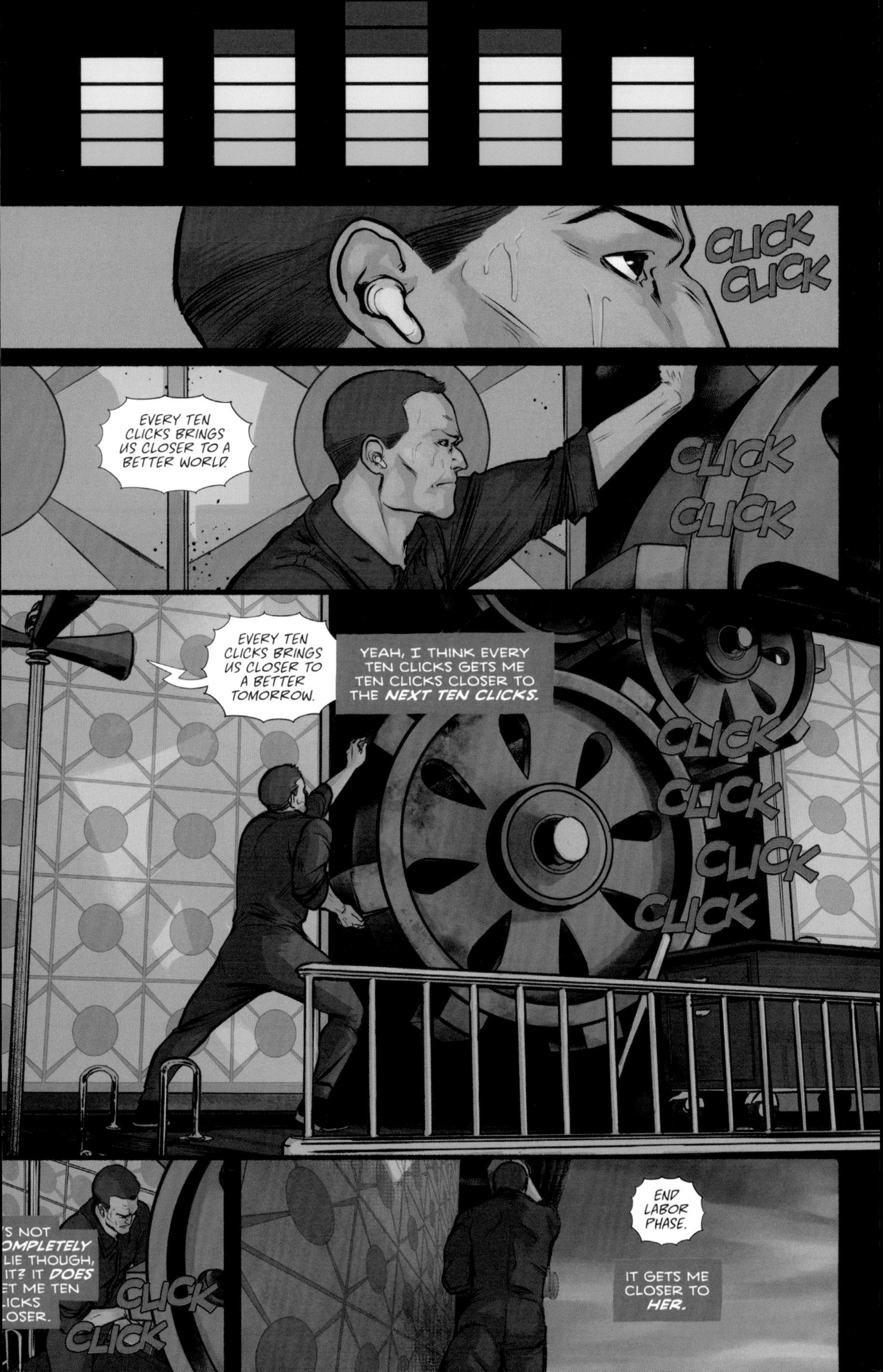
CLICK CLICK
EVERY TEN CLICKS BRINGS US CLOSER TO A BETTER WORLD.
CLICK CLICK
EVERY TEN CLICKS BRINGS US CLOSER TO A BETTER TOMORROW.
YEAH, I THINK EVERY TEN CLICKS GETS ME TEN CLICKS CLOSER TO THE *NEXT TEN CLICKS.*
CLICK CLICK CLICK CLICK
'S NOT *OMPLETELY* LIE THOUGH, IT? IT *DOES* ET ME TEN LICKS LOSER.
CLICK CLICK
END LABOR PHASE.
IT GETS ME CLOSER TO *HER.*

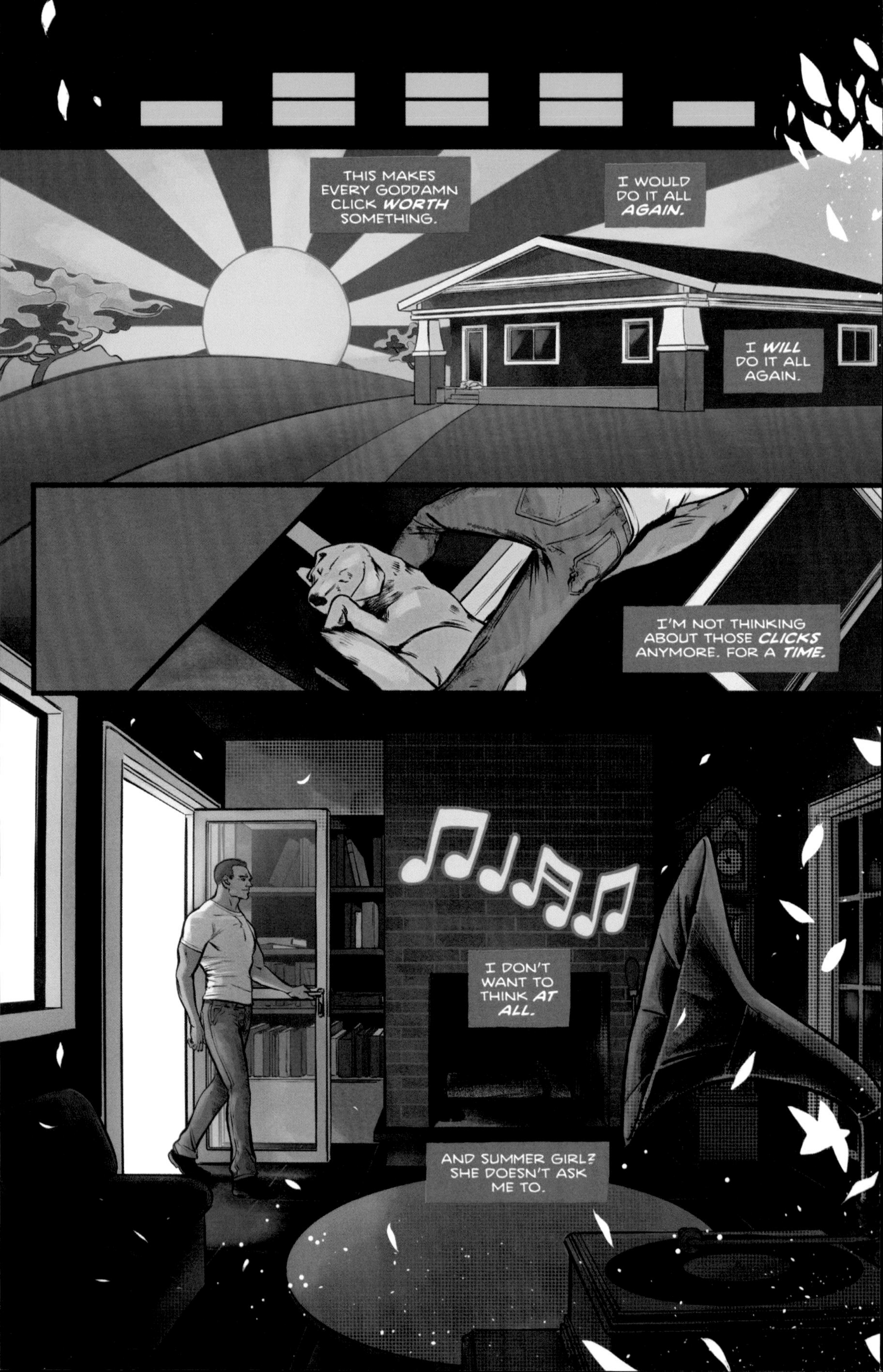
THIS MAKES EVERY GODDAMN CLICK WORTH SOMETHING.
I WOULD DO IT ALL AGAIN.
I WILL DO IT ALL AGAIN.
I'M NOT THINKING ABOUT THOSE CLICKS ANYMORE. FOR A TIME.
I DON'T WANT TO THINK AT ALL.
AND SUMMER GIRL? SHE DOESN'T ASK ME TO.

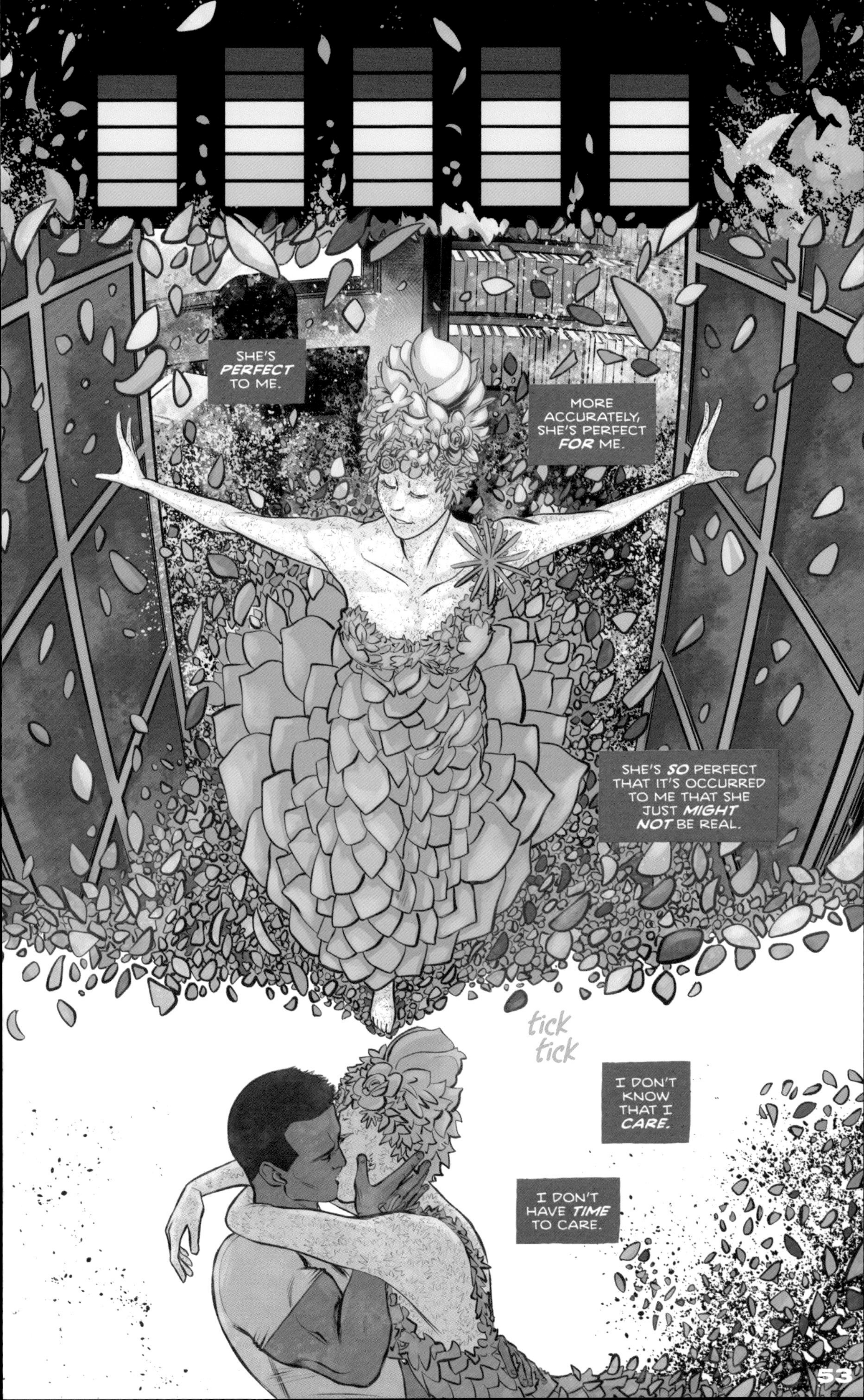

SHE'S PERFECT TO ME.
MORE ACCURATELY, SHE'S PERFECT FOR ME.
SHE'S SO PERFECT THAT IT'S OCCURRED TO ME THAT SHE JUST MIGHT NOT BE REAL.
tick tick
I DON'T KNOW THAT I CARE.
I DON'T HAVE TIME TO CARE.

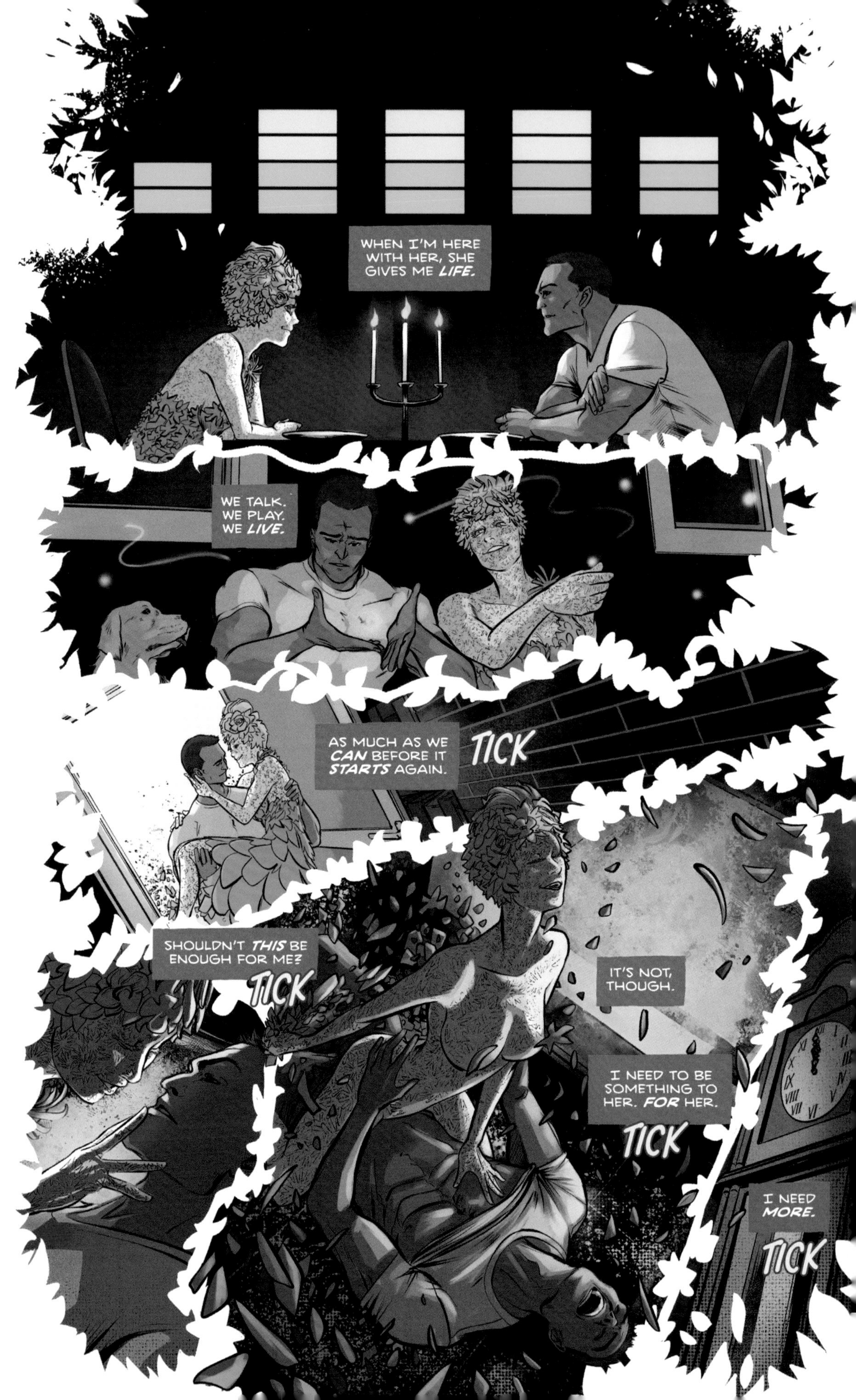
WHEN I'M HERE WITH HER, SHE GIVES ME LIFE.
WE TALK. WE PLAY. WE LIVE.
AS MUCH AS WE CAN BEFORE IT STARTS AGAIN.
TICK
SHOULDN'T THIS BE ENOUGH FOR ME?
TICK
IT'S NOT, THOUGH.
I NEED TO BE SOMETHING TO HER. FOR HER.
TICK
I NEED MORE.
TICK

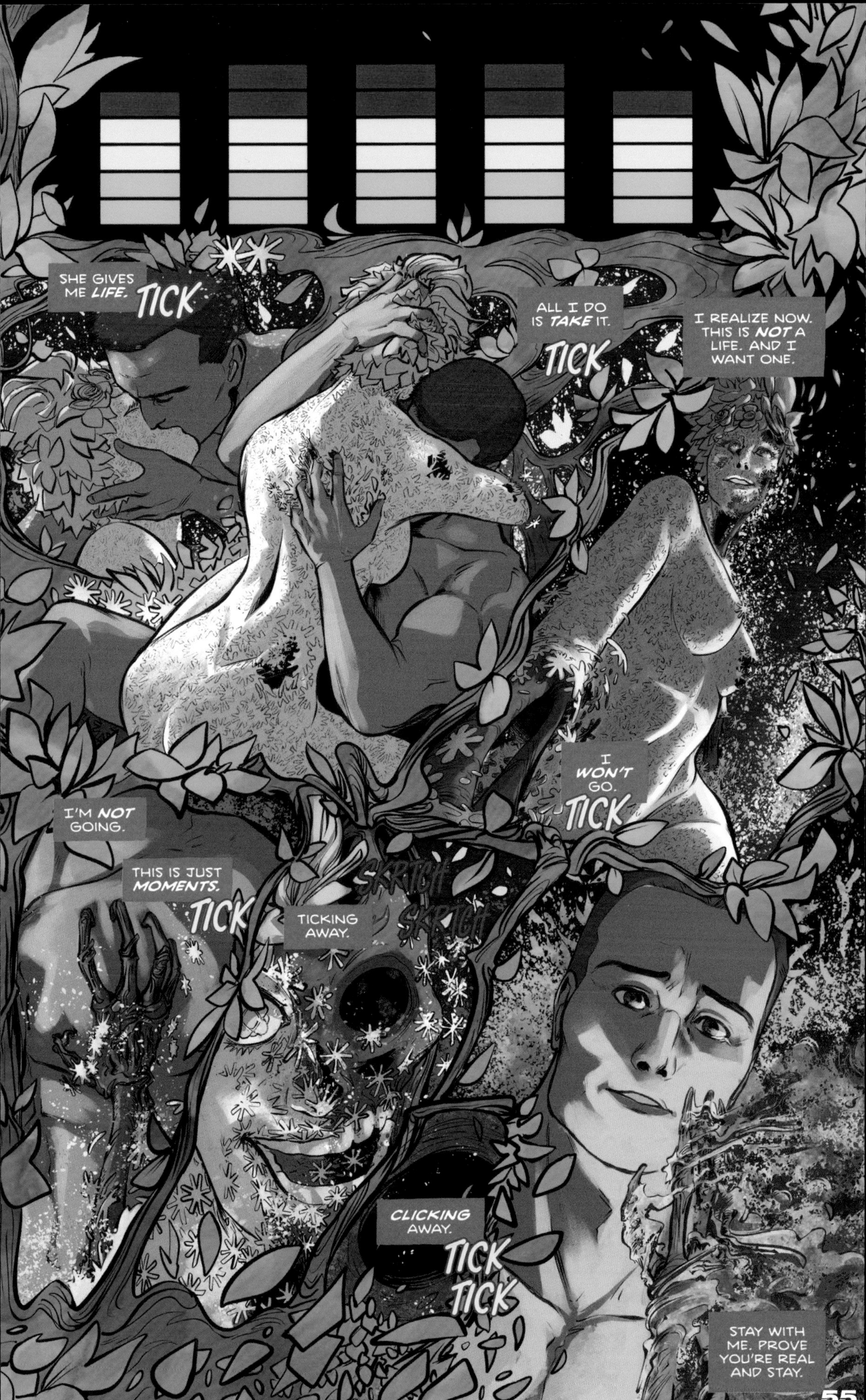
SHE GIVES ME *LIFE.*
TICK
ALL I DO IS *TAKE* IT.
TICK
I REALIZE NOW. THIS IS *NOT* A LIFE. AND I WANT ONE.
I *WON'T* GO.
TICK
I'M *NOT* GOING.
THIS IS JUST *MOMENTS.*
TICK
TICKING AWAY.
SKRTCH
SKRTCH
CLICKING AWAY.
TICK
TICK
STAY WITH ME. PROVE YOU'RE REAL AND STAY.

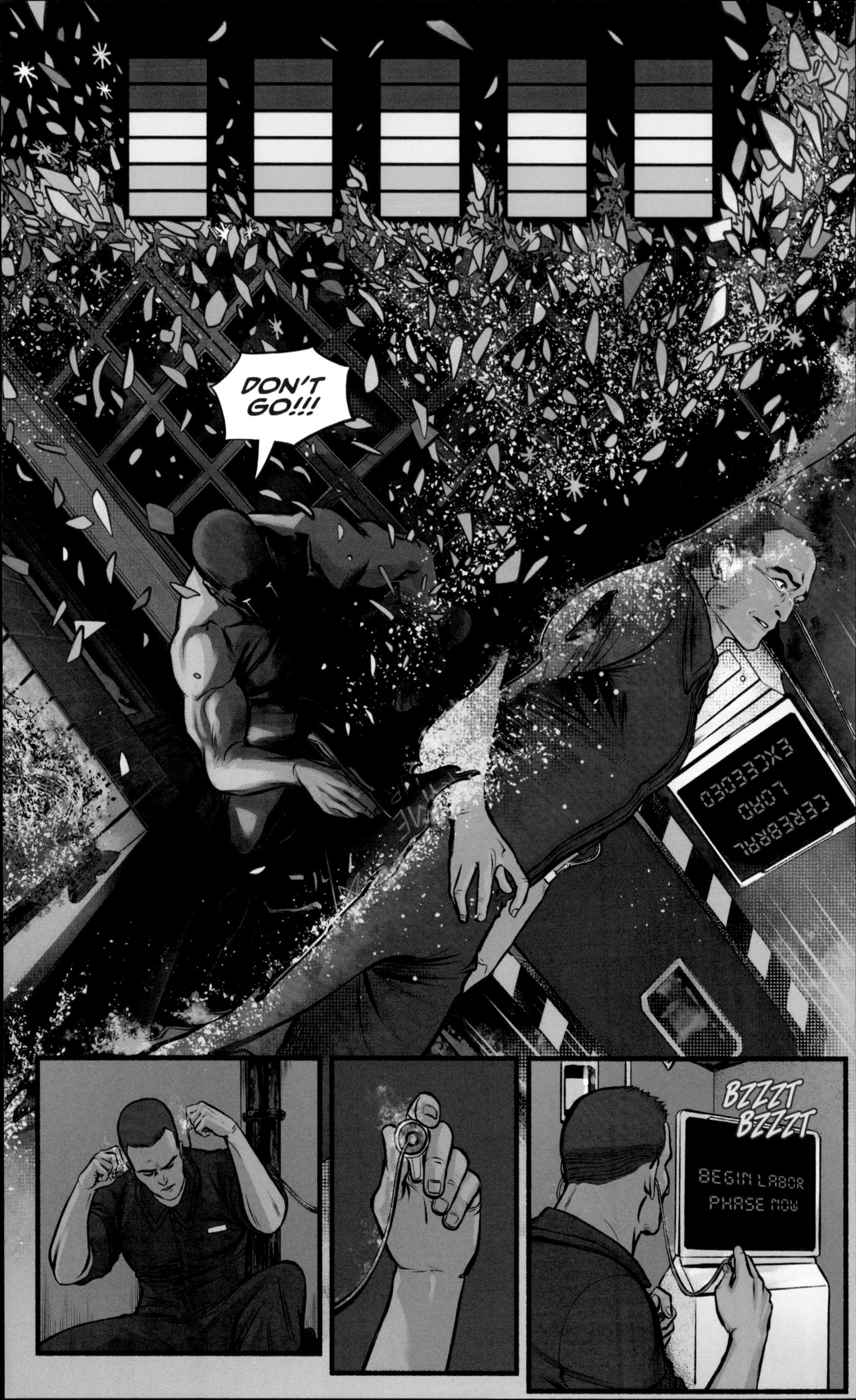
DON'T GO!!!
CEREBRAL LOAD EXCEEDED
BZZZT
BZZZT
BEGIN LABOR PHASE NOW

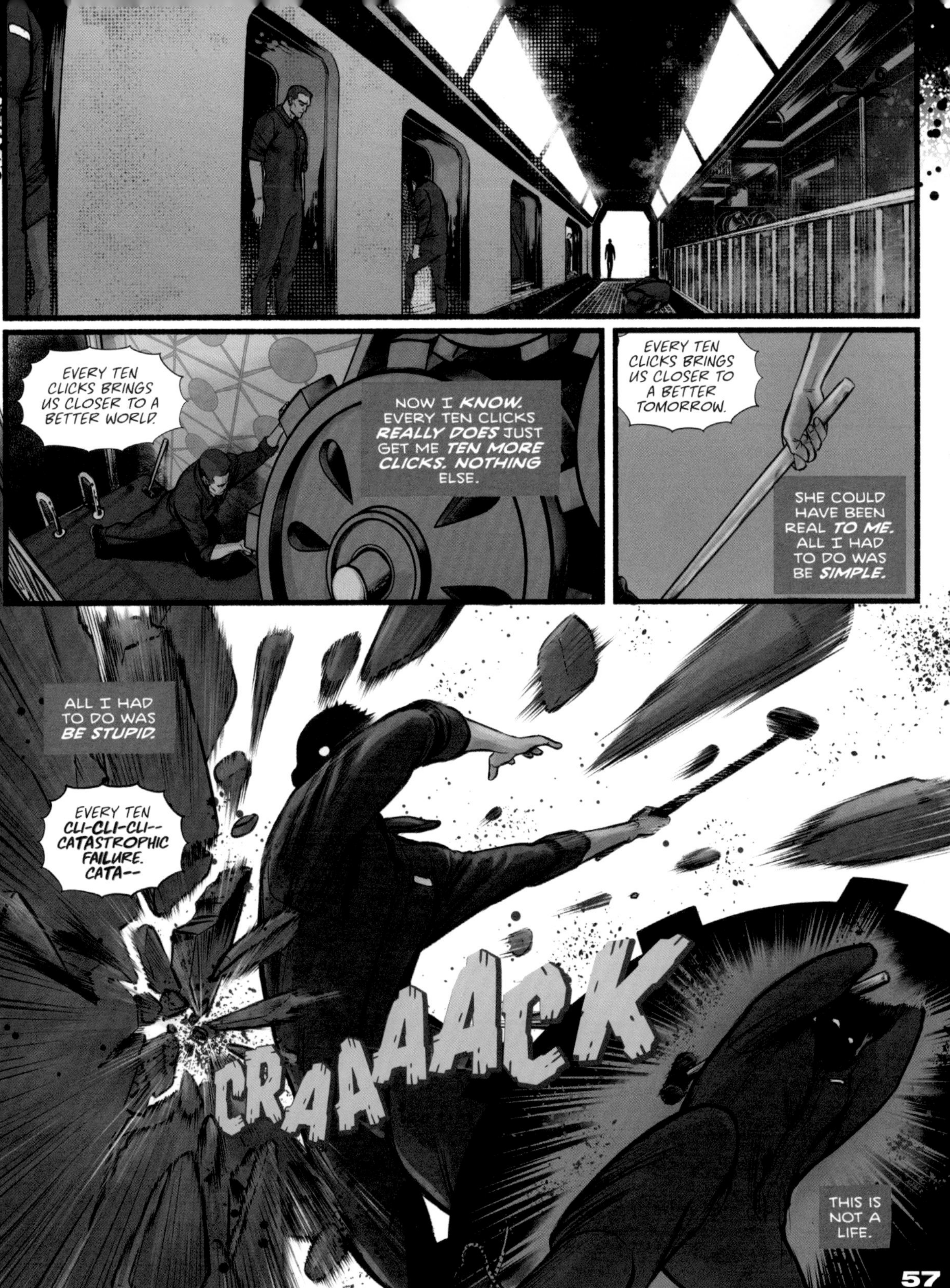

EVERY TEN CLICKS BRINGS US CLOSER TO A BETTER WORLD.
NOW I KNOW. EVERY TEN CLICKS REALLY DOES JUST GET ME TEN MORE CLICKS. NOTHING ELSE.
EVERY TEN CLICKS BRINGS US CLOSER TO A BETTER TOMORROW.
SHE COULD HAVE BEEN REAL TO ME. ALL I HAD TO DO WAS BE SIMPLE.
ALL I HAD TO DO WAS BE STUPID.
EVERY TEN CLI-CLI-CLI-- CATASTROPHIC FAILURE. CATA--
CRAAAACK
THIS IS NOT A LIFE.

DON'T MISTAKE LACK

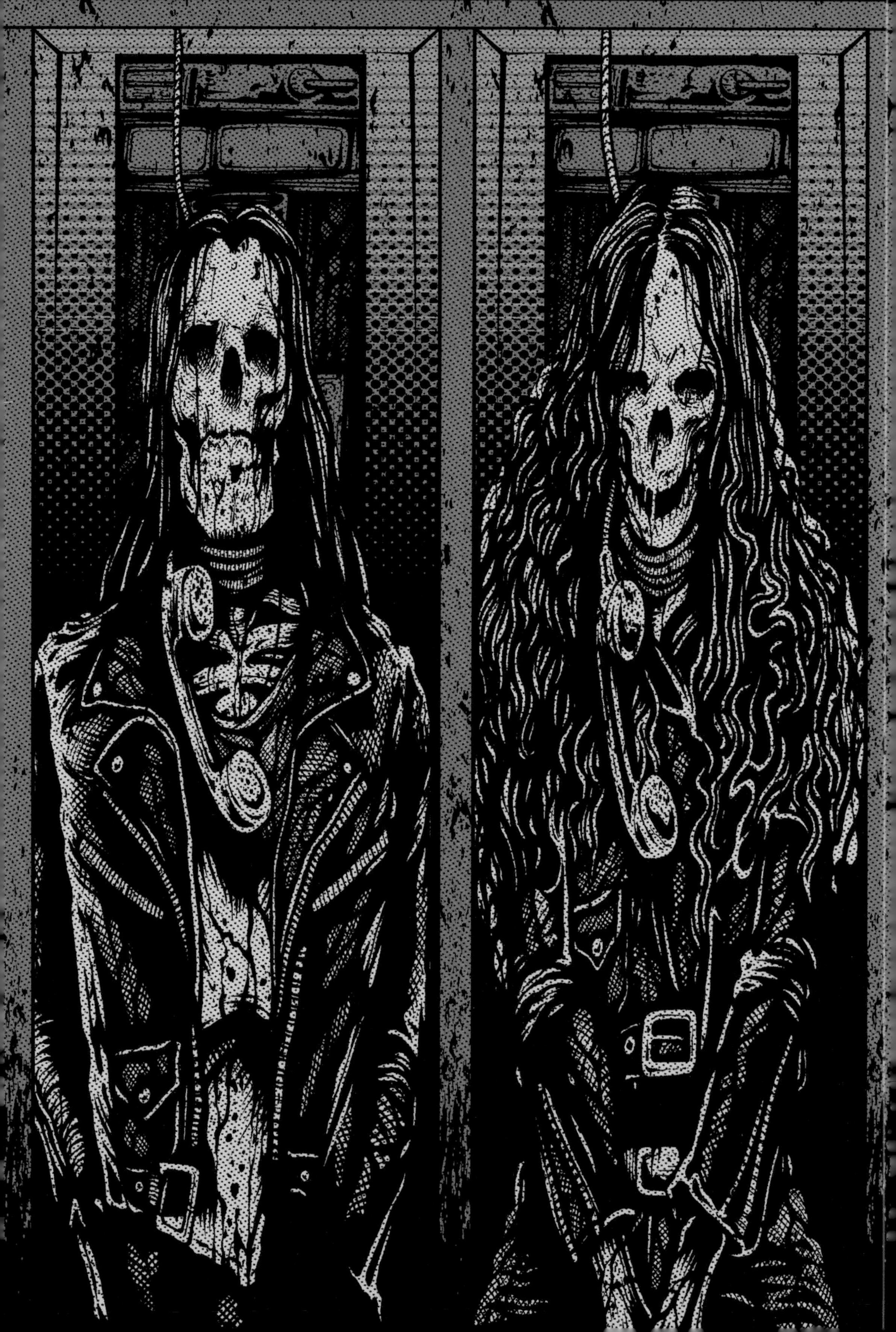

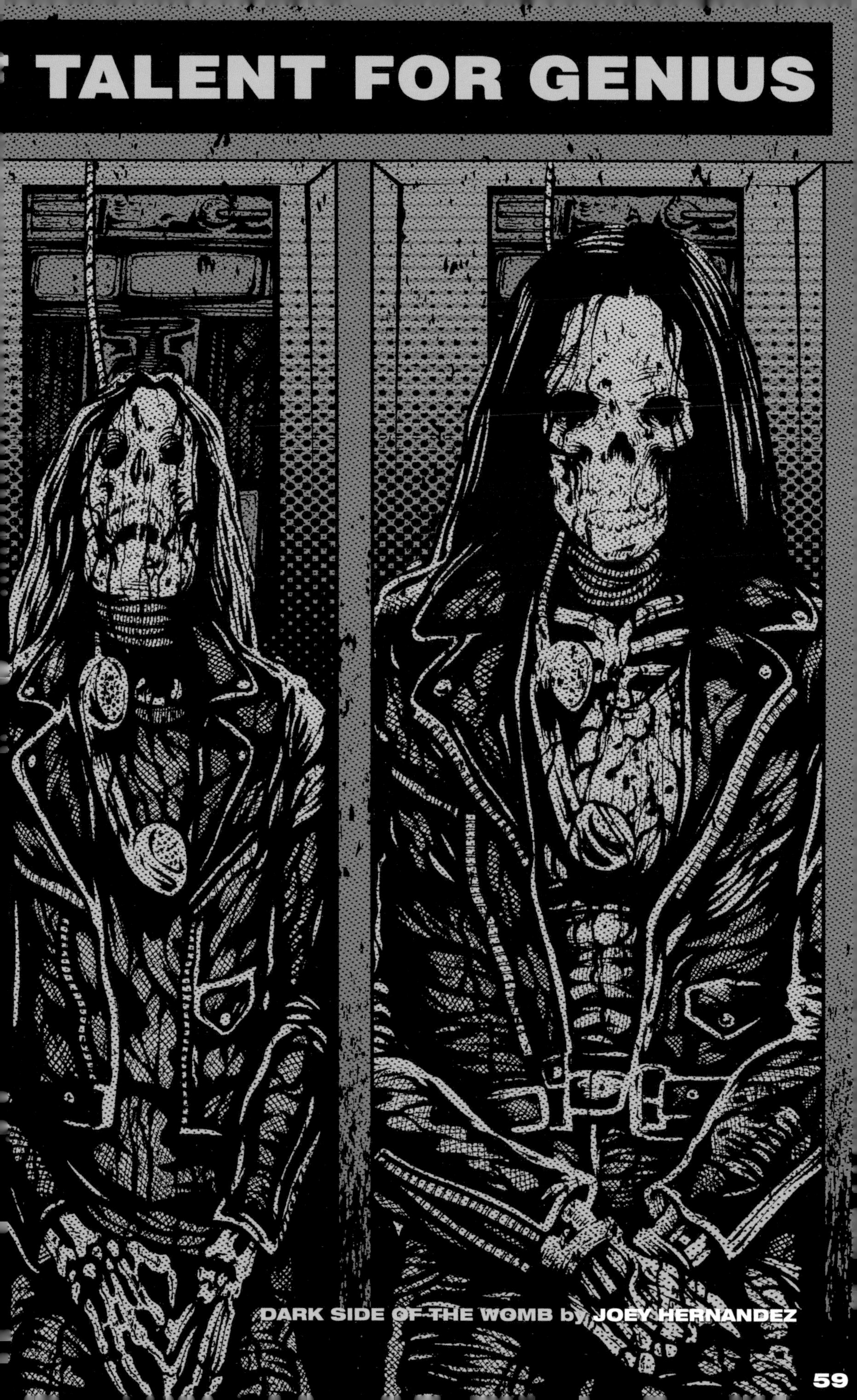
TALENT FOR GENIUS
DARK SIDE OF THE WOMB by JOEY HERNANDEZ

WE HATE EVERYONE

WRITER AND ARTIST: ALAN ROBERT
COLORIST: JAY FOTOS

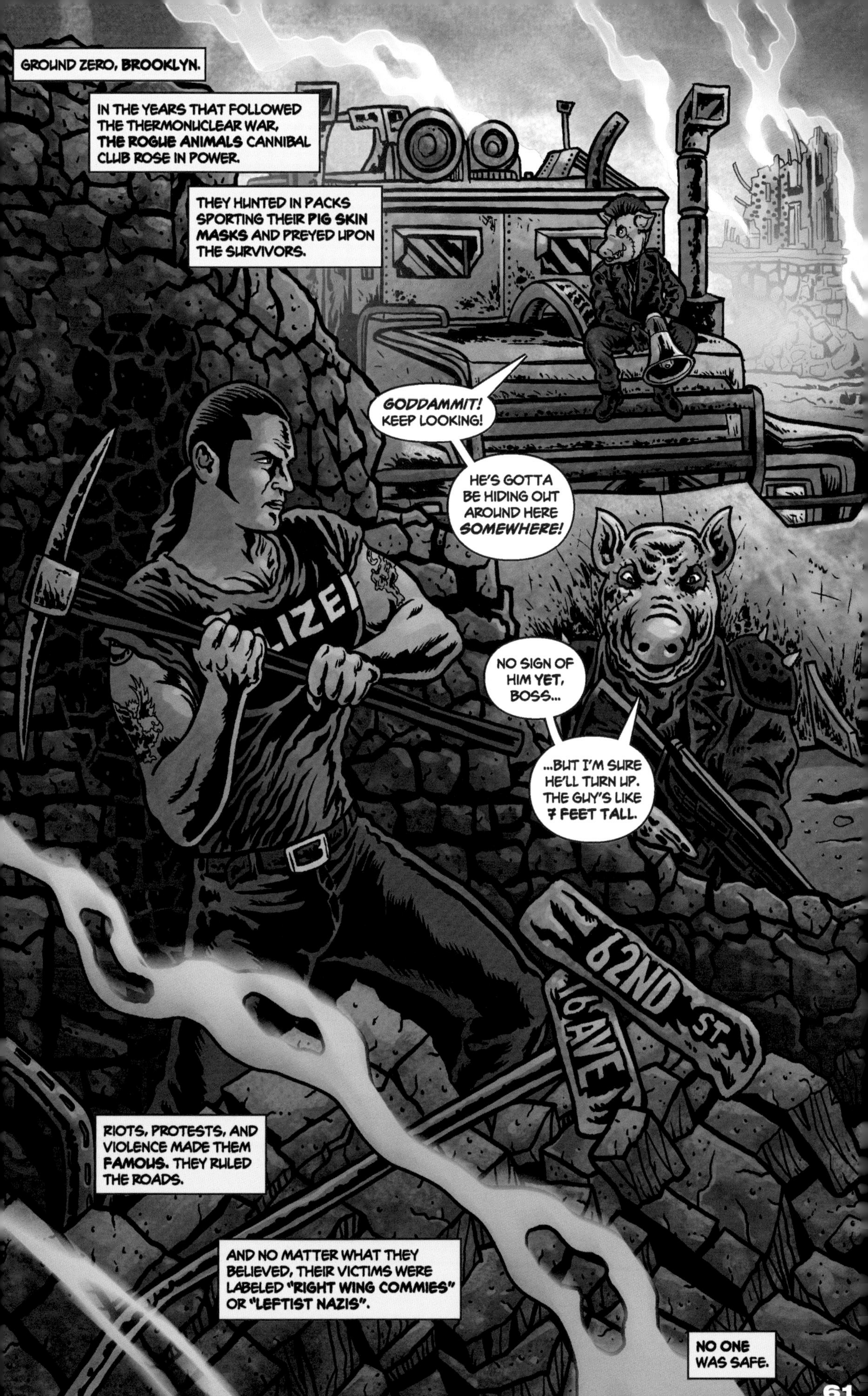

GROUND ZERO, **BROOKLYN.**
IN THE YEARS THAT FOLLOWED THE THERMONUCLEAR WAR, **THE ROGUE ANIMALS** CANNIBAL CLUB ROSE IN POWER.
THEY HUNTED IN PACKS SPORTING THEIR **PIG SKIN MASKS** AND PREYED UPON THE SURVIVORS.
GODDAMMIT! KEEP LOOKING!
HE'S GOTTA BE HIDING OUT AROUND HERE *SOMEWHERE!*
NO SIGN OF HIM YET, BOSS...
...BUT I'M SURE HE'LL TURN UP. THE GUY'S LIKE **7 FEET TALL.**
62ND ST
16 AVE
RIOTS, PROTESTS, AND VIOLENCE MADE THEM **FAMOUS.** THEY RULED THE ROADS.
AND NO MATTER WHAT THEY BELIEVED, THEIR VICTIMS WERE LABELED **"RIGHT WING COMMIES"** OR **"LEFTIST NAZIS".**
NO ONE WAS SAFE.

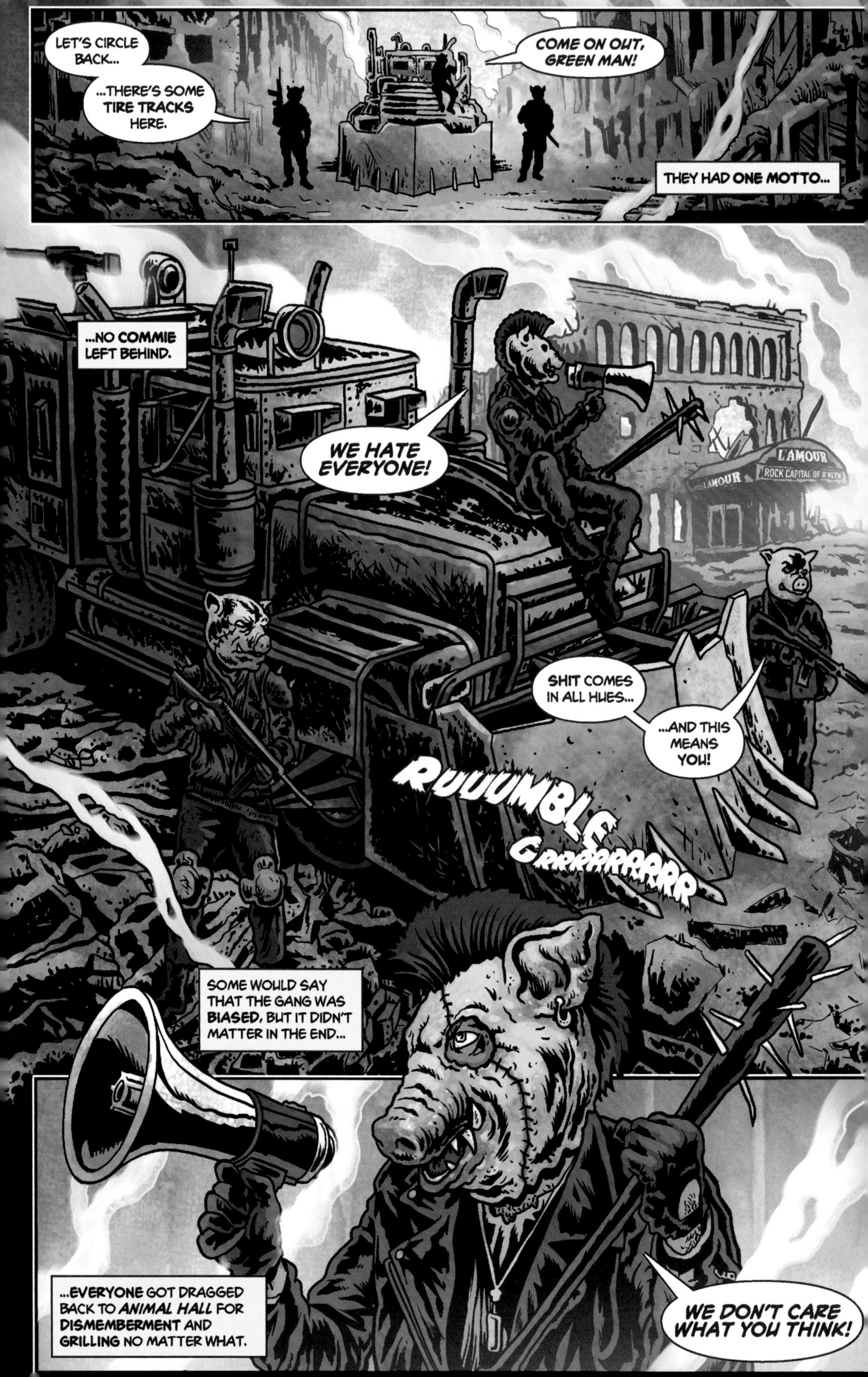
LET'S CIRCLE BACK...
...THERE'S SOME TIRE TRACKS HERE.
COME ON OUT, GREEN MAN!
THEY HAD ONE MOTTO...
...NO COMMIE LEFT BEHIND.
WE HATE EVERYONE!
L'AMOUR
ROCK CAPITAL OF B'KLYN
L'AMOUR
SHIT COMES IN ALL HUES...
...AND THIS MEANS YOU!
RUUUMBLE
GRRRRRRRRR
SOME WOULD SAY THAT THE GANG WAS BIASED, BUT IT DIDN'T MATTER IN THE END...
...EVERYONE GOT DRAGGED BACK TO ANIMAL HALL FOR DISMEMBERMENT AND GRILLING NO MATTER WHAT.
WE DON'T CARE WHAT YOU THINK!

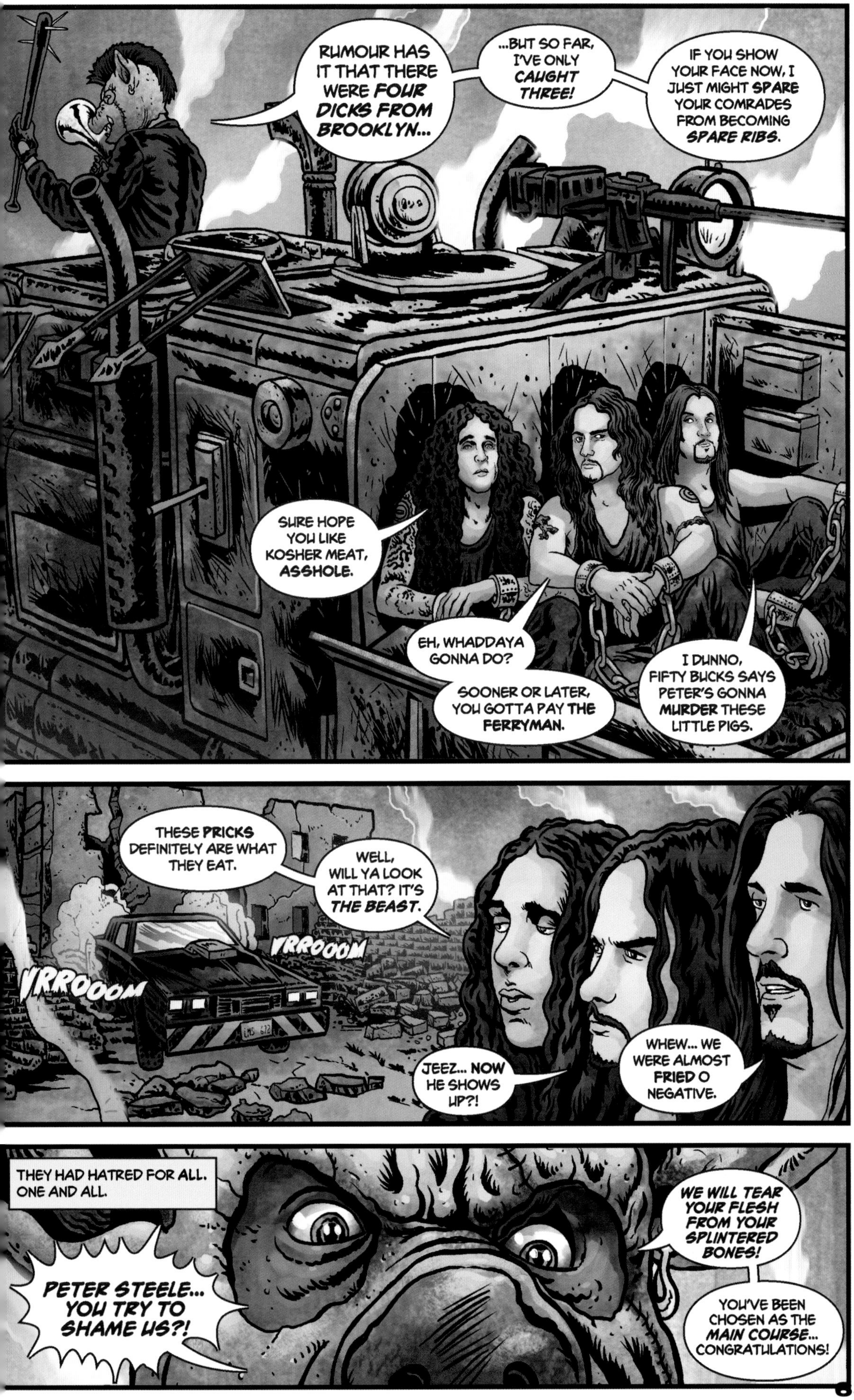
RUMOUR HAS IT THAT THERE WERE FOUR DICKS FROM BROOKLYN...
...BUT SO FAR, I'VE ONLY CAUGHT THREE!
IF YOU SHOW YOUR FACE NOW, I JUST MIGHT SPARE YOUR COMRADES FROM BECOMING SPARE RIBS.
SURE HOPE YOU LIKE KOSHER MEAT, ASSHOLE.
EH, WHADDAYA GONNA DO?
SOONER OR LATER, YOU GOTTA PAY THE FERRYMAN.
I DUNNO, FIFTY BUCKS SAYS PETER'S GONNA MURDER THESE LITTLE PIGS.
THESE PRICKS DEFINITELY ARE WHAT THEY EAT.
WELL, WILL YA LOOK AT THAT? IT'S THE BEAST.
VRROOOM
VRROOOM
JEEZ... NOW HE SHOWS UP?!
WHEW... WE WERE ALMOST FRIED O NEGATIVE.
THEY HAD HATRED FOR ALL. ONE AND ALL.
PETER STEELE... YOU TRY TO SHAME US?!
WE WILL TEAR YOUR FLESH FROM YOUR SPLINTERED BONES!
YOU'VE BEEN CHOSEN AS THE MAIN COURSE... CONGRATULATIONS!

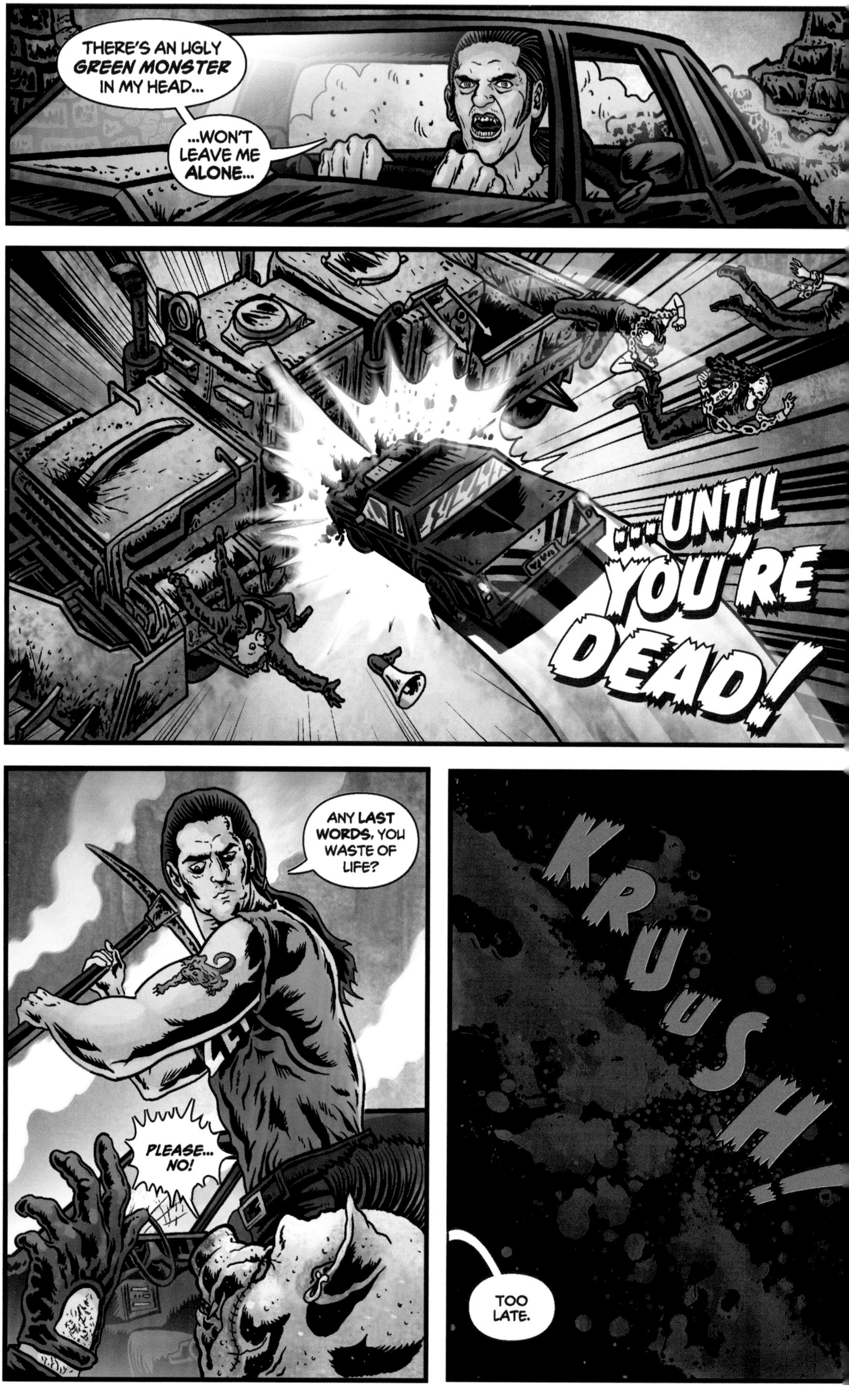
THERE'S AN UGLY GREEN MONSTER IN MY HEAD...
...WON'T LEAVE ME ALONE...
...UNTIL YOU'RE DEAD!
ANY LAST WORDS, YOU WASTE OF LIFE?
PLEASE... NO!
KRUUSH!
TOO LATE.

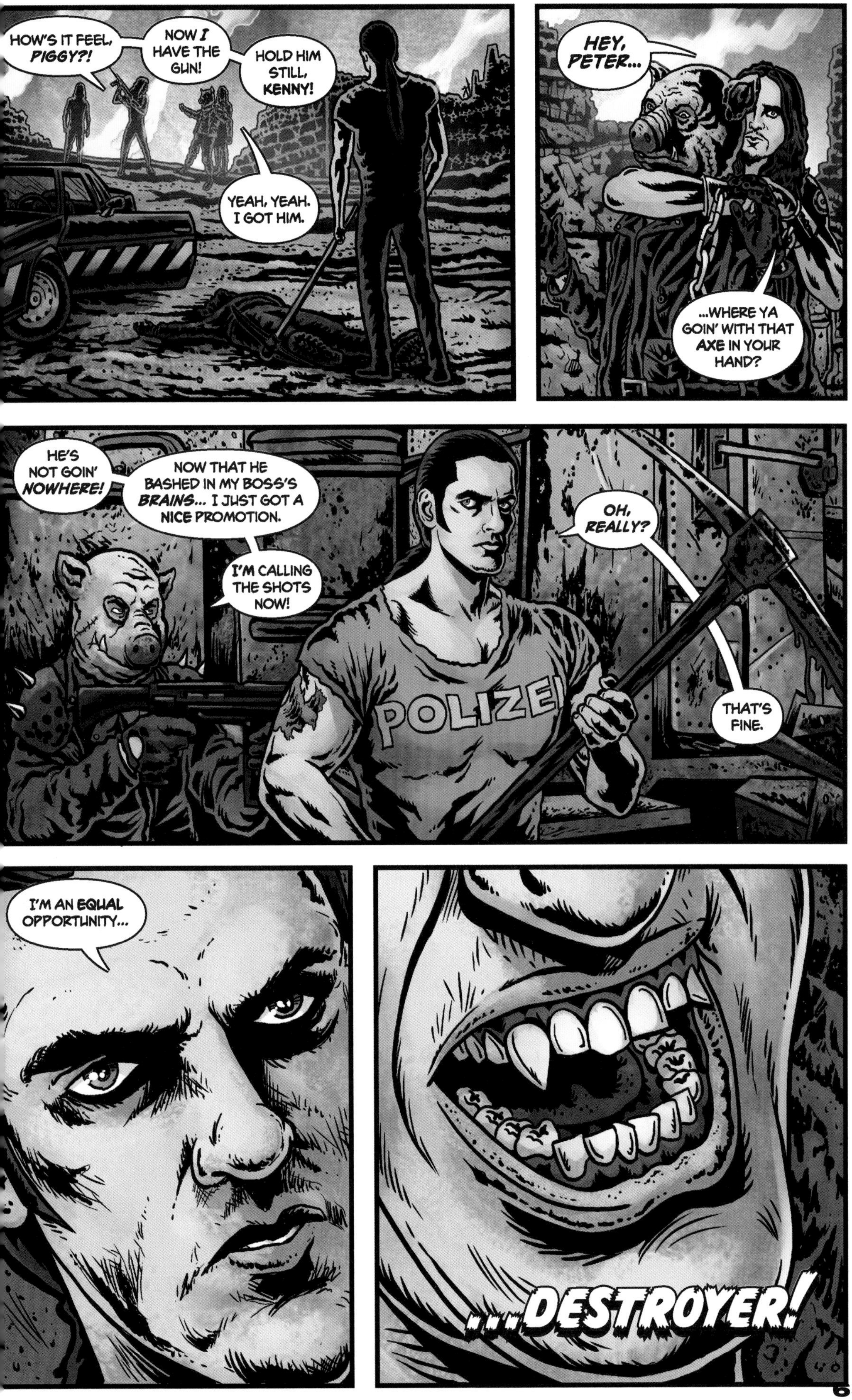
HOW'S IT FEEL, PIGGY?!
NOW I HAVE THE GUN!
HOLD HIM STILL, KENNY!
YEAH, YEAH. I GOT HIM.
HEY, PETER...
...WHERE YA GOIN' WITH THAT AXE IN YOUR HAND?
HE'S NOT GOIN' NOWHERE!
NOW THAT HE BASHED IN MY BOSS'S BRAINS... I JUST GOT A NICE PROMOTION.
I'M CALLING THE SHOTS NOW!
OH, REALLY?
POLIZEI
THAT'S FINE.
I'M AN EQUAL OPPORTUNITY...
...DESTROYER!

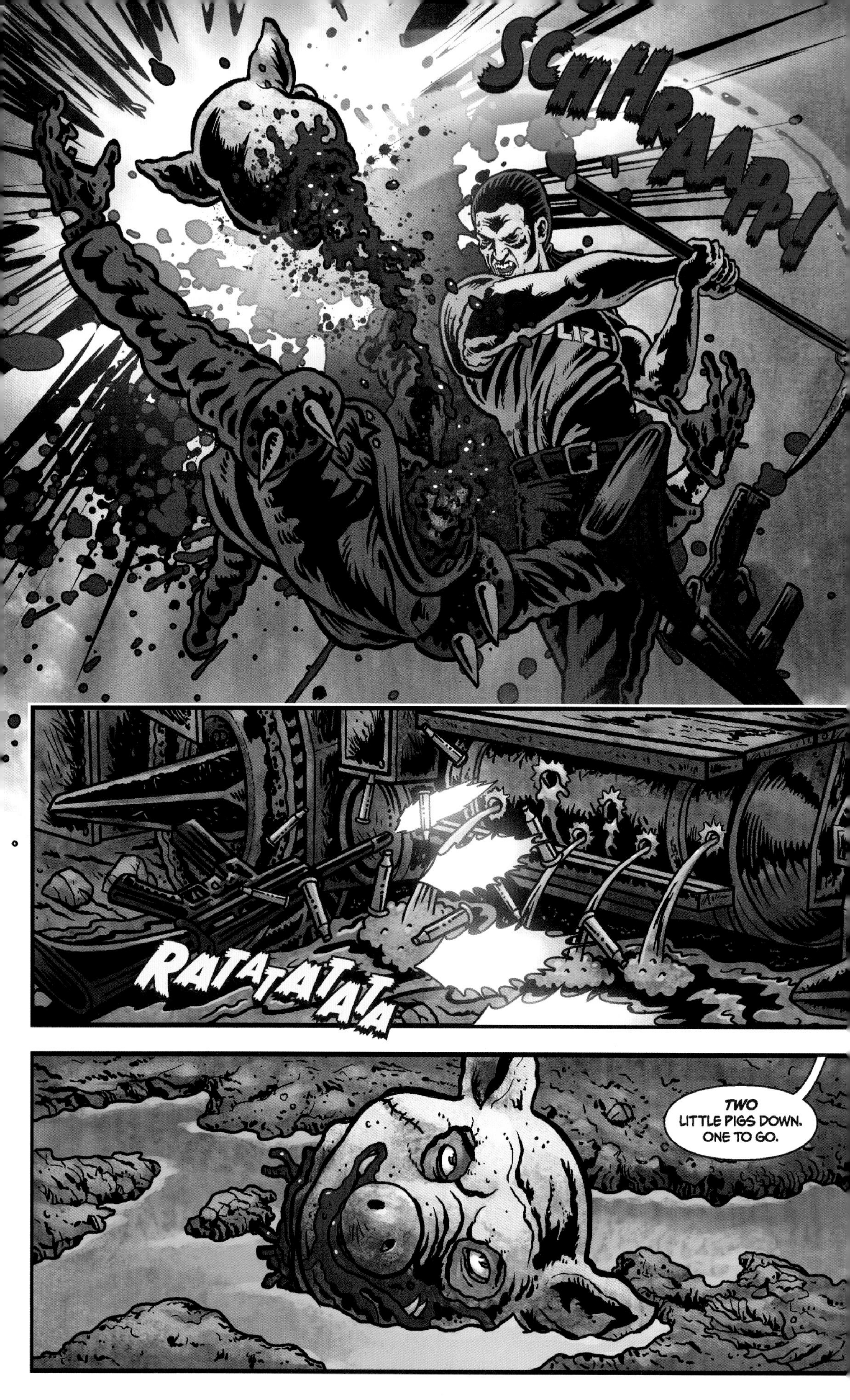
SCHHRAAPP!
RATATATATA
TWO LITTLE PIGS DOWN. ONE TO GO.

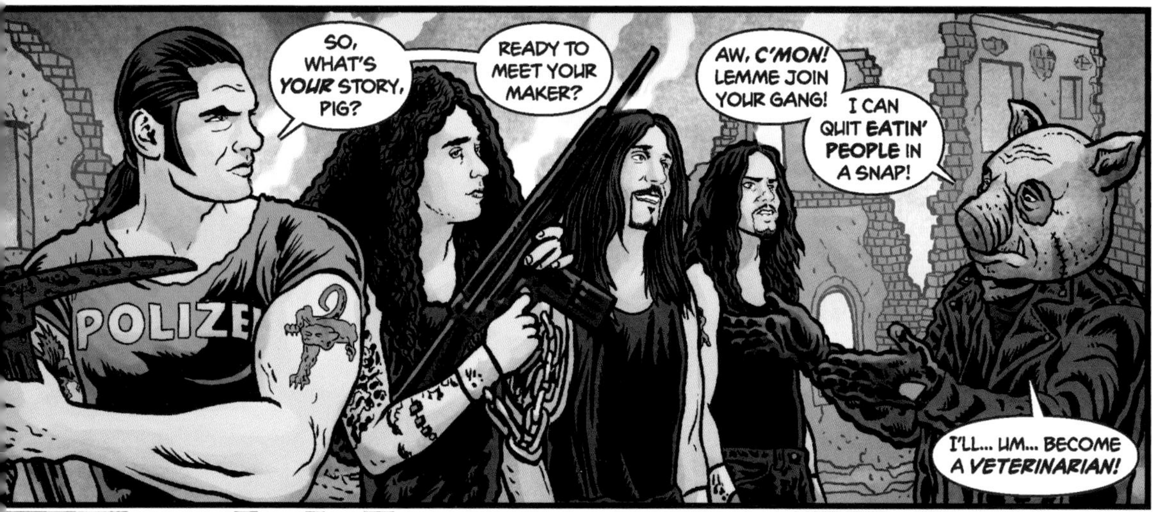
SO, WHAT'S YOUR STORY, PIG?
READY TO MEET YOUR MAKER?
AW, C'MON! LEMME JOIN YOUR GANG!
I CAN QUIT EATIN' PEOPLE IN A SNAP!
I'LL... UM... BECOME A VETERINARIAN!
POLIZEI

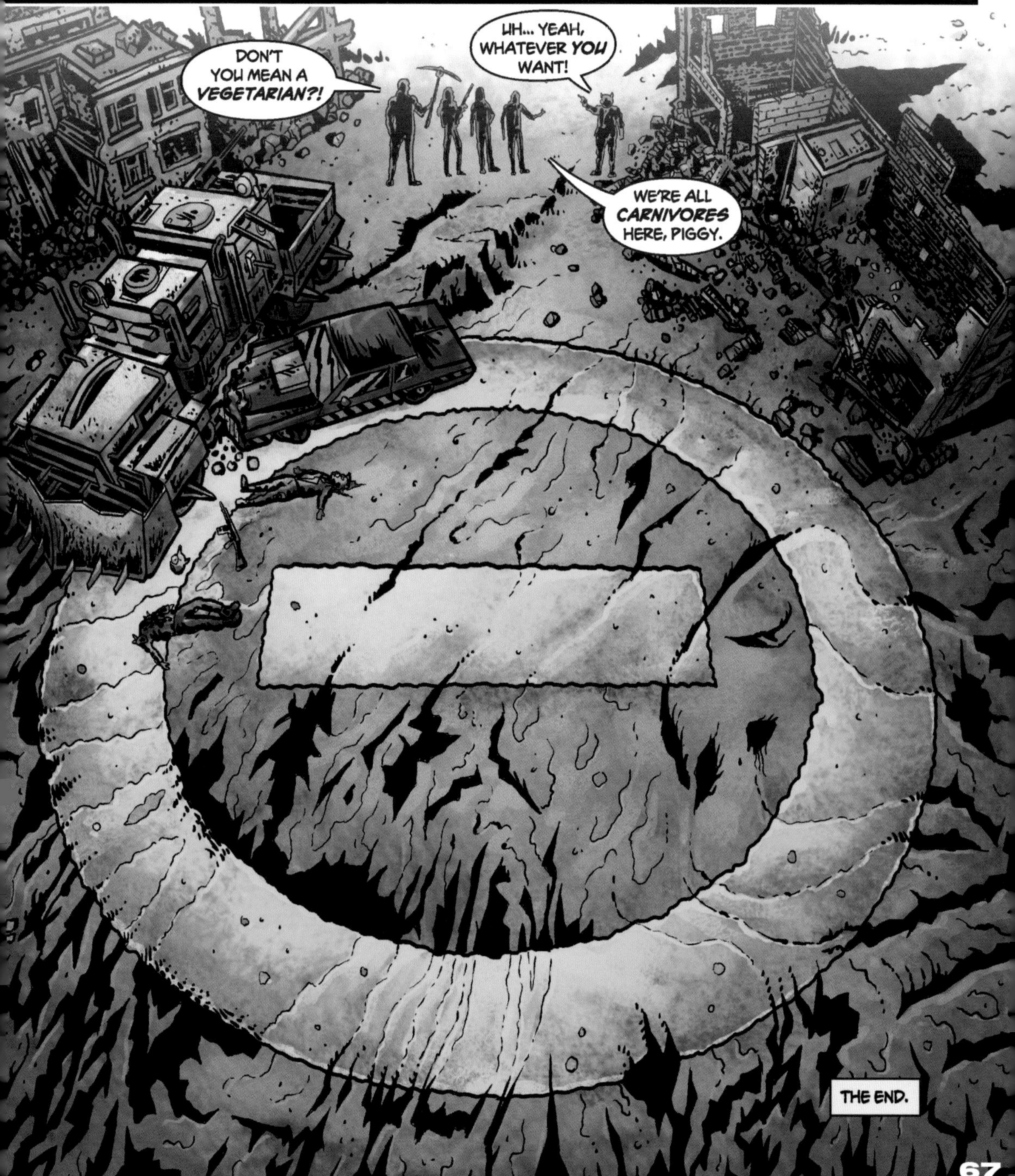
DON'T YOU MEAN A VEGETARIAN?!
UH... YEAH, WHATEVER YOU WANT!
WE'RE ALL CARNIVORES HERE, PIGGY.
THE END.

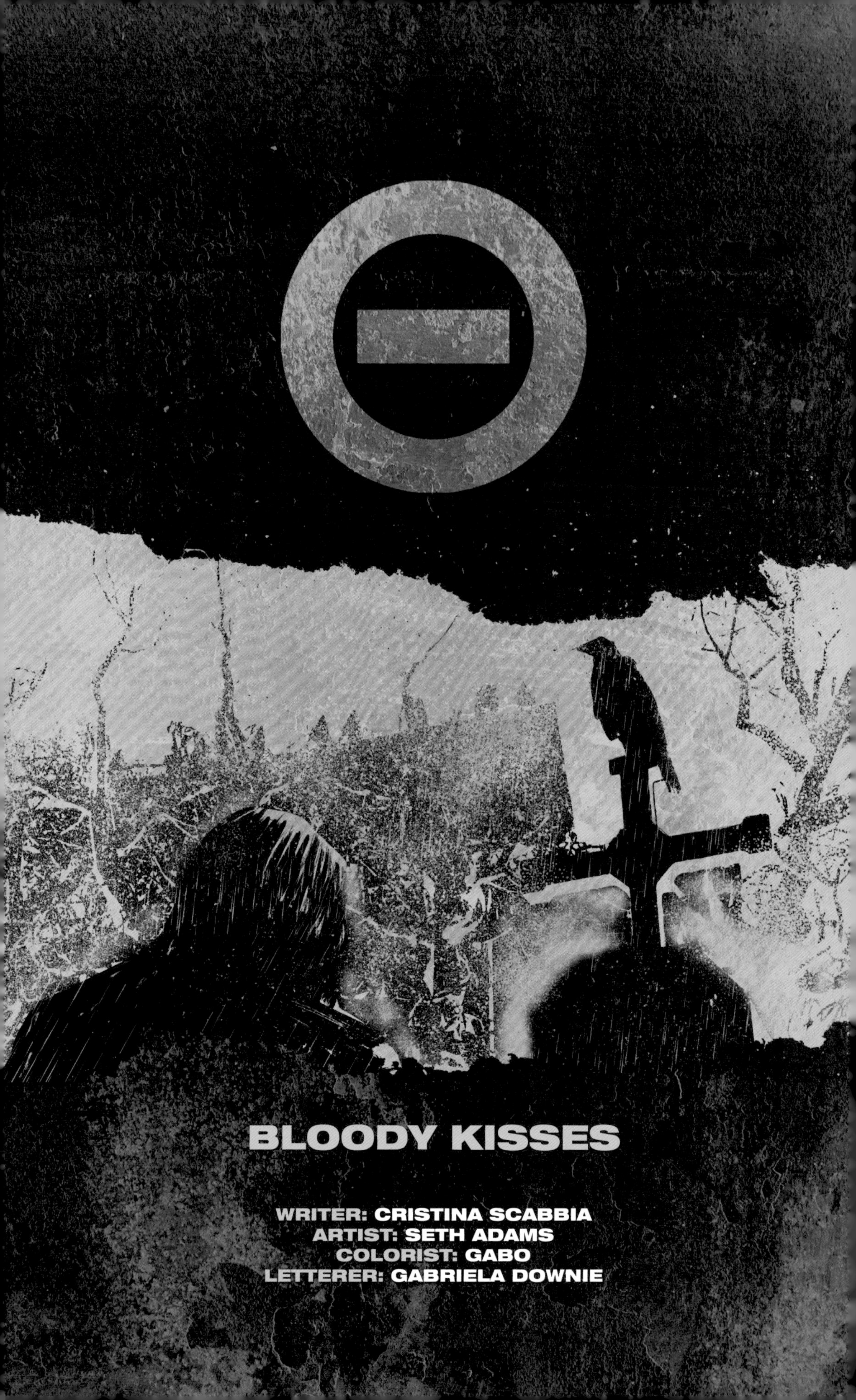
BLOODY KISSES
WRITER: CRISTINA SCABBIA
ARTIST: SETH ADAMS
COLORIST: GABO
LETTERER: GABRIELA DOWNIE

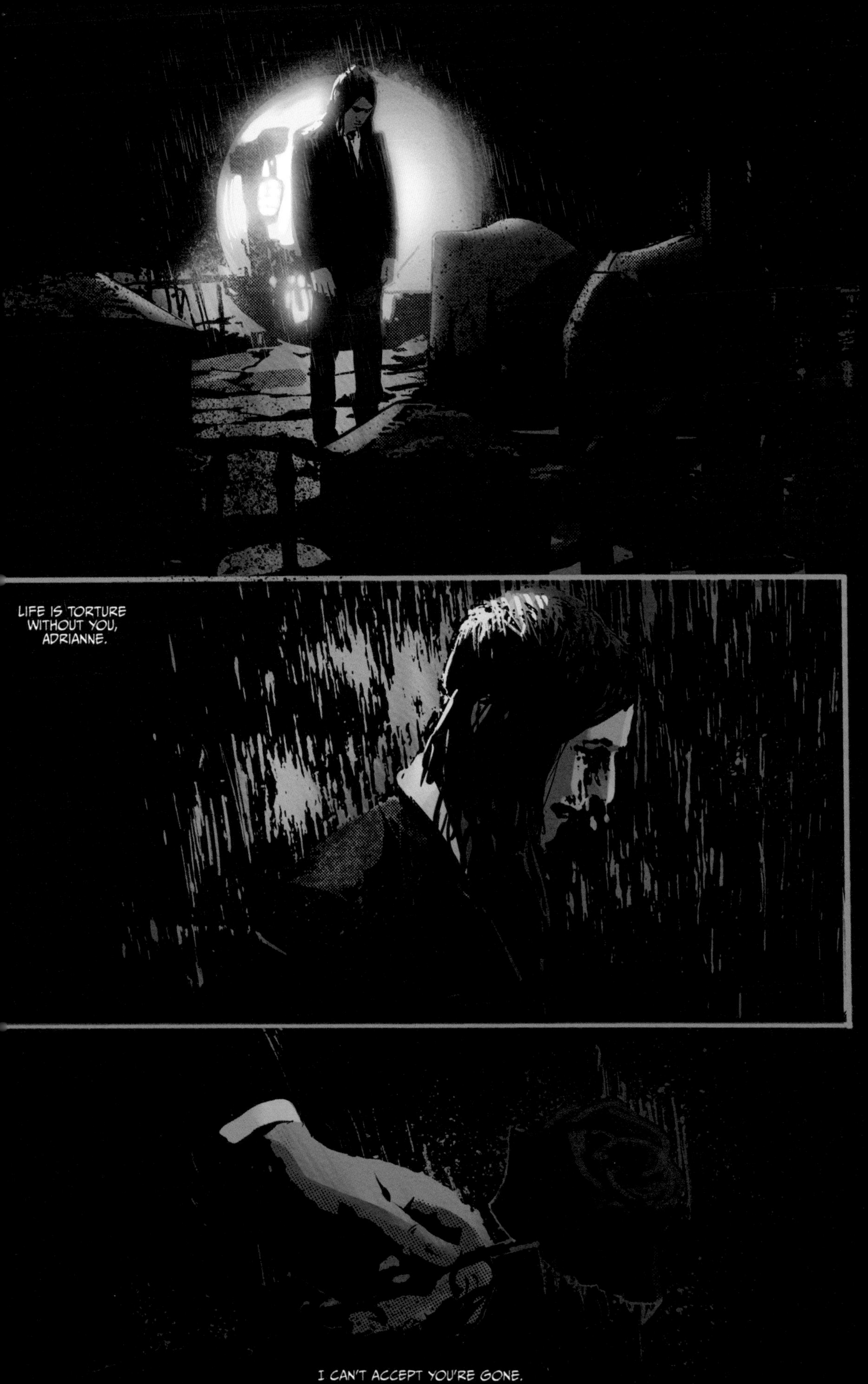
LIFE IS TORTURE WITHOUT YOU, ADRIANNE.
I CAN'T ACCEPT YOU'RE GONE.

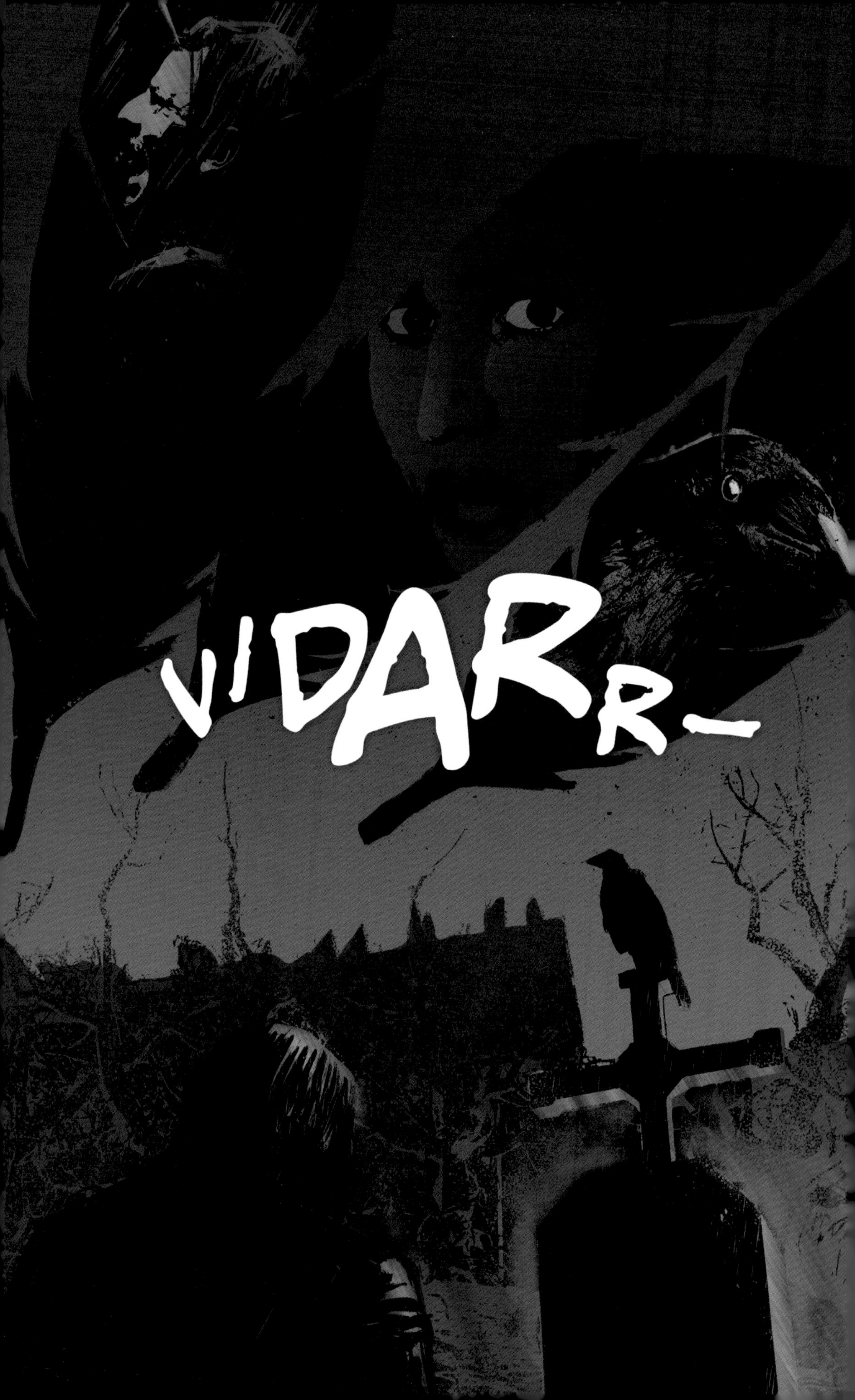
VIDARR

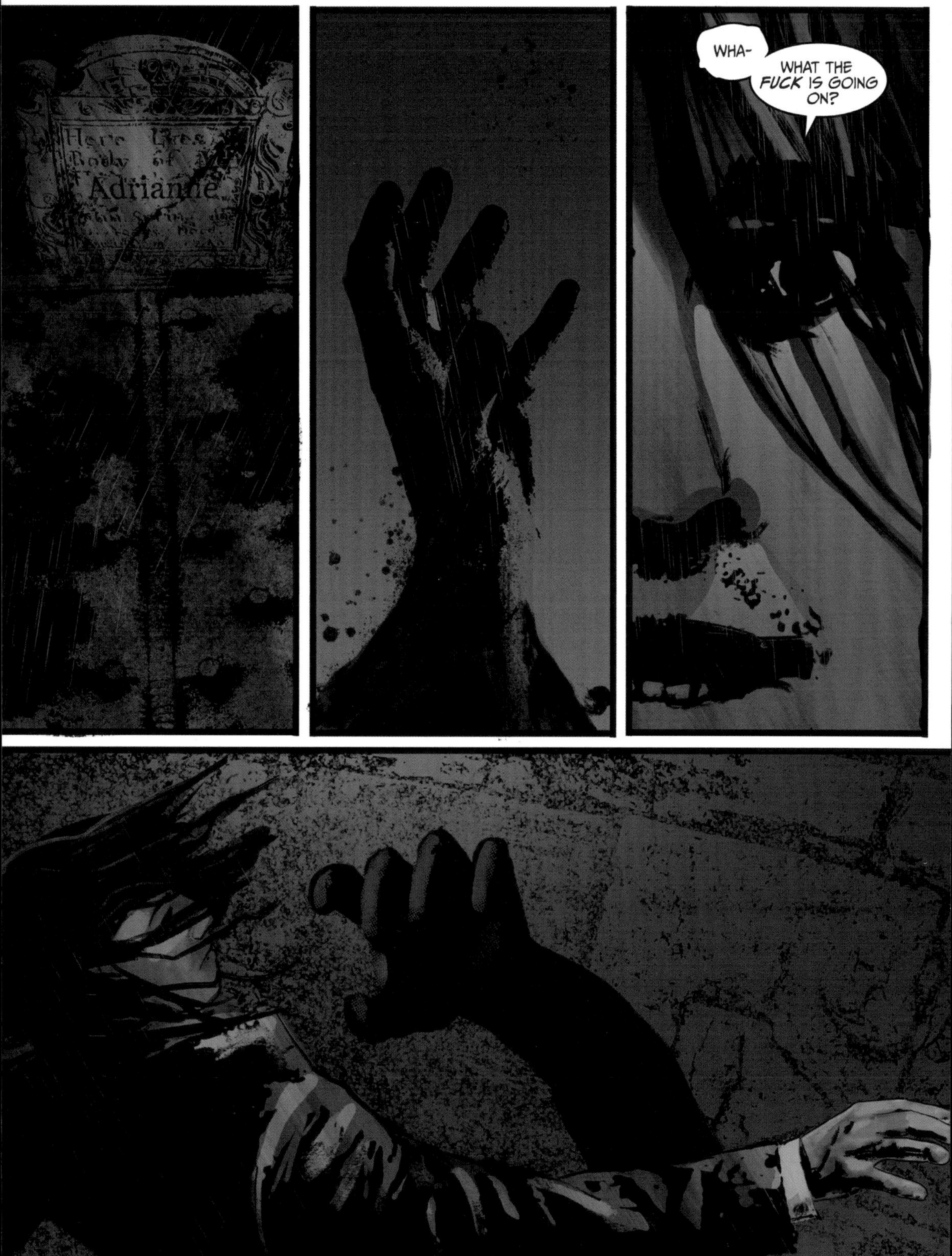
Adrianne
WHA-
WHAT THE *FUCK* IS GOING ON?

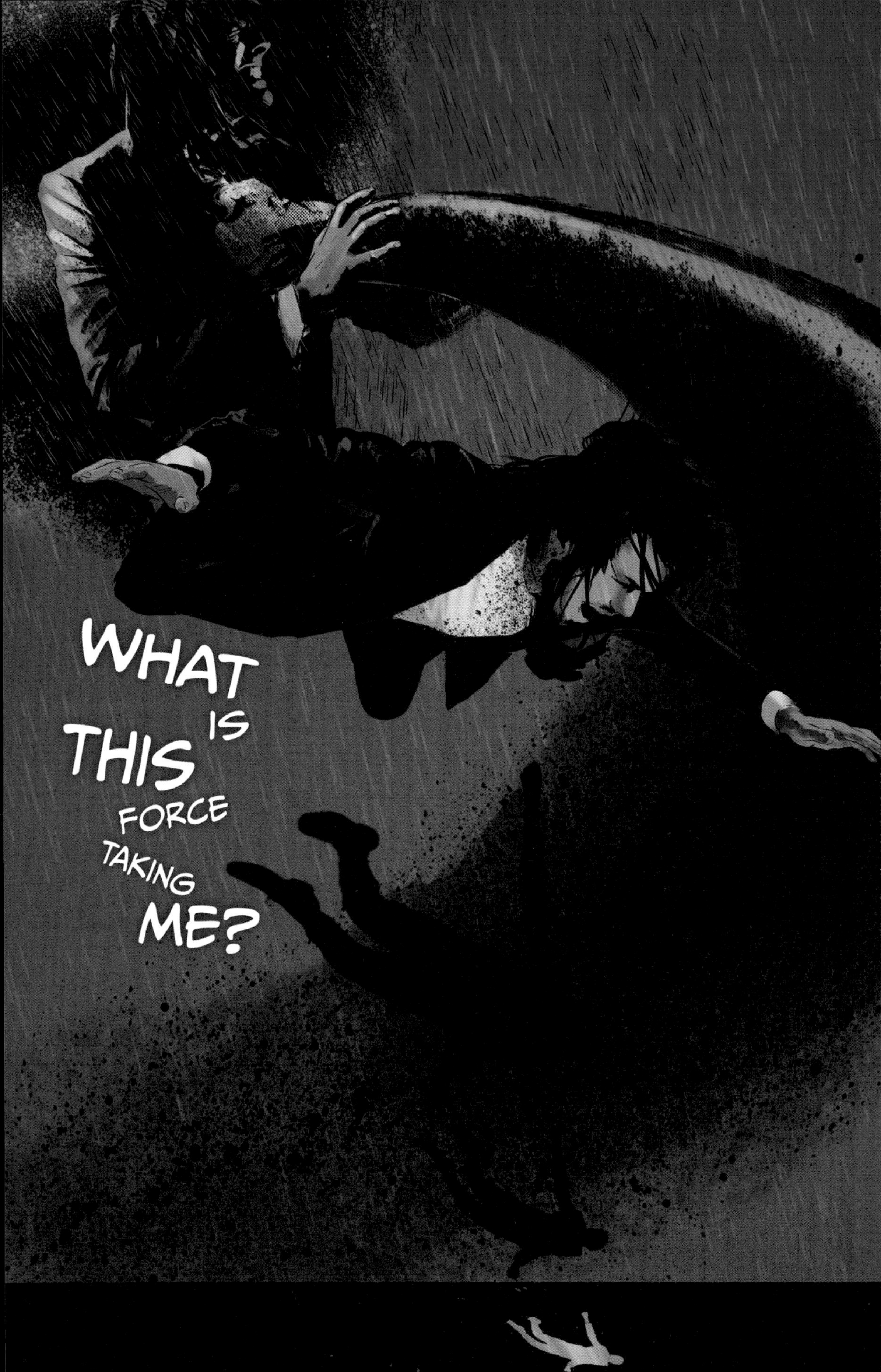
WHAT IS THIS FORCE TAKING ME?

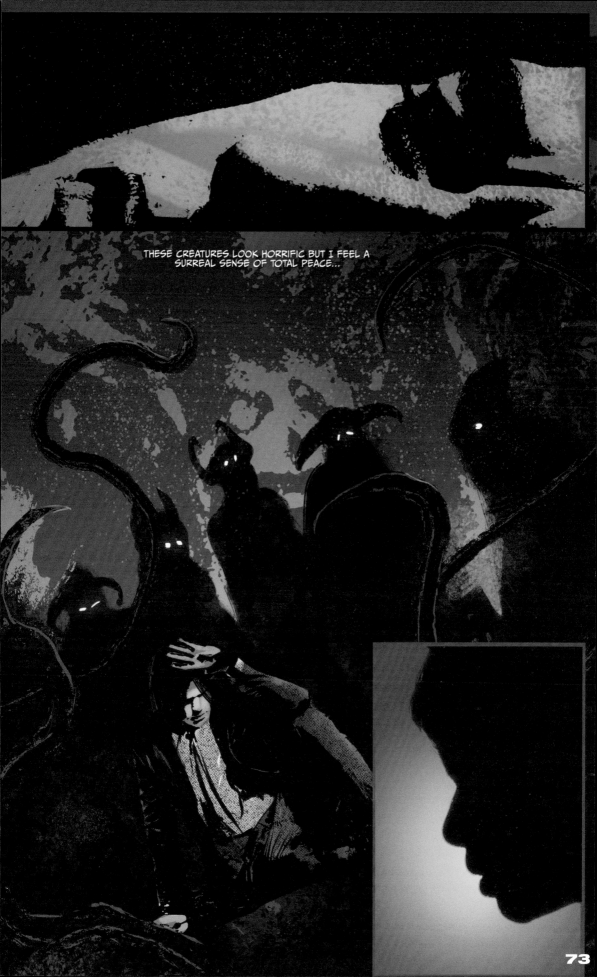

THESE CREATURES LOOK HORRIFIC BUT I FEEL A
SURREAL SENSE OF TOTAL PEACE...

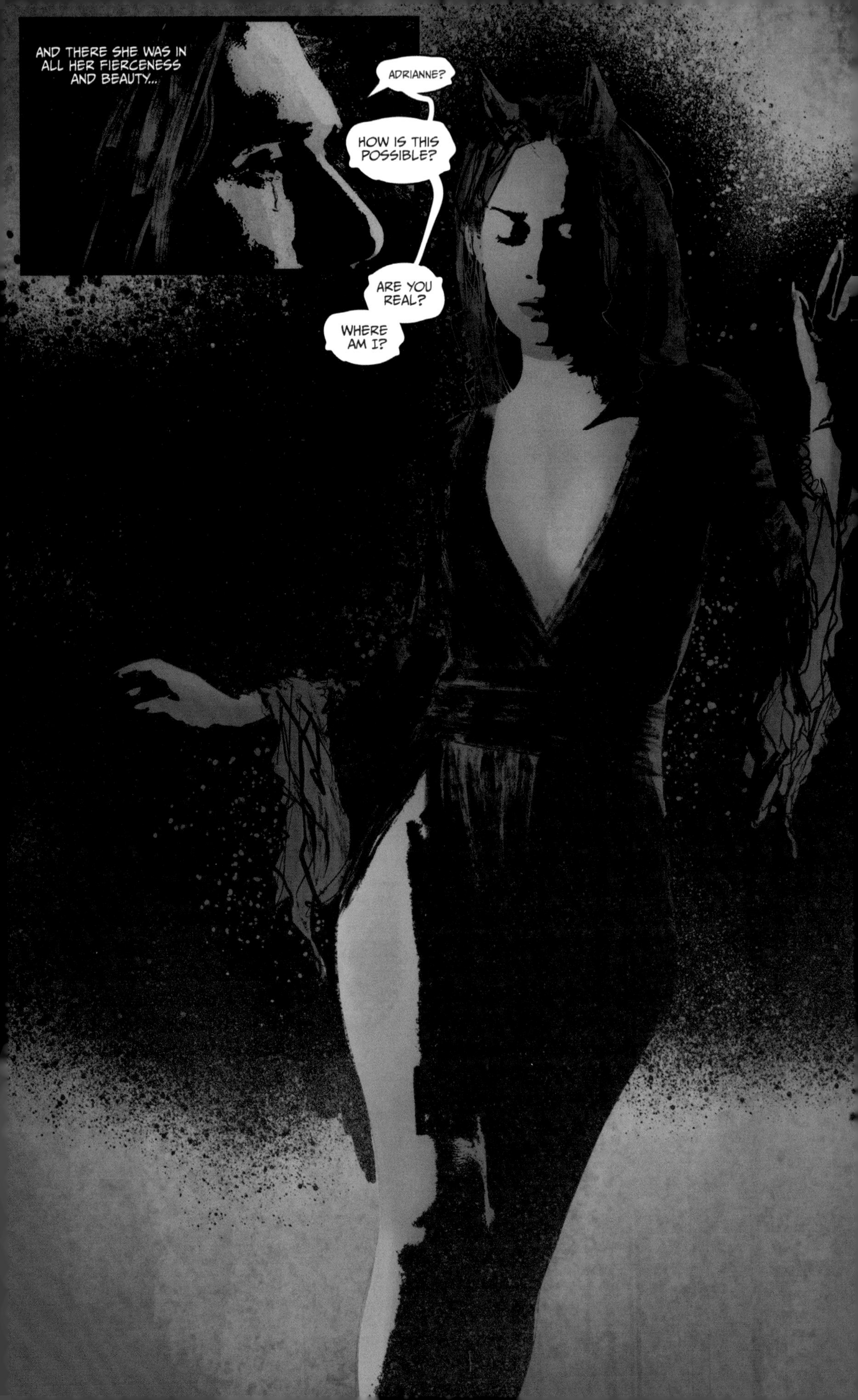
AND THERE SHE WAS IN ALL HER FIERCENESS AND BEAUTY...
ADRIANNE?
HOW IS THIS POSSIBLE?
ARE YOU REAL?
WHERE AM I?

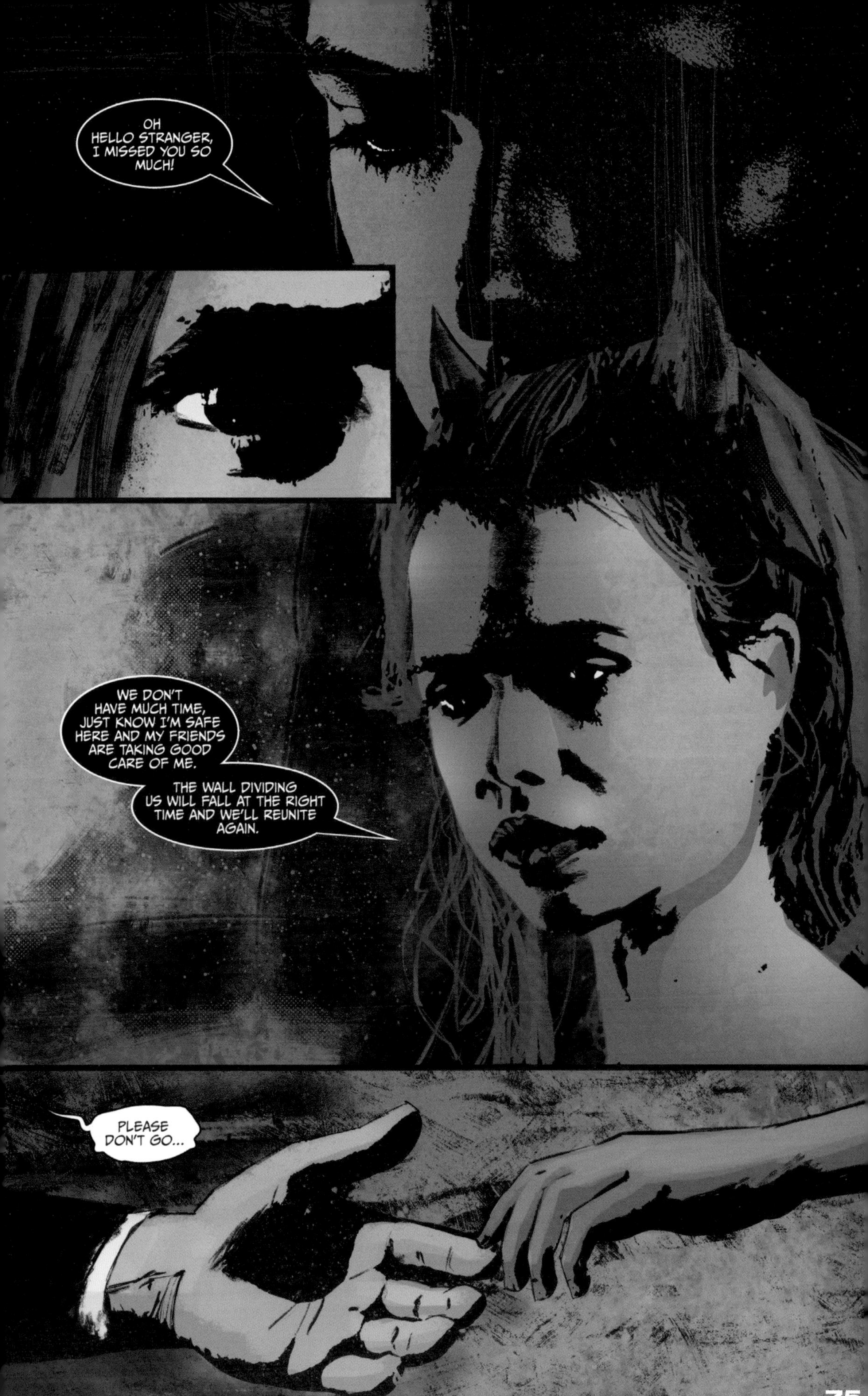
OH HELLO STRANGER, I MISSED YOU SO MUCH!
WE DON'T HAVE MUCH TIME, JUST KNOW I'M SAFE HERE AND MY FRIENDS ARE TAKING GOOD CARE OF ME.
THE WALL DIVIDING US WILL FALL AT THE RIGHT TIME AND WE'LL REUNITE AGAIN.
PLEASE DON'T GO...

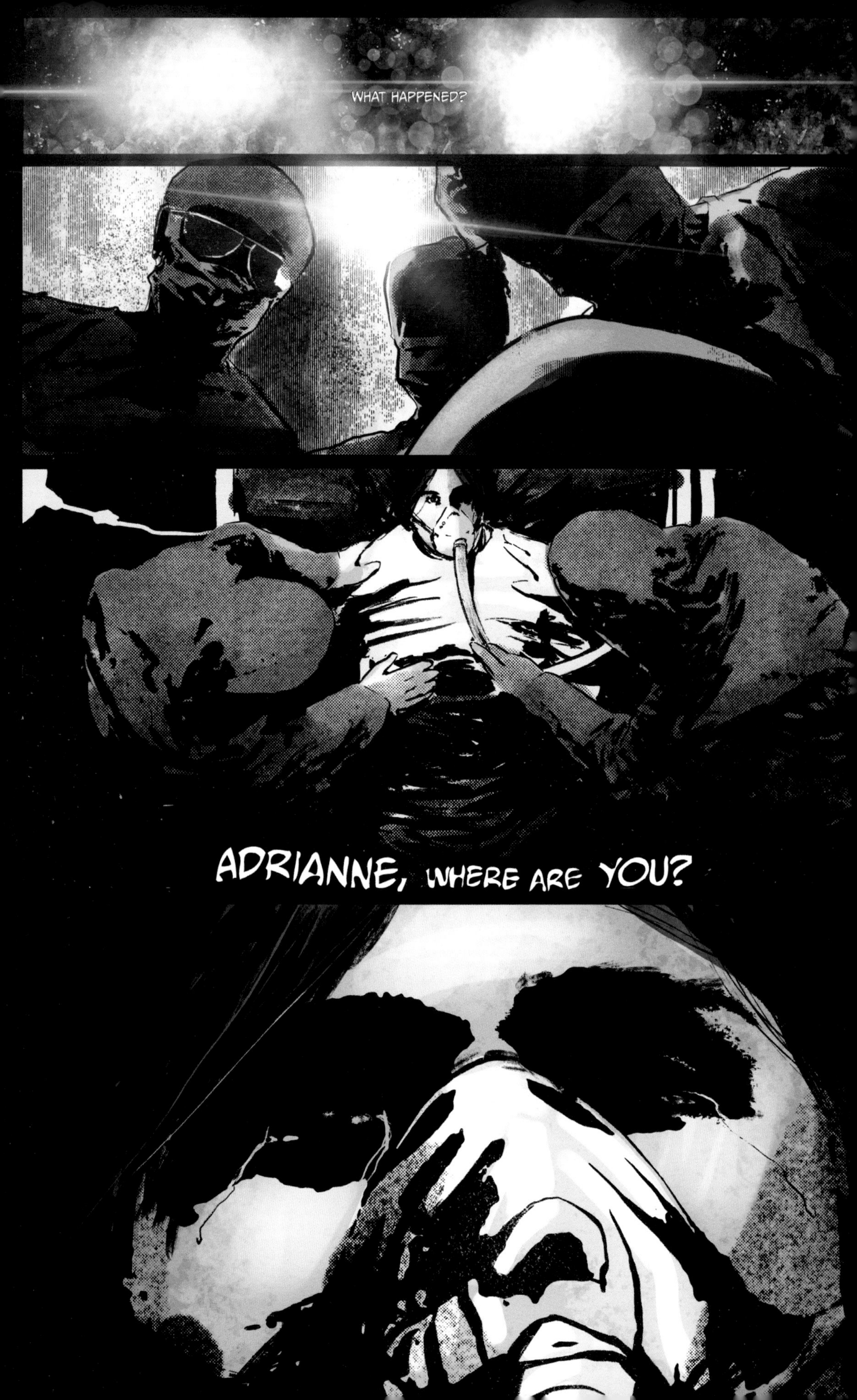
WHAT HAPPENED?
ADRIANNE, WHERE ARE YOU?

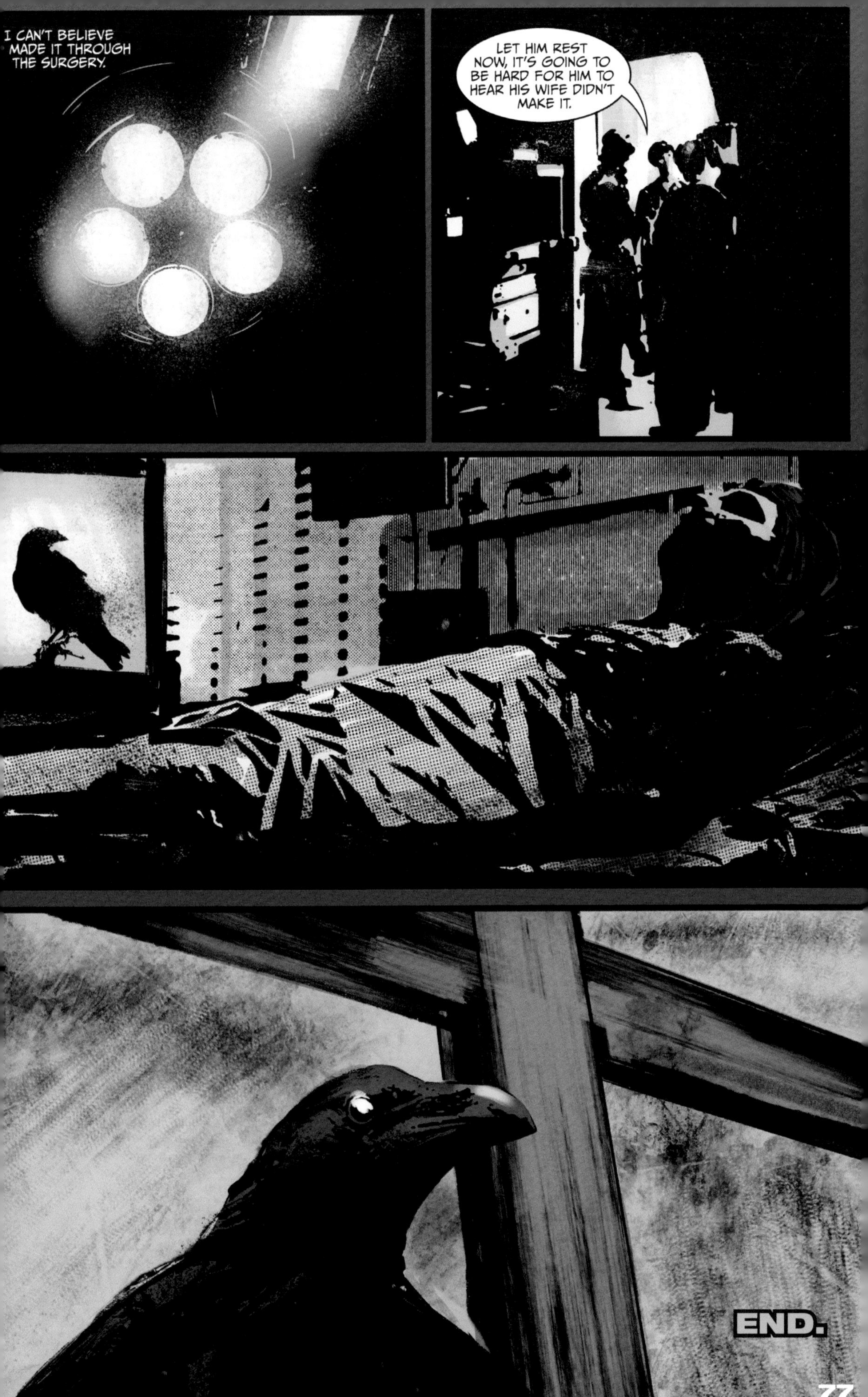
I CAN'T BELIEVE MADE IT THROUGH THE SURGERY.
LET HIM REST NOW, IT'S GOING TO BE HARD FOR HIM TO HEAR HIS WIFE DIDN'T MAKE IT.
END.

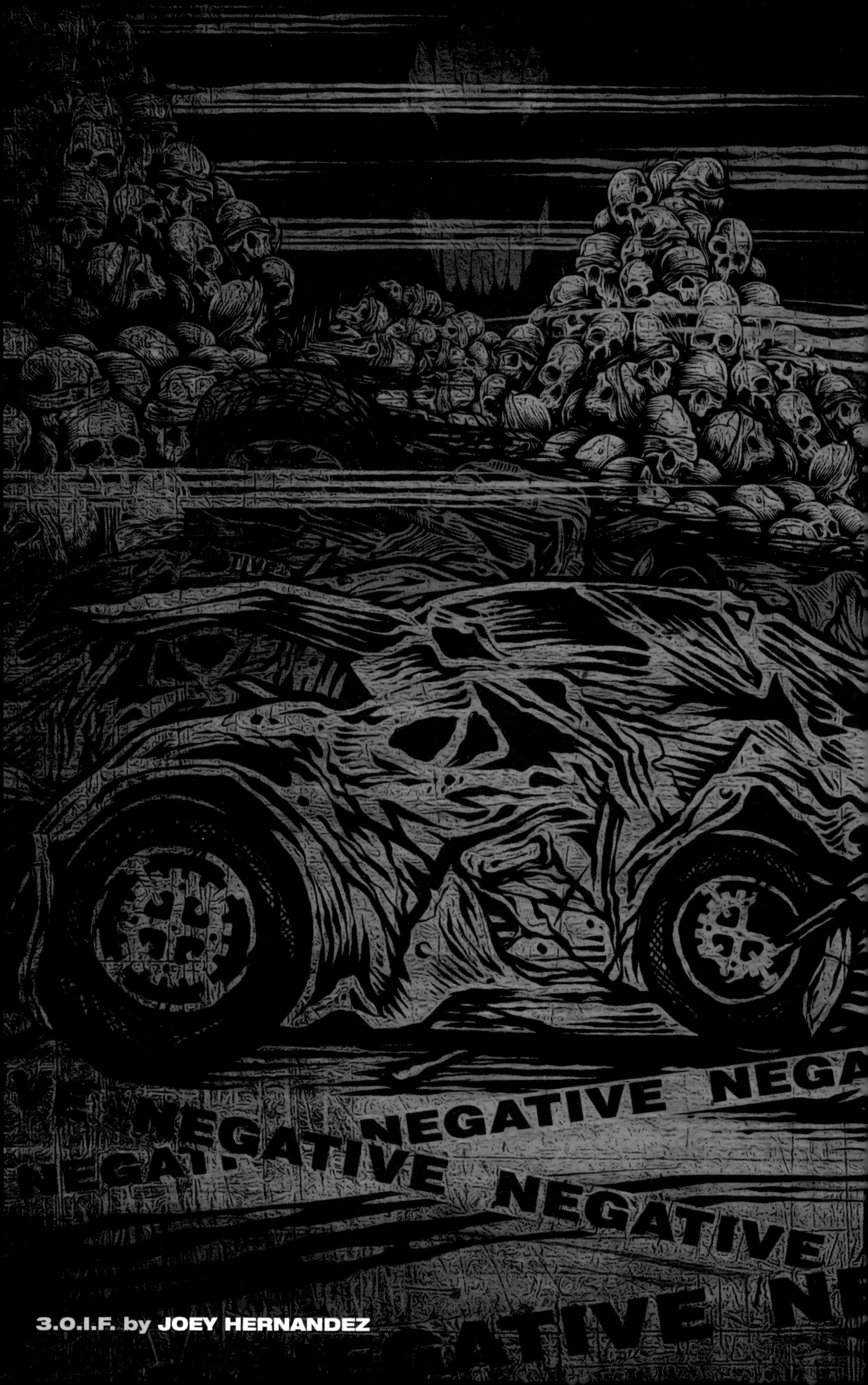
NEGATIVE NEGA
NEGATIVE
NEGATIVE
ATIVE

3.O.I.F. by **JOEY HERNANDEZ**

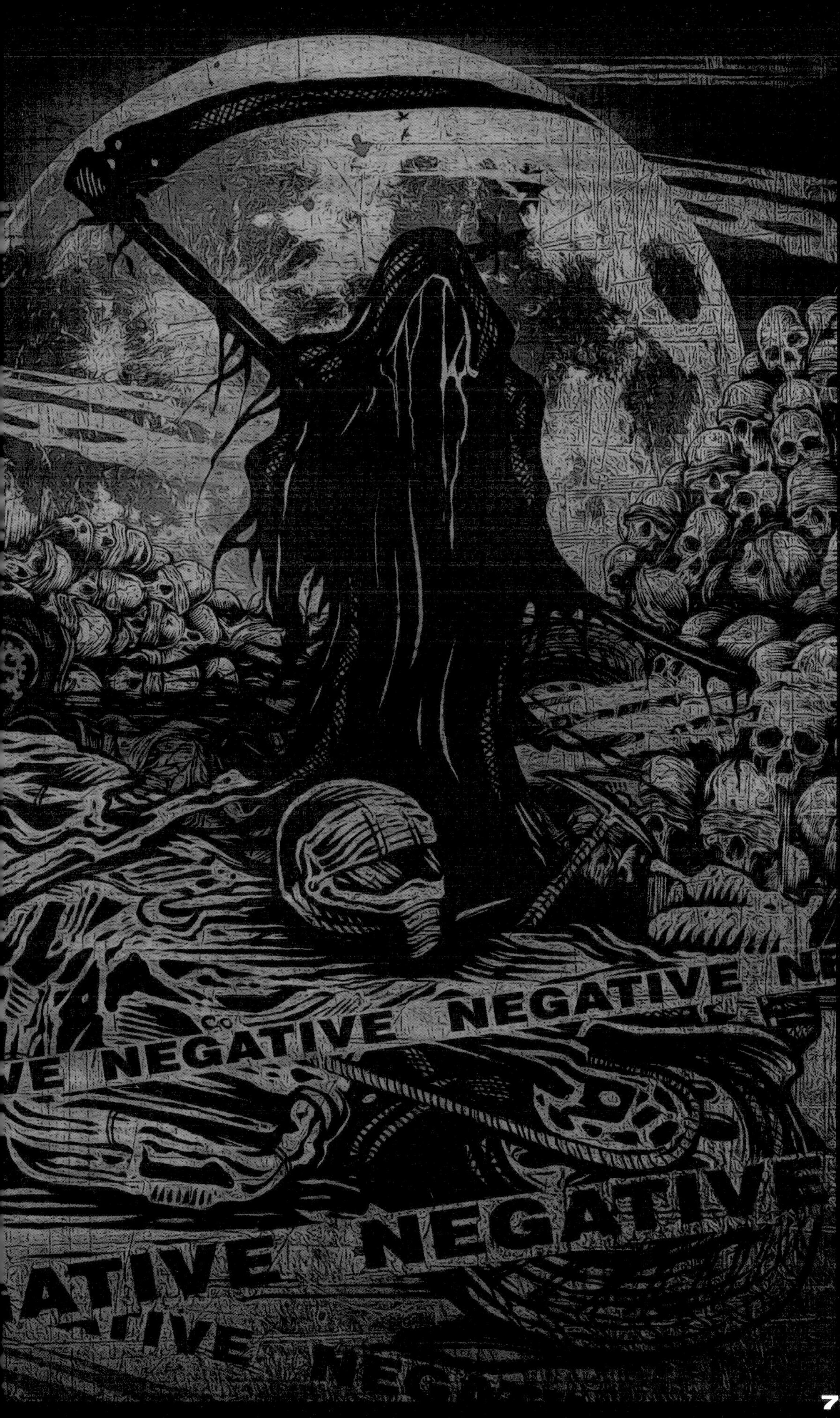
VE NEGATIVE NEGATIVE NE
ATIVE NEGATIVE

TOO LATE: FROZEN

WRITER: ANDY BIERSACK
ARTIST: ARMITANO
COLORIST: FRANCESCA CAROTENUTO
LETTERER: ADAM WOLLET

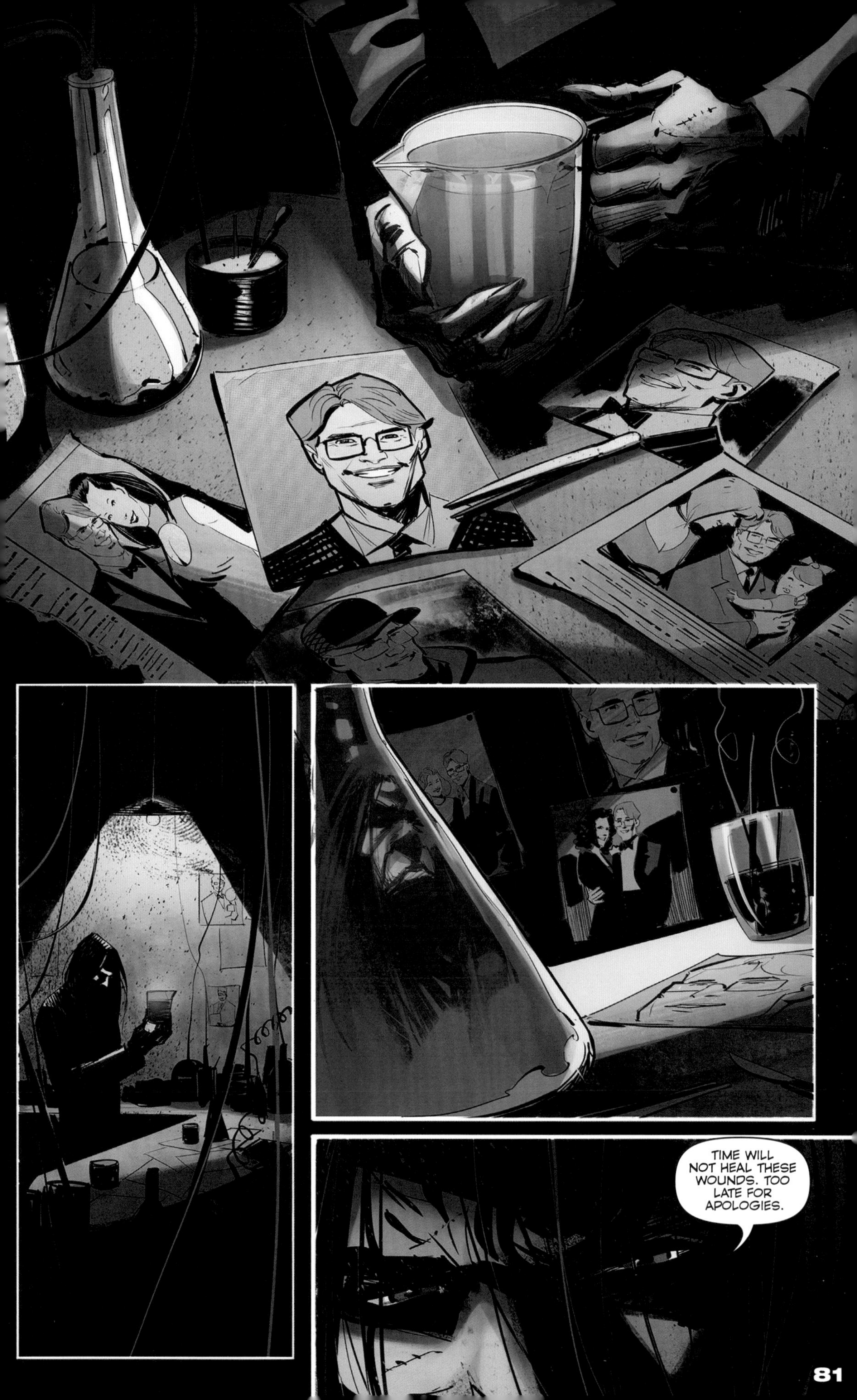
TIME WILL NOT HEAL THESE WOUNDS. TOO LATE FOR APOLOGIES.

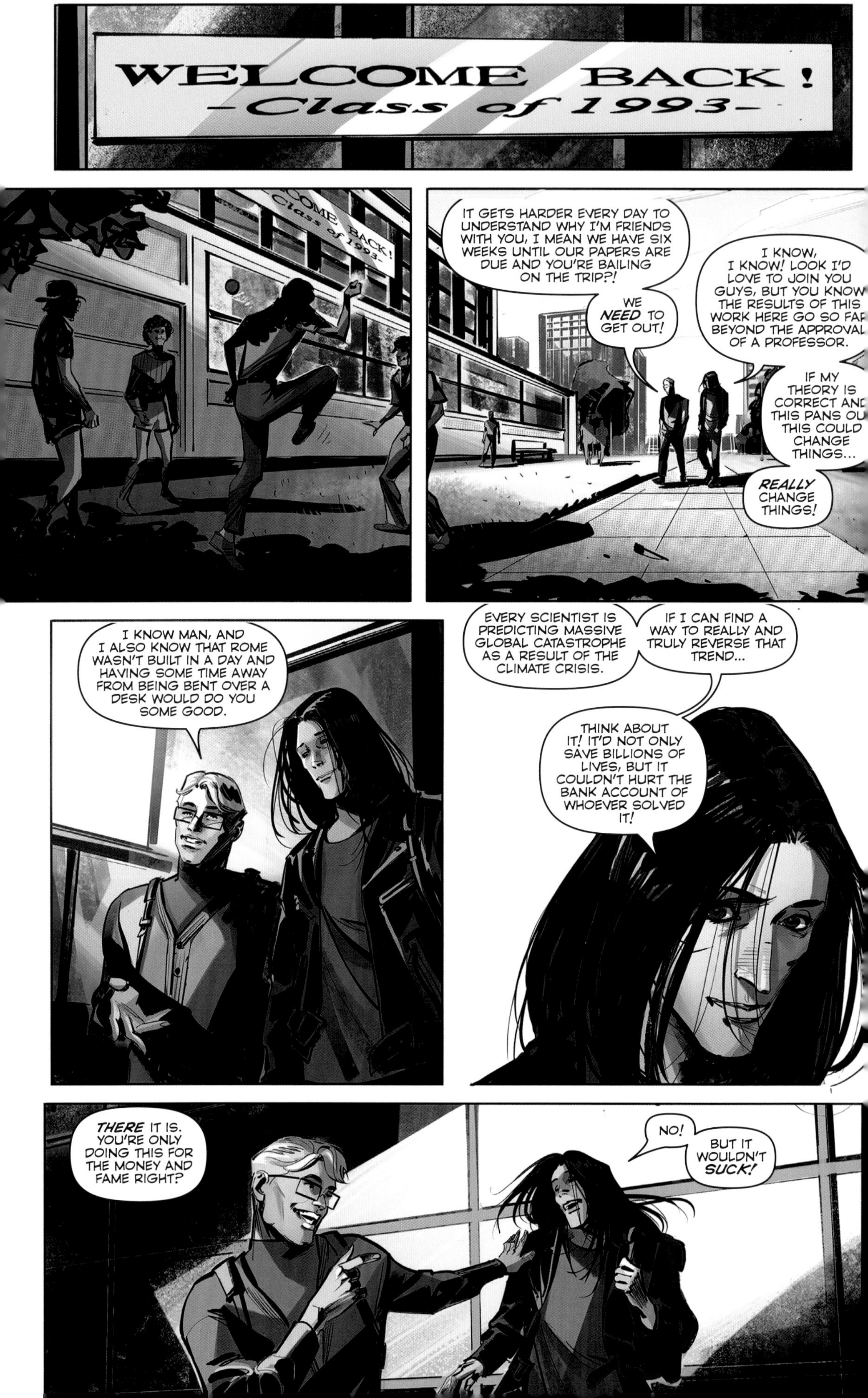
WELCOME BACK!
-Class of 1993-
IT GETS HARDER EVERY DAY TO UNDERSTAND WHY I'M FRIENDS WITH YOU, I MEAN WE HAVE SIX WEEKS UNTIL OUR PAPERS ARE DUE AND YOU'RE BAILING ON THE TRIP?!
WE NEED TO GET OUT!
I KNOW, I KNOW! LOOK I'D LOVE TO JOIN YOU GUYS, BUT YOU KNOW THE RESULTS OF THIS WORK HERE GO SO FAR BEYOND THE APPROVAL OF A PROFESSOR.
IF MY THEORY IS CORRECT AND THIS PANS OUT THIS COULD CHANGE THINGS...
REALLY CHANGE THINGS!
I KNOW MAN, AND I ALSO KNOW THAT ROME WASN'T BUILT IN A DAY AND HAVING SOME TIME AWAY FROM BEING BENT OVER A DESK WOULD DO YOU SOME GOOD.
EVERY SCIENTIST IS PREDICTING MASSIVE GLOBAL CATASTROPHE AS A RESULT OF THE CLIMATE CRISIS.
IF I CAN FIND A WAY TO REALLY AND TRULY REVERSE THAT TREND...
THINK ABOUT IT! IT'D NOT ONLY SAVE BILLIONS OF LIVES, BUT IT COULDN'T HURT THE BANK ACCOUNT OF WHOEVER SOLVED IT!
THERE IT IS. YOU'RE ONLY DOING THIS FOR THE MONEY AND FAME RIGHT?
NO!
BUT IT WOULDN'T SUCK!

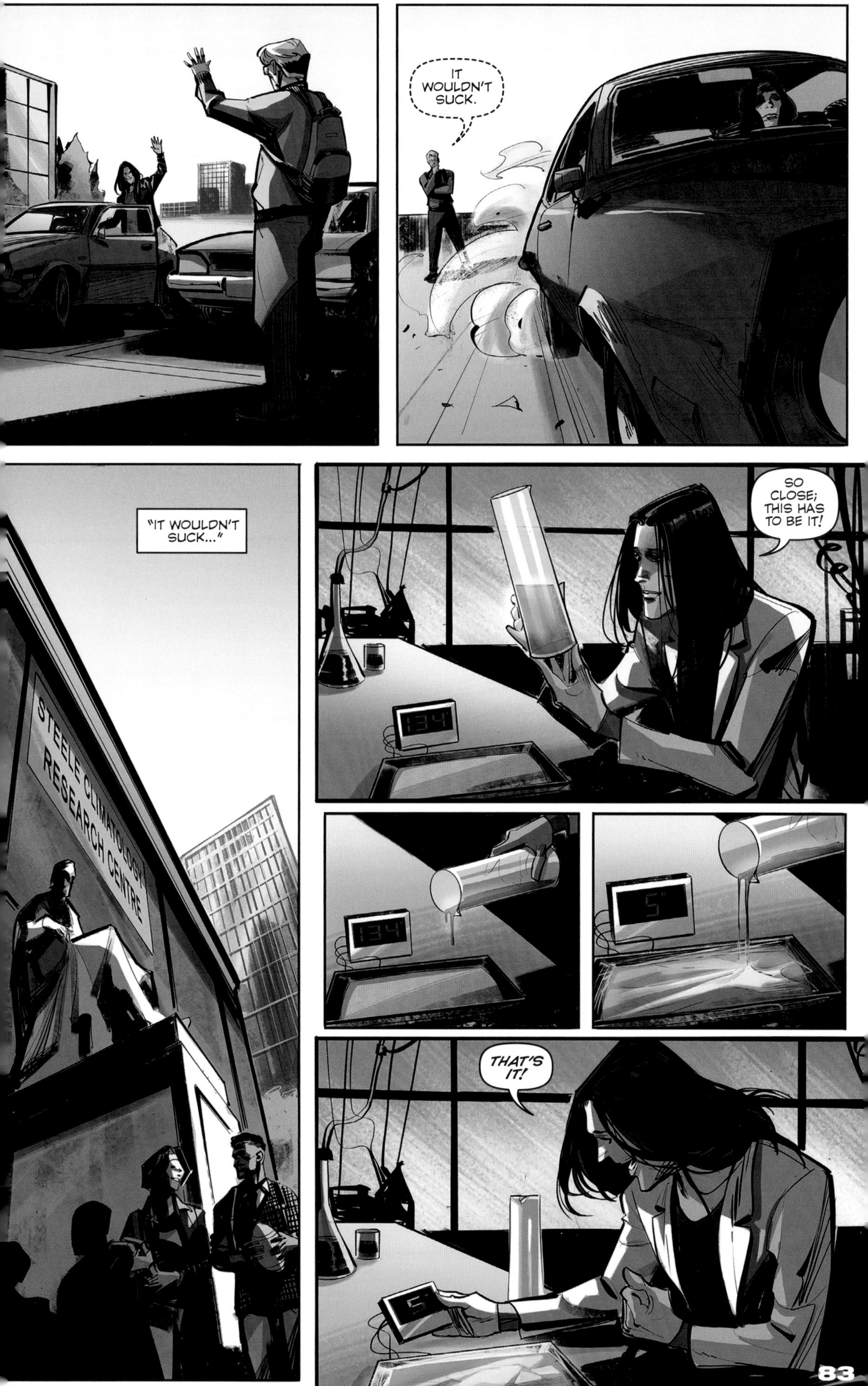
IT WOULDN'T SUCK.
"IT WOULDN'T SUCK..."
SO CLOSE; THIS HAS TO BE IT!
THAT'S IT!
STEELE CLIMATOLOGY RESEARCH CENTRE

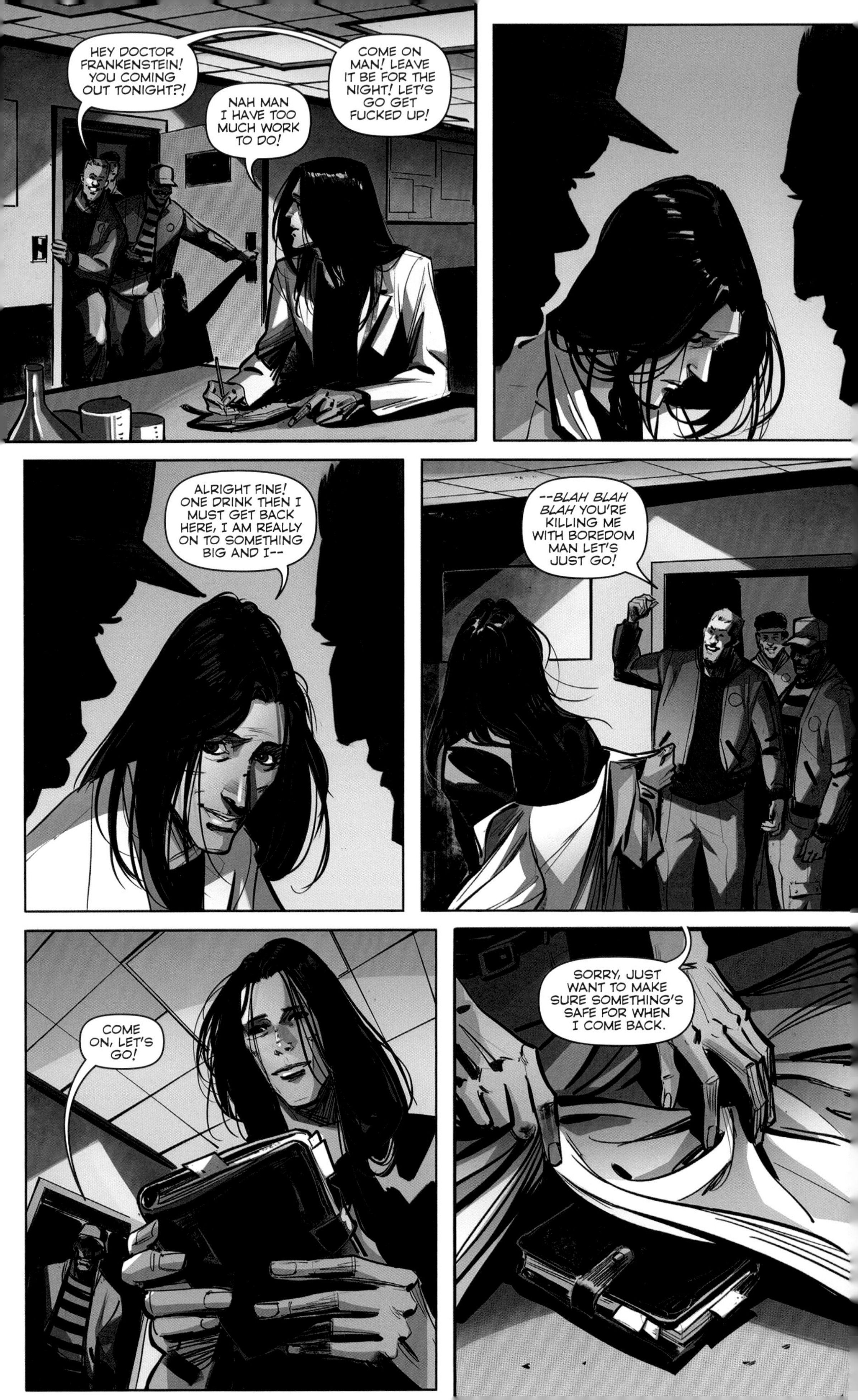
HEY DOCTOR FRANKENSTEIN! YOU COMING OUT TONIGHT?!
NAH MAN I HAVE TOO MUCH WORK TO DO!
COME ON MAN! LEAVE IT BE FOR THE NIGHT! LET'S GO GET FUCKED UP!
ALRIGHT FINE! ONE DRINK THEN I MUST GET BACK HERE, I AM REALLY ON TO SOMETHING BIG AND I--
--*BLAH BLAH BLAH* YOU'RE KILLING ME WITH BOREDOM MAN LET'S JUST GO!
COME ON, LET'S GO!
SORRY, JUST WANT TO MAKE SURE SOMETHING'S SAFE FOR WHEN I COME BACK.

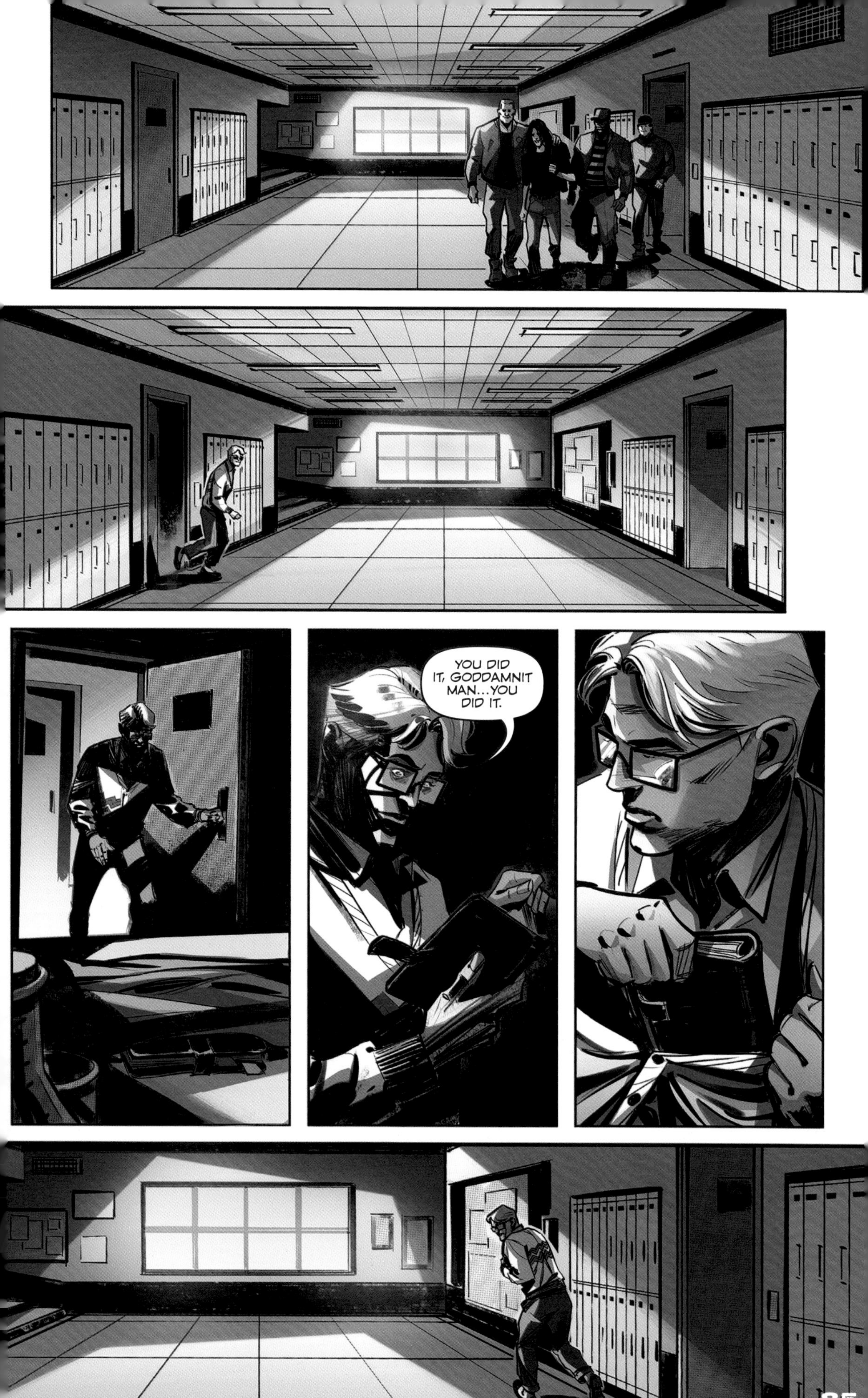
YOU DID IT, GODDAMNIT MAN...YOU DID IT.

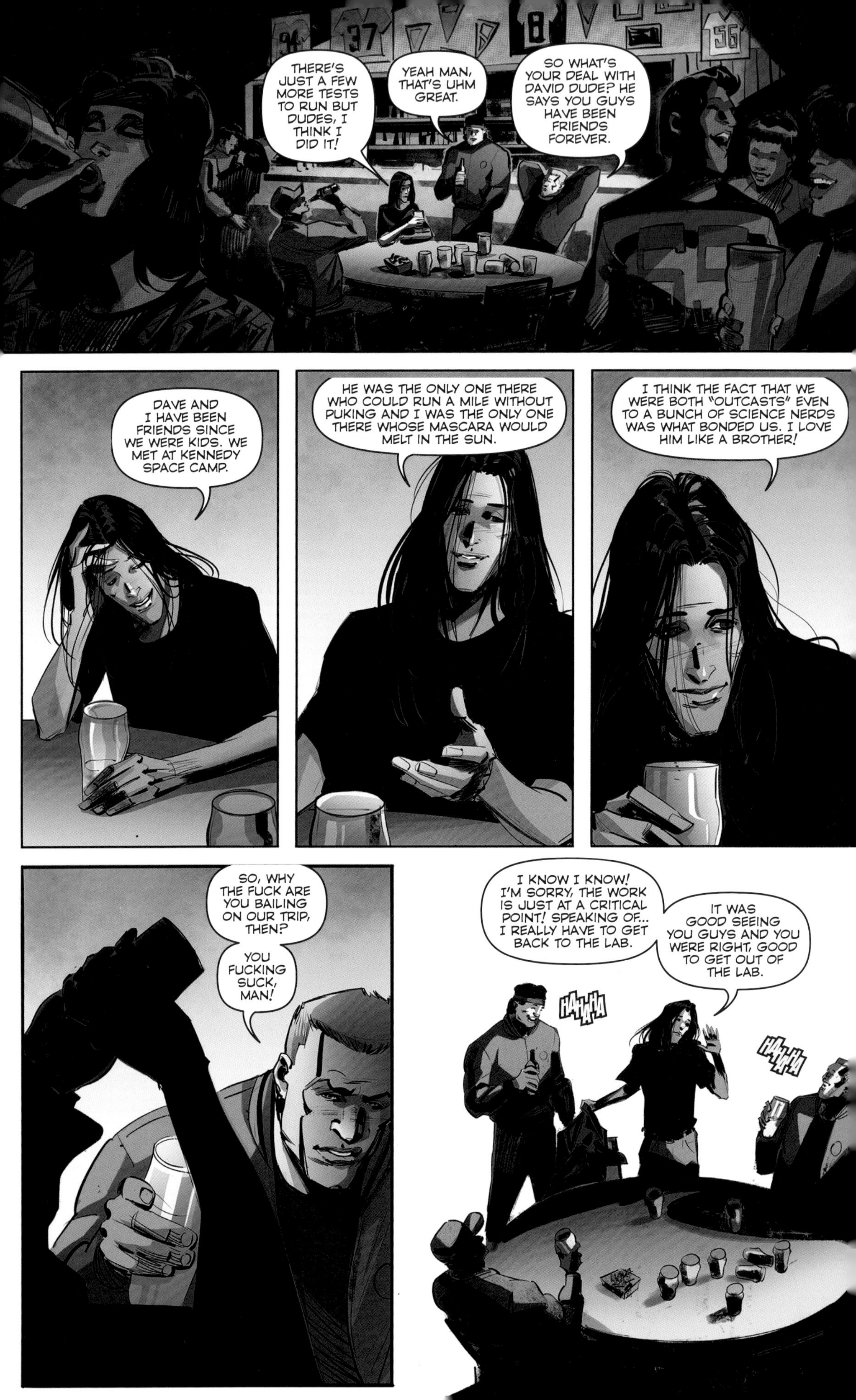

THERE'S JUST A FEW MORE TESTS TO RUN BUT DUDES, I THINK I DID IT!
YEAH MAN, THAT'S UHM GREAT.
SO WHAT'S YOUR DEAL WITH DAVID DUDE? HE SAYS YOU GUYS HAVE BEEN FRIENDS FOREVER.
DAVE AND I HAVE BEEN FRIENDS SINCE WE WERE KIDS. WE MET AT KENNEDY SPACE CAMP.
HE WAS THE ONLY ONE THERE WHO COULD RUN A MILE WITHOUT PUKING AND I WAS THE ONLY ONE THERE WHOSE MASCARA WOULD MELT IN THE SUN.
I THINK THE FACT THAT WE WERE BOTH "OUTCASTS" EVEN TO A BUNCH OF SCIENCE NERDS WAS WHAT BONDED US. I LOVE HIM LIKE A BROTHER!
SO, WHY THE FUCK ARE YOU BAILING ON OUR TRIP, THEN?
YOU FUCKING SUCK, MAN!
I KNOW I KNOW! I'M SORRY, THE WORK IS JUST AT A CRITICAL POINT! SPEAKING OF... I REALLY HAVE TO GET BACK TO THE LAB.
IT WAS GOOD SEEING YOU GUYS AND YOU WERE RIGHT, GOOD TO GET OUT OF THE LAB.
HAHAHA
HAHAHA

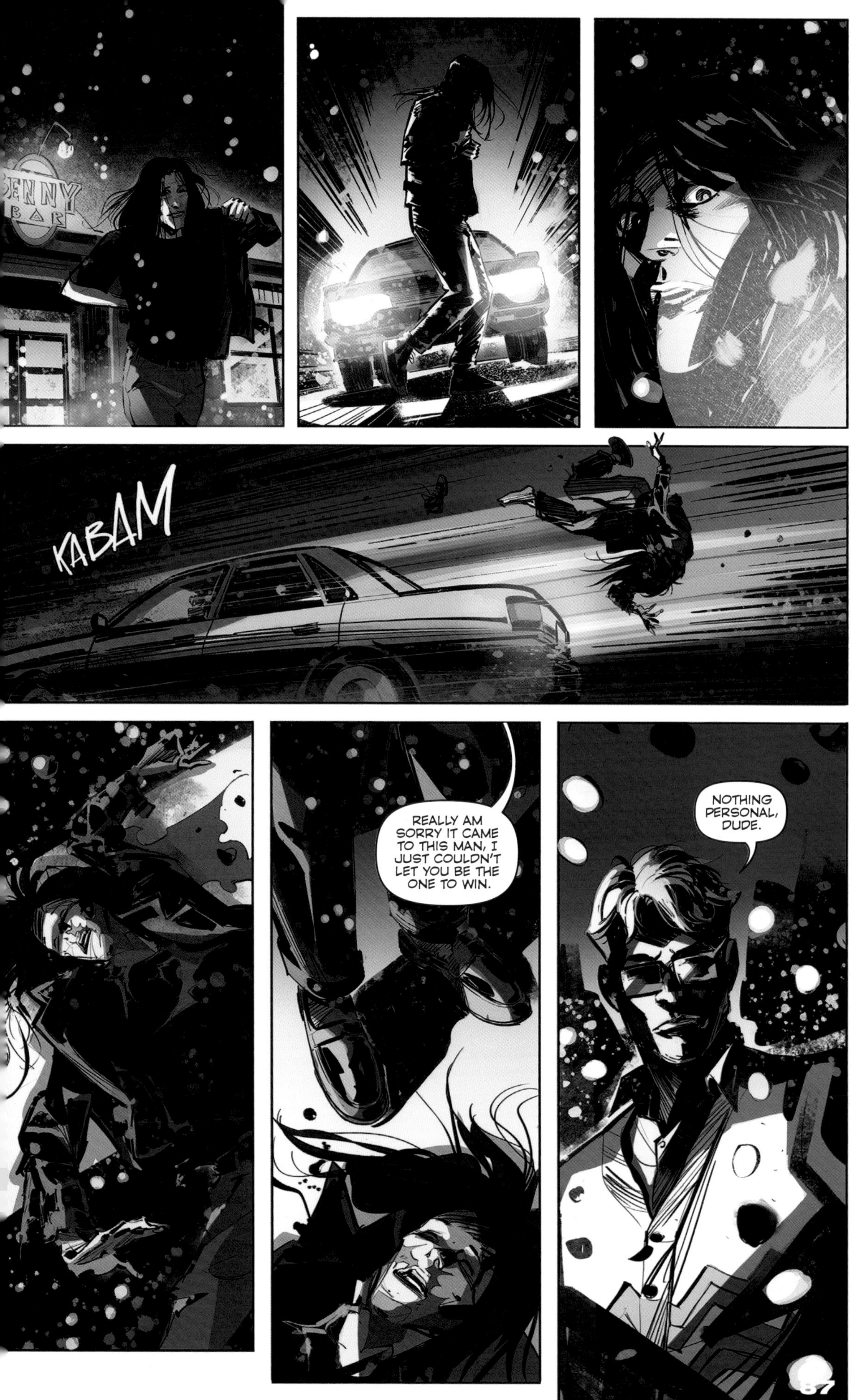
ENNY
BAR
KABAM
REALLY AM SORRY IT CAME TO THIS MAN, I JUST COULDN'T LET YOU BE THE ONE TO WIN.
NOTHING PERSONAL, DUDE.

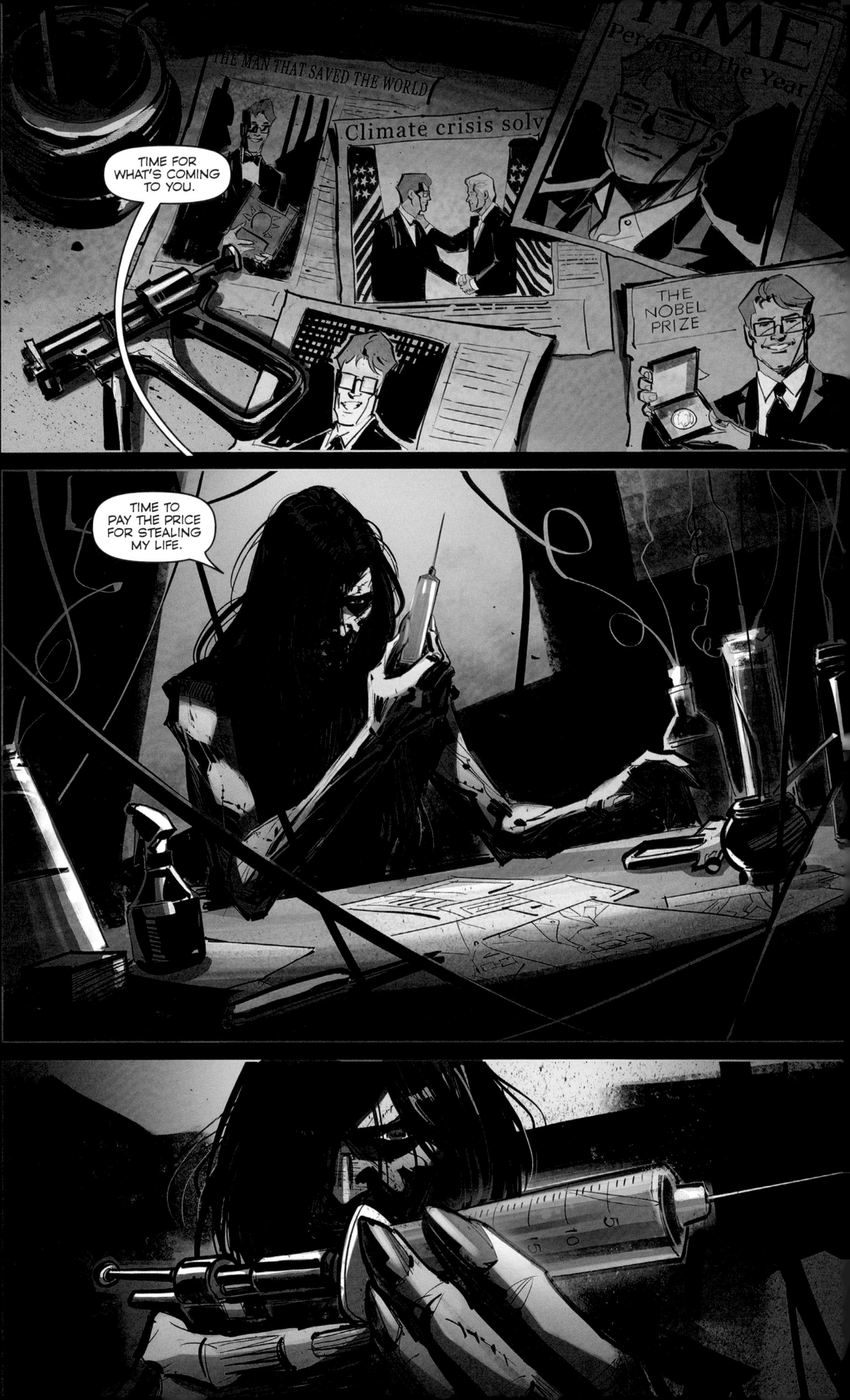
THE MAN THAT SAVED THE WORLD
Climate crisis solv
TIME
Person of the Year
THE NOBEL PRIZE
TIME FOR WHAT'S COMING TO YOU.
TIME TO PAY THE PRICE FOR STEALING MY LIFE.

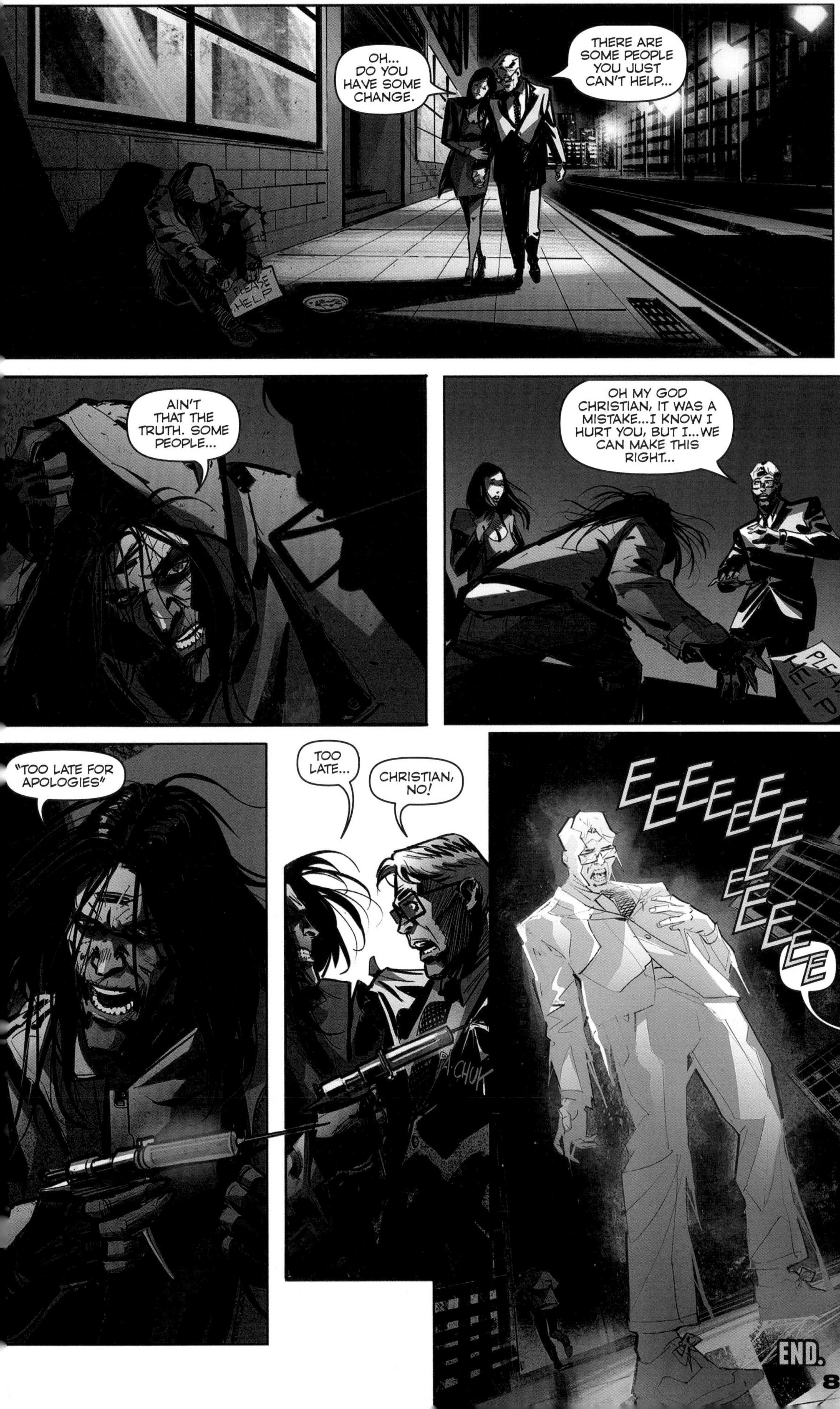
OH... DO YOU HAVE SOME CHANGE.
THERE ARE SOME PEOPLE YOU JUST CAN'T HELP...
PLEASE HELP
AIN'T THAT THE TRUTH. SOME PEOPLE...
OH MY GOD CHRISTIAN, IT WAS A MISTAKE...I KNOW I HURT YOU, BUT I...WE CAN MAKE THIS RIGHT...
PLEASE HELP
"TOO LATE FOR APOLOGIES"
TOO LATE...
CHRISTIAN, NO!
PA-CHUK
EEEEEEEEEEEEEE
END.

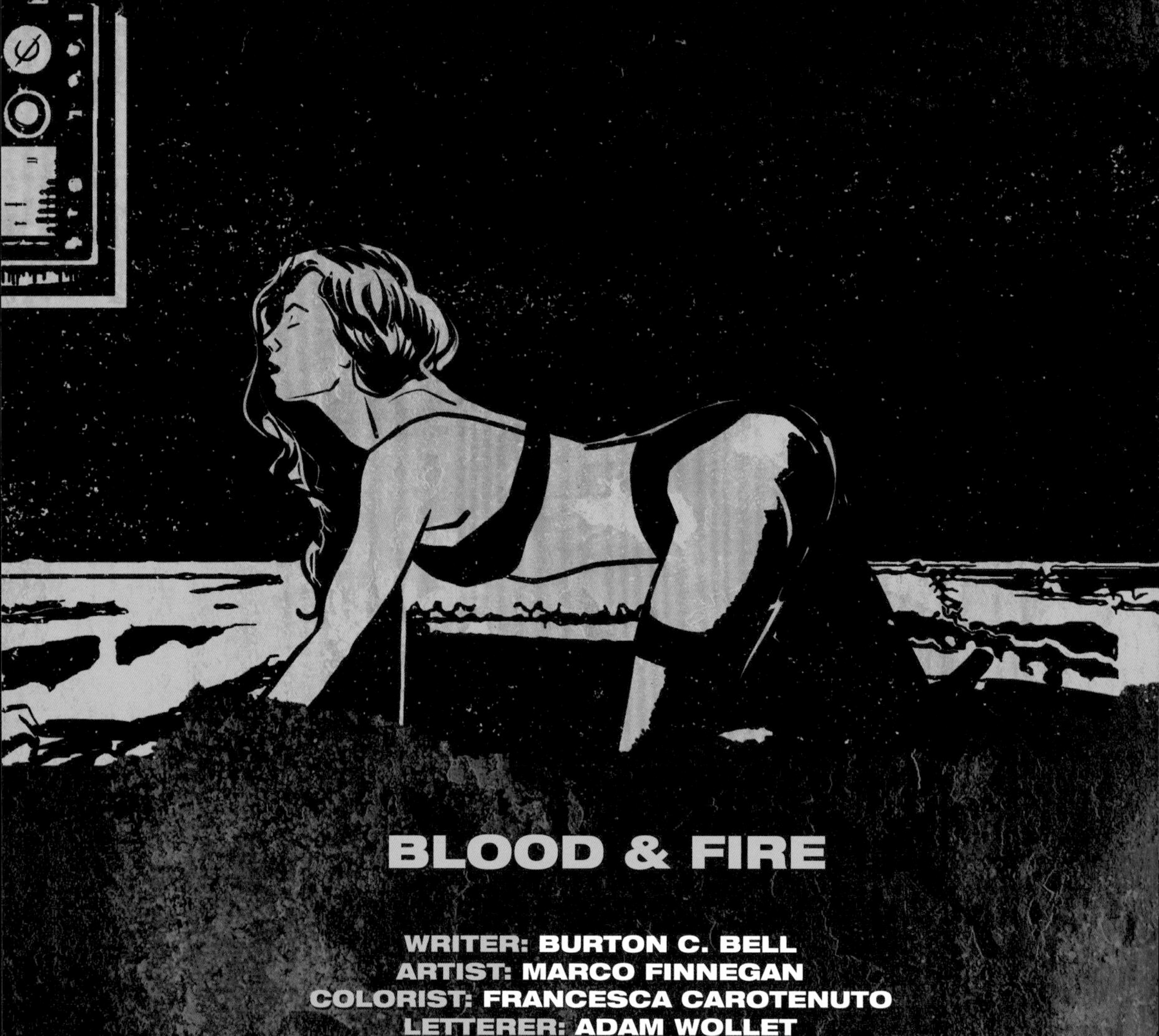

BLOOD & FIRE

WRITER: BURTON C. BELL
ARTIST: MARCO FINNEGAN
COLORIST: FRANCESCA CAROTENUTO
LETTERER: ADAM WOLLET

Based on actual events between 1993 and 1994, a series of savage murders plagued the northeast United States. Nine victims in total. All victims were adult, white males. All men were found alone, stripped of their clothing and brutally murdered, with forensic evidence indicating sexual activity prior to death. As time progressed all the bodies were found 1 month apart in vicinities of all female strip clubs. The police were never able to produce any significant leads, nor determine any rational motive. No one has ever been charged for these crimes. All the cases have been classified homicides, and to this day remain cold cases

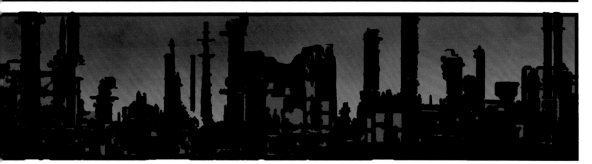

Desperate longing has lifted the veil over your secrecy, and it is your insatiable lust that has forsaken you with a river of blood pulsing from the mouths of your innocent victims, leading me to this fraction of Hell. This thirst that drives you will never be satiated, and this suffering will not end until you are vanquished from this terrestrial plane.

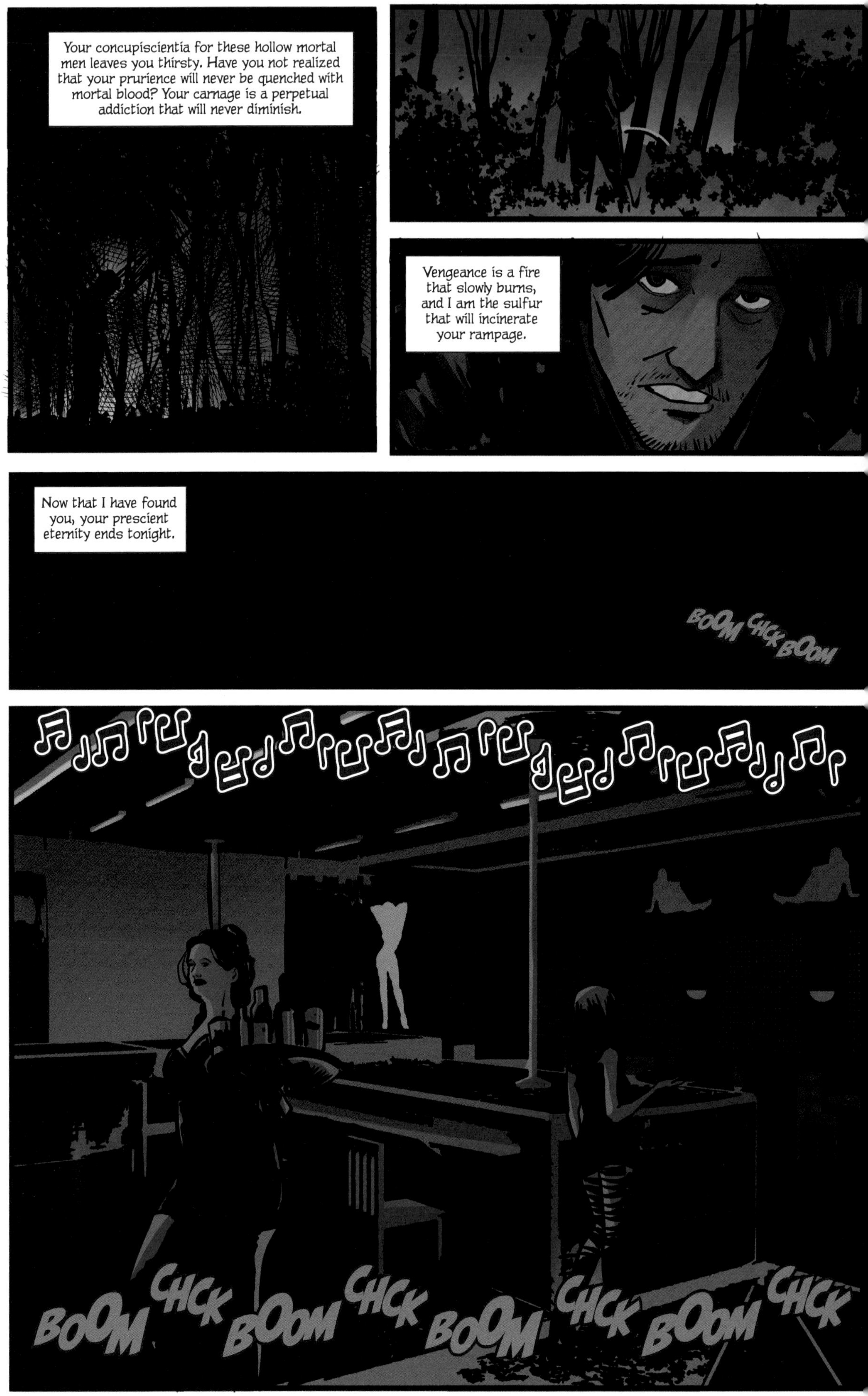

Your concupiscientia for these hollow mortal men leaves you thirsty. Have you not realized that your prurience will never be quenched with mortal blood? Your carnage is a perpetual addiction that will never diminish.
Vengeance is a fire that slowly burns, and I am the sulfur that will incinerate your rampage.
Now that I have found you, your prescient eternity ends tonight.
BOOM CHCK BOOM
BOOM CHCK BOOM CHCK BOOM CHCK BOOM CHCK

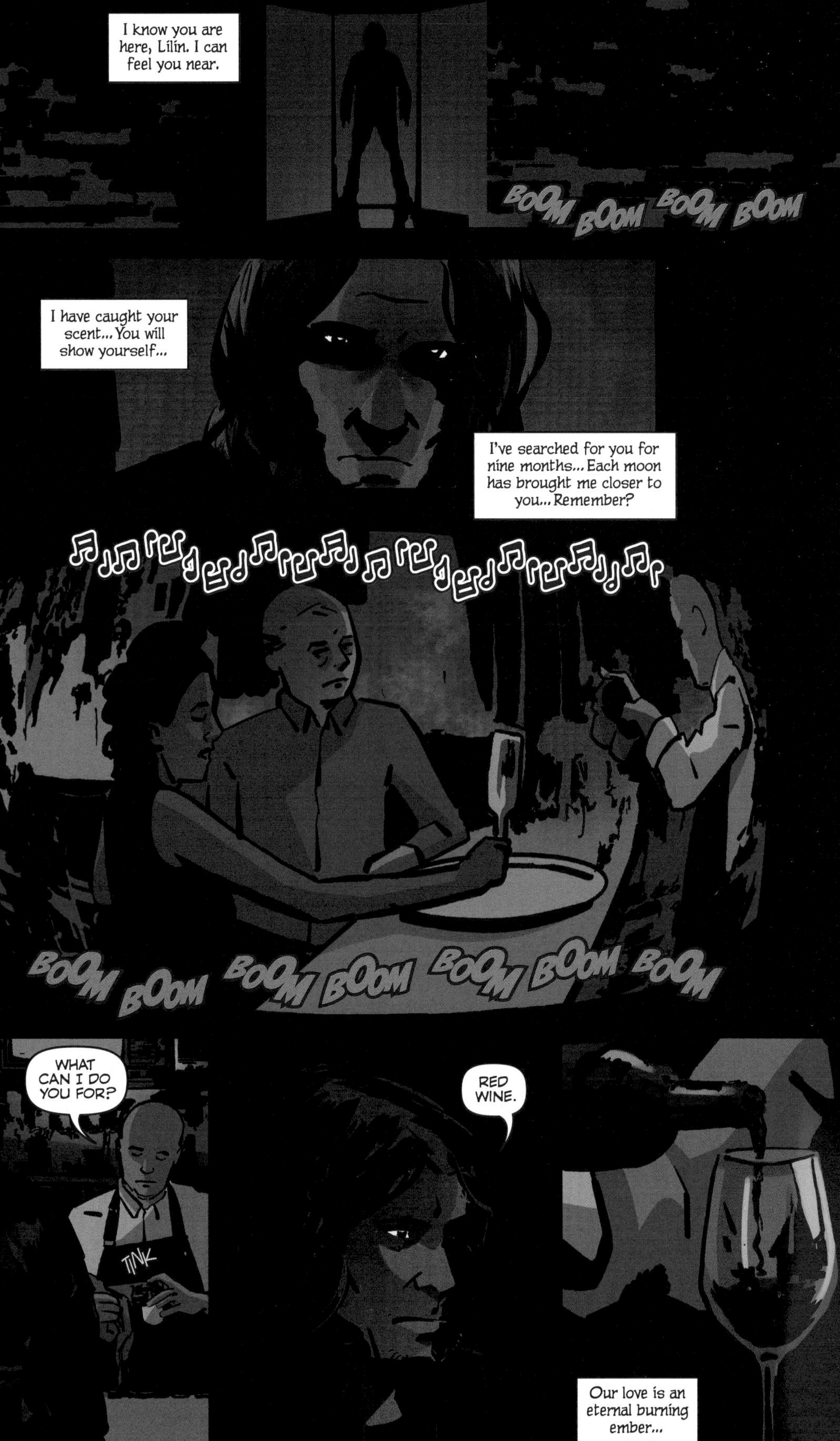

I know you are here, Lilin. I can feel you near.
BOOM BOOM BOOM BOOM
I have caught your scent... You will show yourself...
I've searched for you for nine months... Each moon has brought me closer to you... Remember?
BOOM BOOM BOOM BOOM BOOM BOOM BOOM
WHAT CAN I DO YOU FOR?
TINK
RED WINE.
Our love is an eternal burning ember...

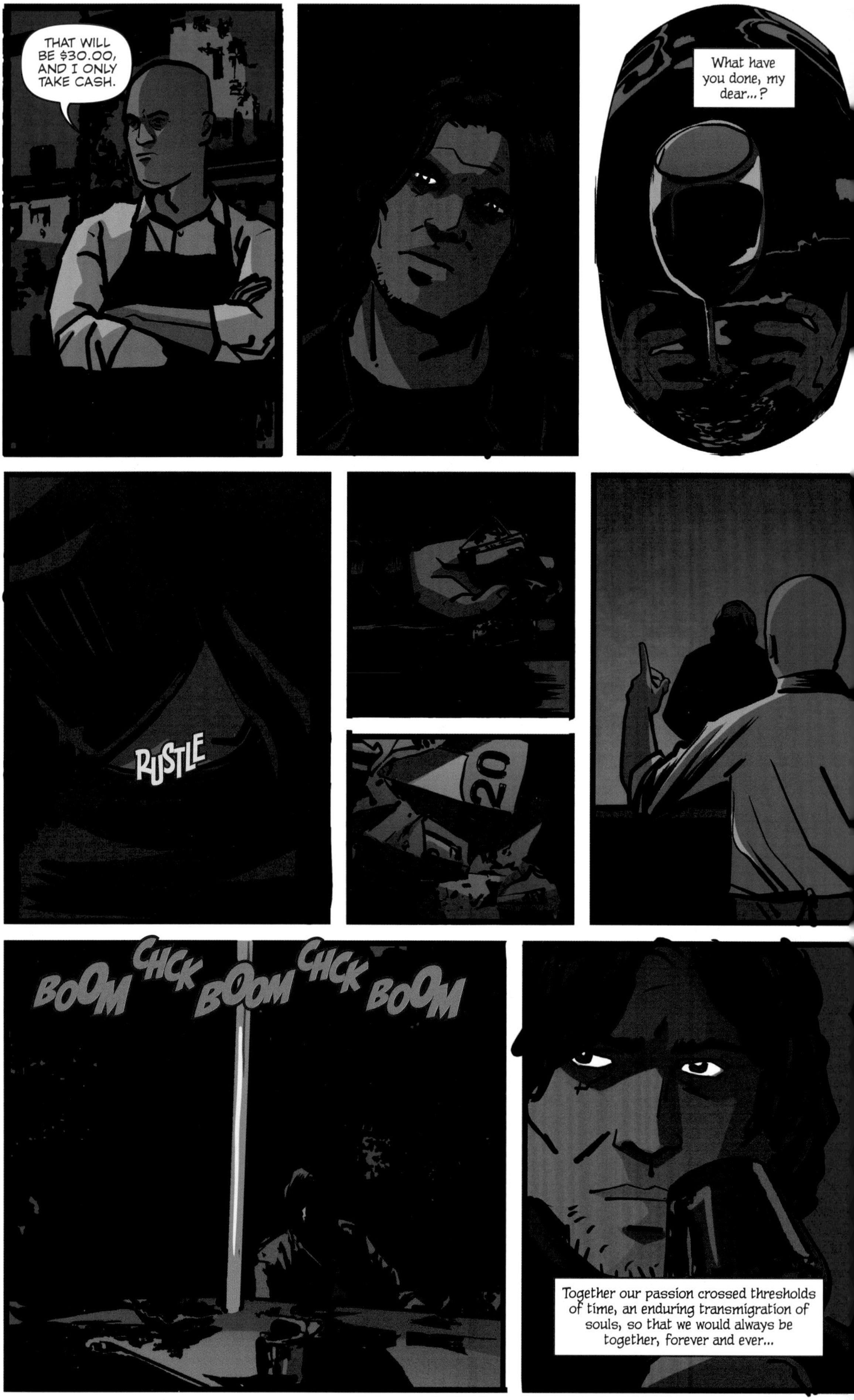

THAT WILL BE $30.00, AND I ONLY TAKE CASH.
What have you done, my dear...?
RUSTLE
20
BOOM CHCK BOOM CHCK BOOM
Together our passion crossed thresholds of time, an enduring transmigration of souls, so that we would always be together, forever and ever...

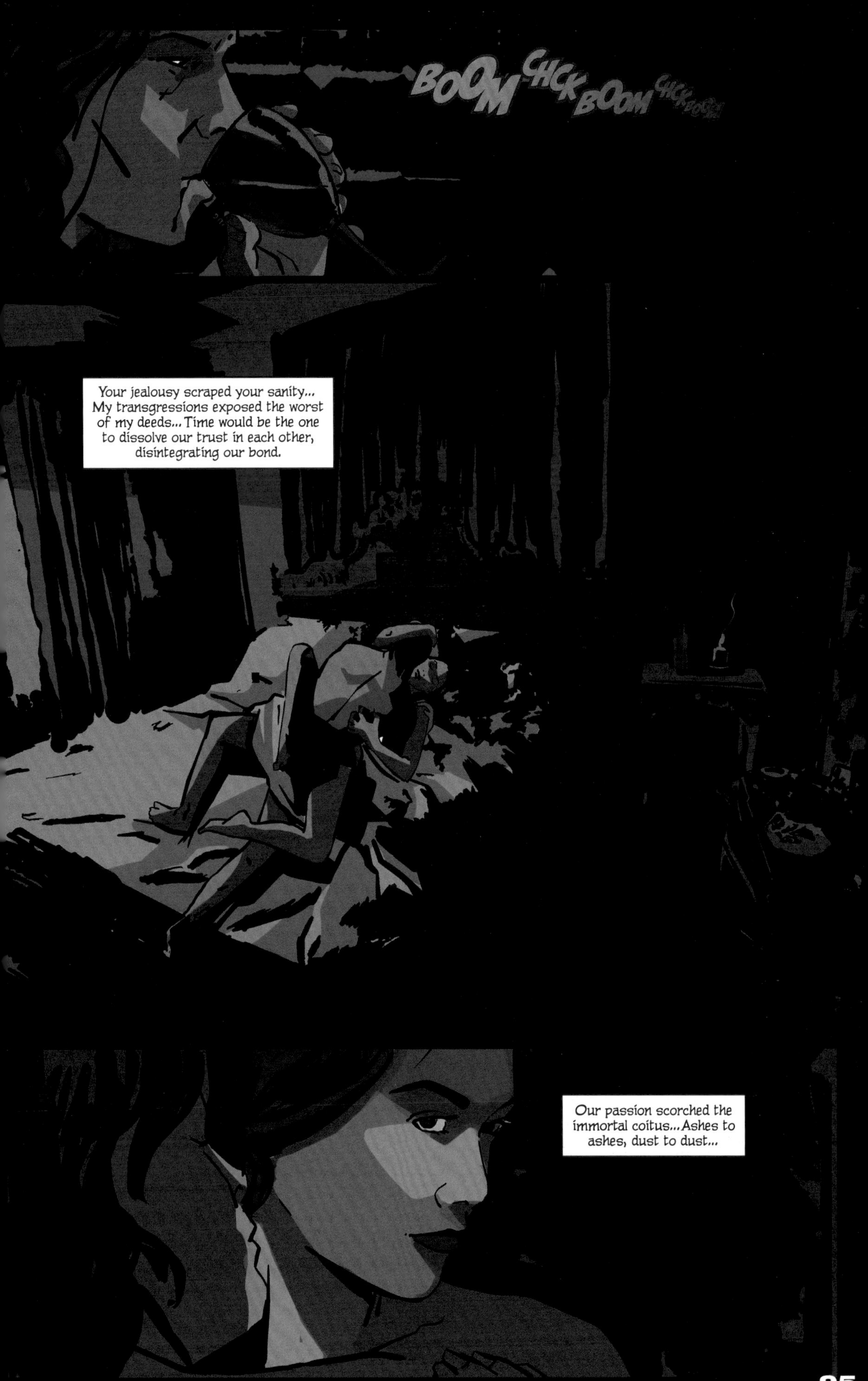
BOOM CHCK BOOM CHCK
Your jealousy scraped your sanity... My transgressions exposed the worst of my deeds... Time would be the one to dissolve our trust in each other, disintegrating our bond.
Our passion scorched the immortal coitus... Ashes to ashes, dust to dust...

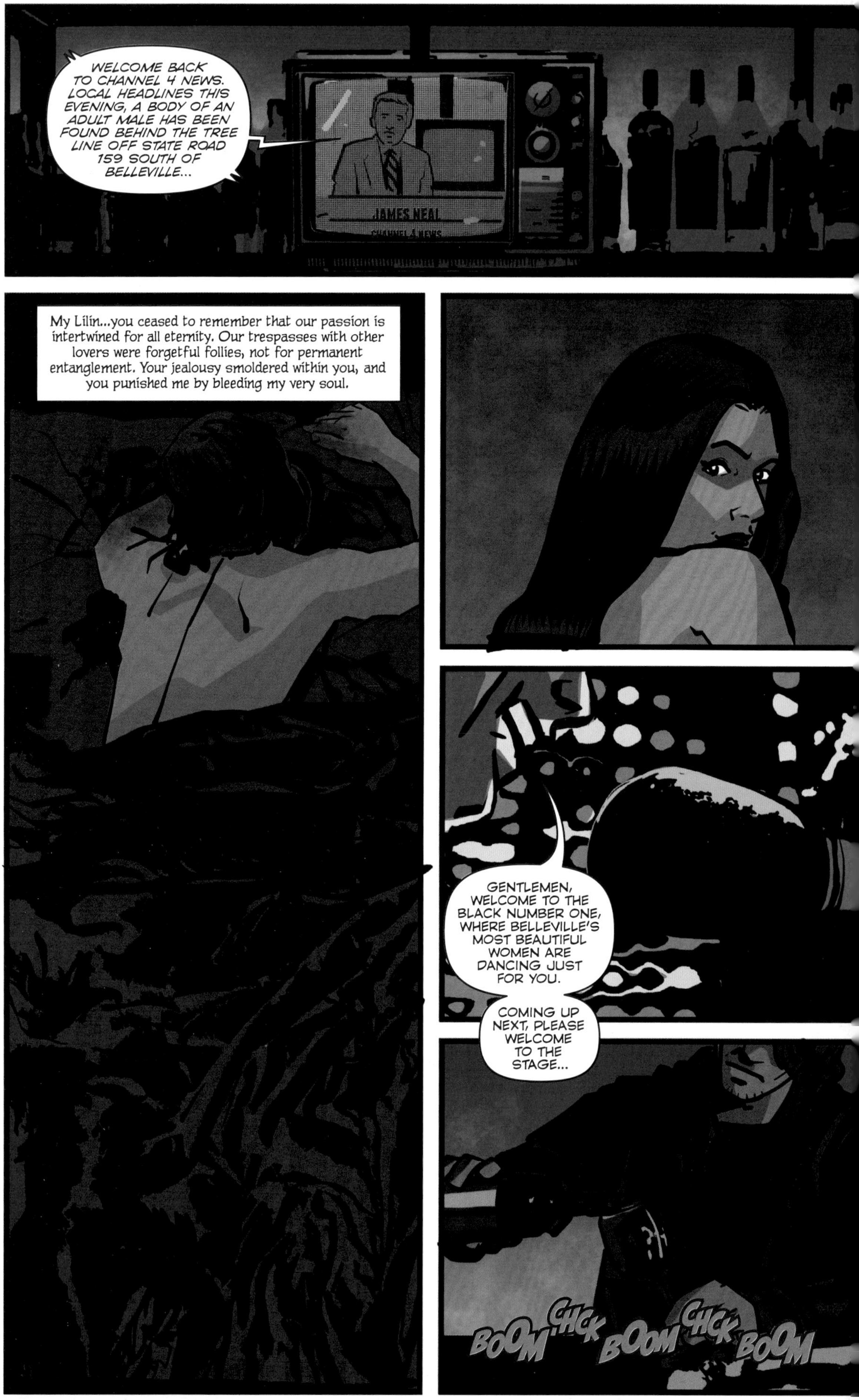
WELCOME BACK TO CHANNEL 4 NEWS. LOCAL HEADLINES THIS EVENING, A BODY OF AN ADULT MALE HAS BEEN FOUND BEHIND THE TREE LINE OFF STATE ROAD 159 SOUTH OF BELLEVILLE...
JAMES NEAL
My Lilin...you ceased to remember that our passion is intertwined for all eternity. Our trespasses with other lovers were forgetful follies, not for permanent entanglement. Your jealousy smoldered within you, and you punished me by bleeding my very soul.
GENTLEMEN, WELCOME TO THE BLACK NUMBER ONE, WHERE BELLEVILLE'S MOST BEAUTIFUL WOMEN ARE DANCING JUST FOR YOU.
COMING UP NEXT, PLEASE WELCOME TO THE STAGE...
BOOM CHCK BOOM CHCK BOOM

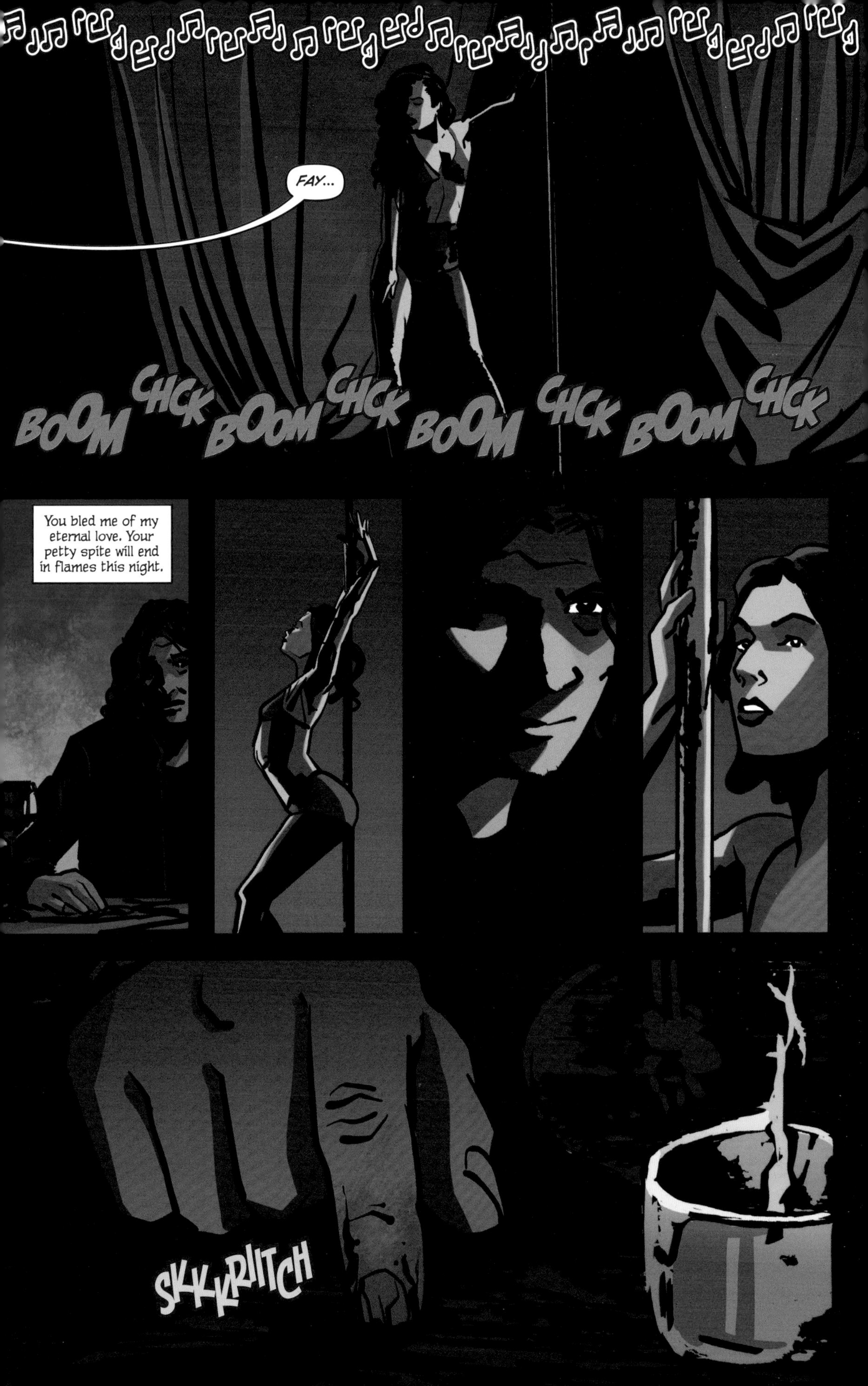
FAY...
BOOM CHCK BOOM CHCK BOOM CHCK BOOM CHCK
You bled me of my eternal love. Your petty spite will end in flames this night.
SKKKRIITCH

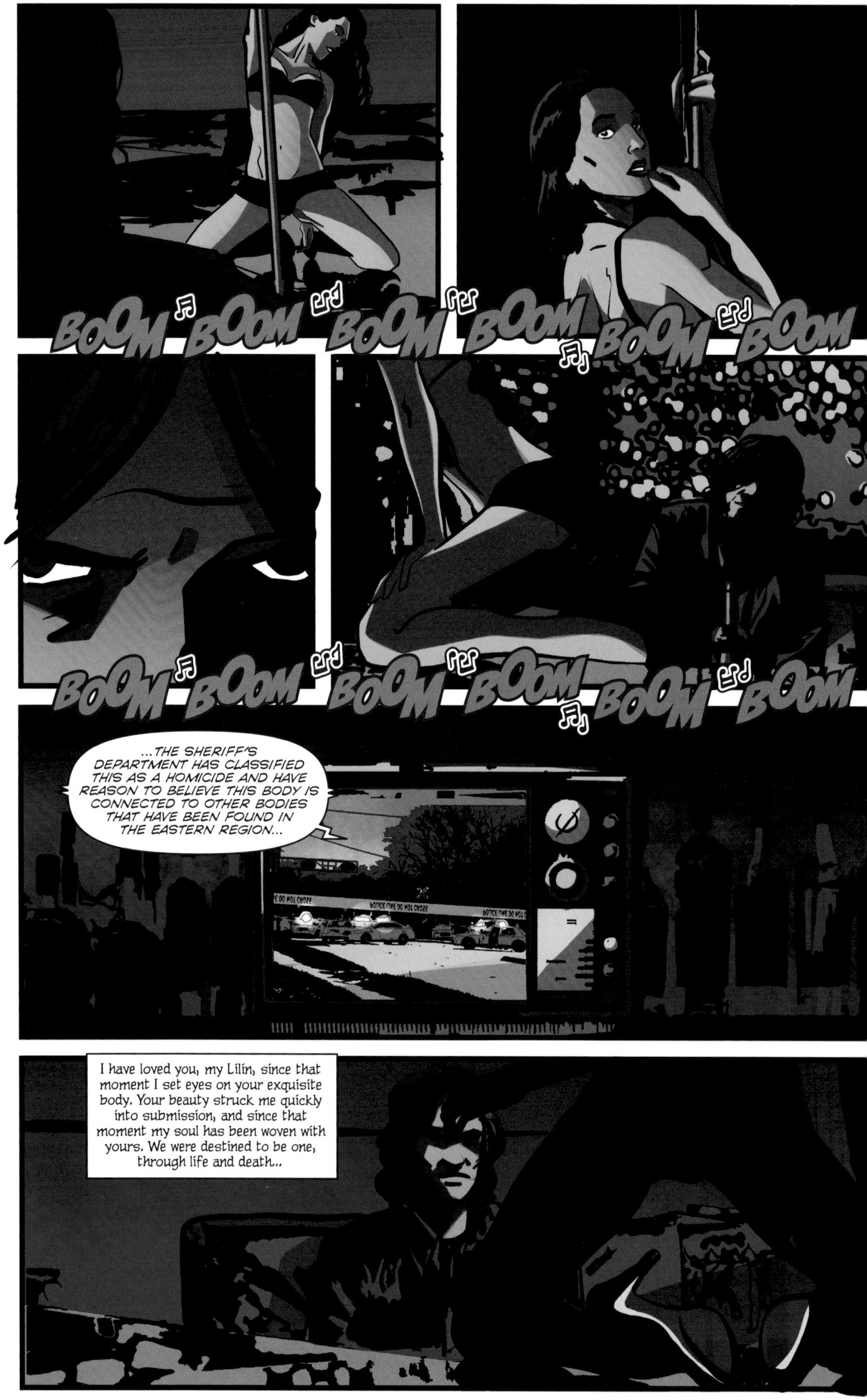
BOOM BOOM BOOM BOOM BOOM BOOM
BOOM BOOM BOOM BOOM BOOM BOOM
...THE SHERIFF'S DEPARTMENT HAS CLASSIFIED THIS AS A HOMICIDE AND HAVE REASON TO BELIEVE THIS BODY IS CONNECTED TO OTHER BODIES THAT HAVE BEEN FOUND IN THE EASTERN REGION...
I have loved you, my Lilin, since that moment I set eyes on your exquisite body. Your beauty struck me quickly into submission, and since that moment my soul has been woven with yours. We were destined to be one, through life and death...

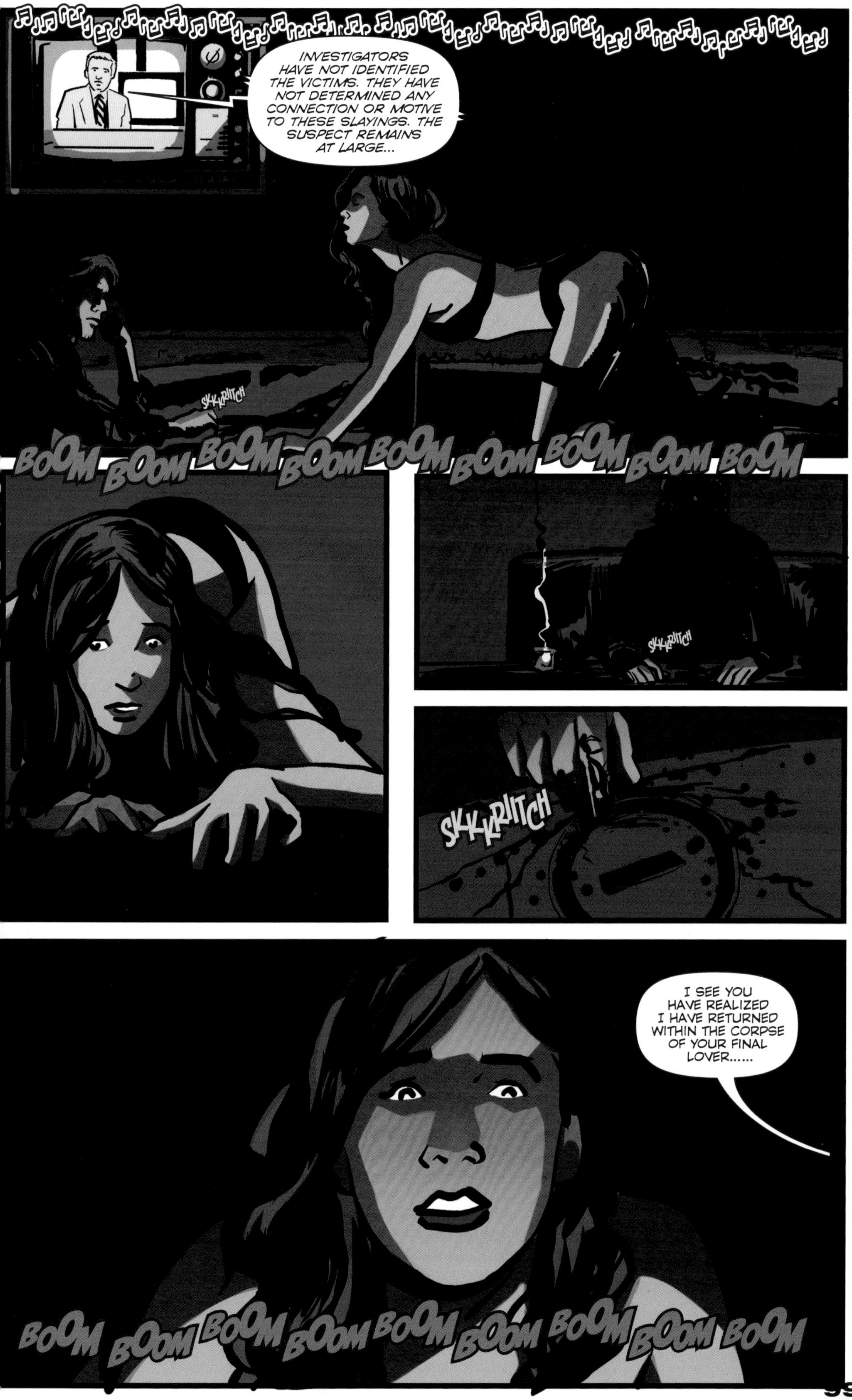
INVESTIGATORS HAVE NOT IDENTIFIED THE VICTIMS. THEY HAVE NOT DETERMINED ANY CONNECTION OR MOTIVE TO THESE SLAYINGS. THE SUSPECT REMAINS AT LARGE...
SKKKRIITCH
BOOM BOOM BOOM BOOM BOOM BOOM BOOM BOOM BOOM
SKKKRIITCH
SKKKRIITCH
I SEE YOU HAVE REALIZED I HAVE RETURNED WITHIN THE CORPSE OF YOUR FINAL LOVER......
BOOM BOOM BOOM BOOM BOOM BOOM BOOM BOOM BOOM

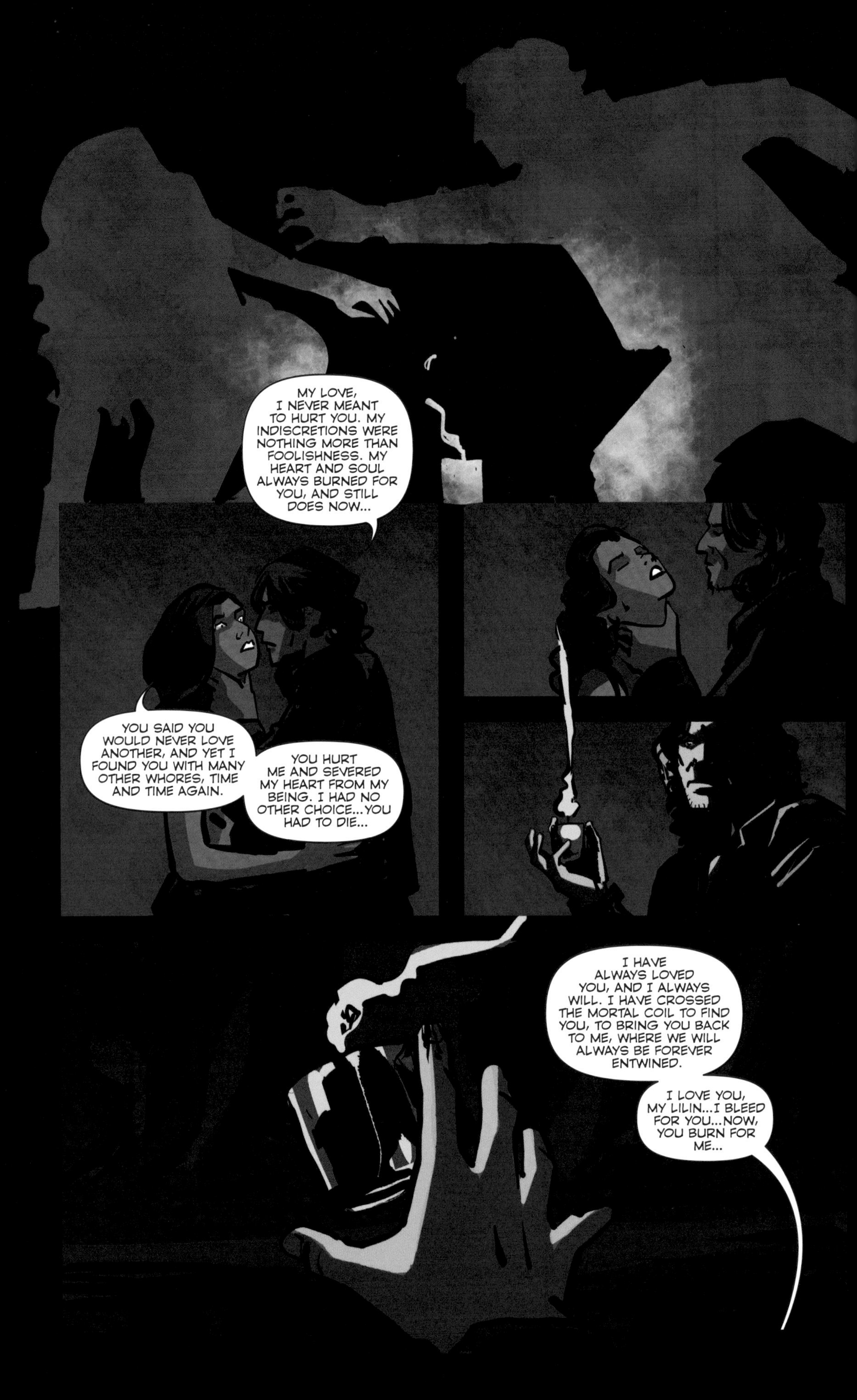
MY LOVE, I NEVER MEANT TO HURT YOU. MY INDISCRETIONS WERE NOTHING MORE THAN FOOLISHNESS. MY HEART AND SOUL ALWAYS BURNED FOR YOU, AND STILL DOES NOW...
YOU SAID YOU WOULD NEVER LOVE ANOTHER, AND YET I FOUND YOU WITH MANY OTHER WHORES, TIME AND TIME AGAIN.
YOU HURT ME AND SEVERED MY HEART FROM MY BEING. I HAD NO OTHER CHOICE...YOU HAD TO DIE...
I HAVE ALWAYS LOVED YOU, AND I ALWAYS WILL. I HAVE CROSSED THE MORTAL COIL TO FIND YOU, TO BRING YOU BACK TO ME, WHERE WE WILL ALWAYS BE FOREVER ENTWINED.
I LOVE YOU, MY LILIN...I BLEED FOR YOU...NOW, YOU BURN FOR ME...

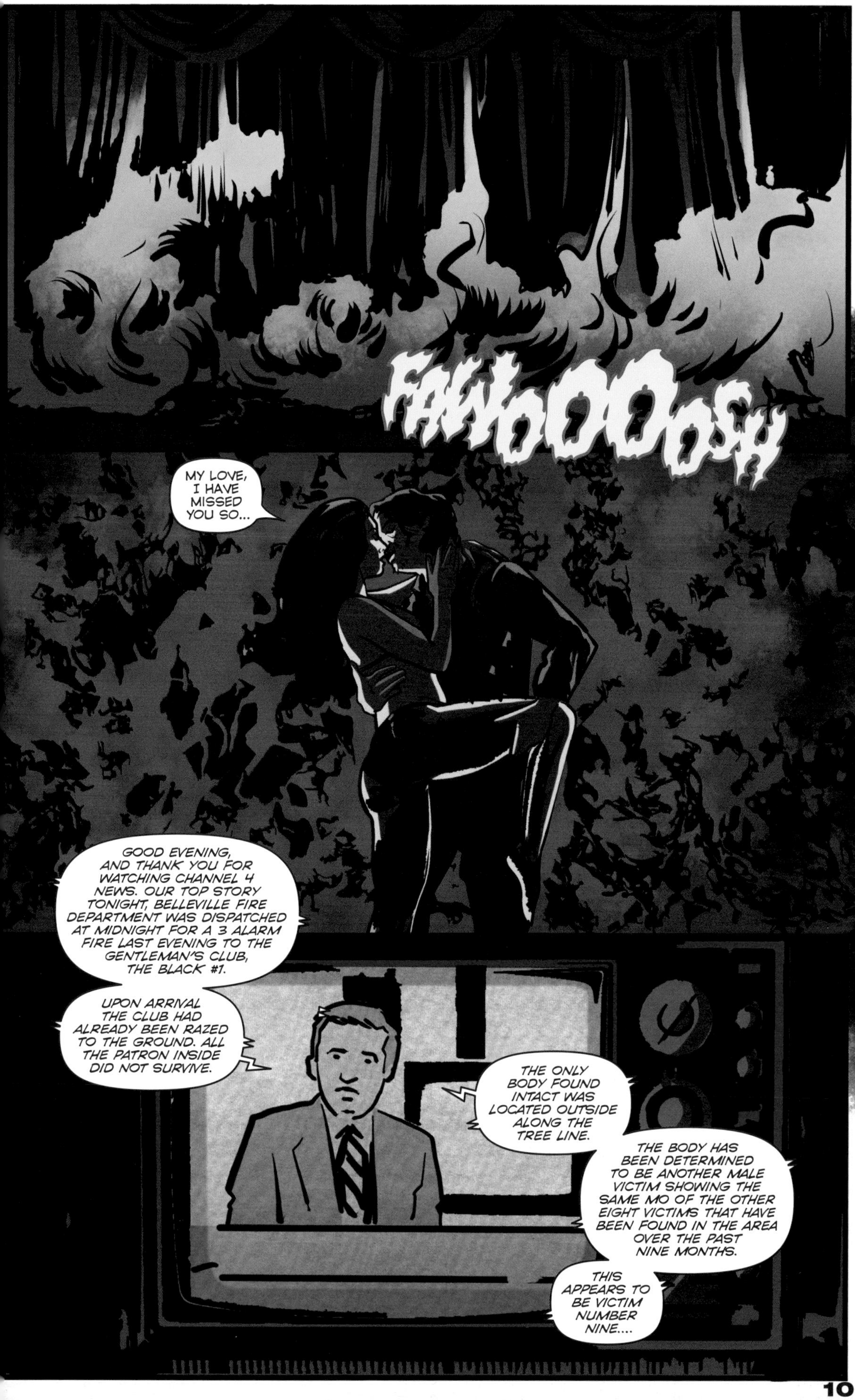
FAWOOOOSH
MY LOVE, I HAVE MISSED YOU SO...
GOOD EVENING, AND THANK YOU FOR WATCHING CHANNEL 4 NEWS. OUR TOP STORY TONIGHT, BELLEVILLE FIRE DEPARTMENT WAS DISPATCHED AT MIDNIGHT FOR A 3 ALARM FIRE LAST EVENING TO THE GENTLEMAN'S CLUB, THE BLACK #1.
UPON ARRIVAL THE CLUB HAD ALREADY BEEN RAZED TO THE GROUND. ALL THE PATRON INSIDE DID NOT SURVIVE.
THE ONLY BODY FOUND INTACT WAS LOCATED OUTSIDE ALONG THE TREE LINE.
THE BODY HAS BEEN DETERMINED TO BE ANOTHER MALE VICTIM SHOWING THE SAME MO OF THE OTHER EIGHT VICTIMS THAT HAVE BEEN FOUND IN THE AREA OVER THE PAST NINE MONTHS.
THIS APPEARS TO BE VICTIM NUMBER NINE....

CAN'T LOSE YOU

WRITER: ROY BURDINE
ARTIST: NICK MARINKOVICH
COLORIST: SIMON D'ANGELO
LETTERER: GABRIELA DOWNIE

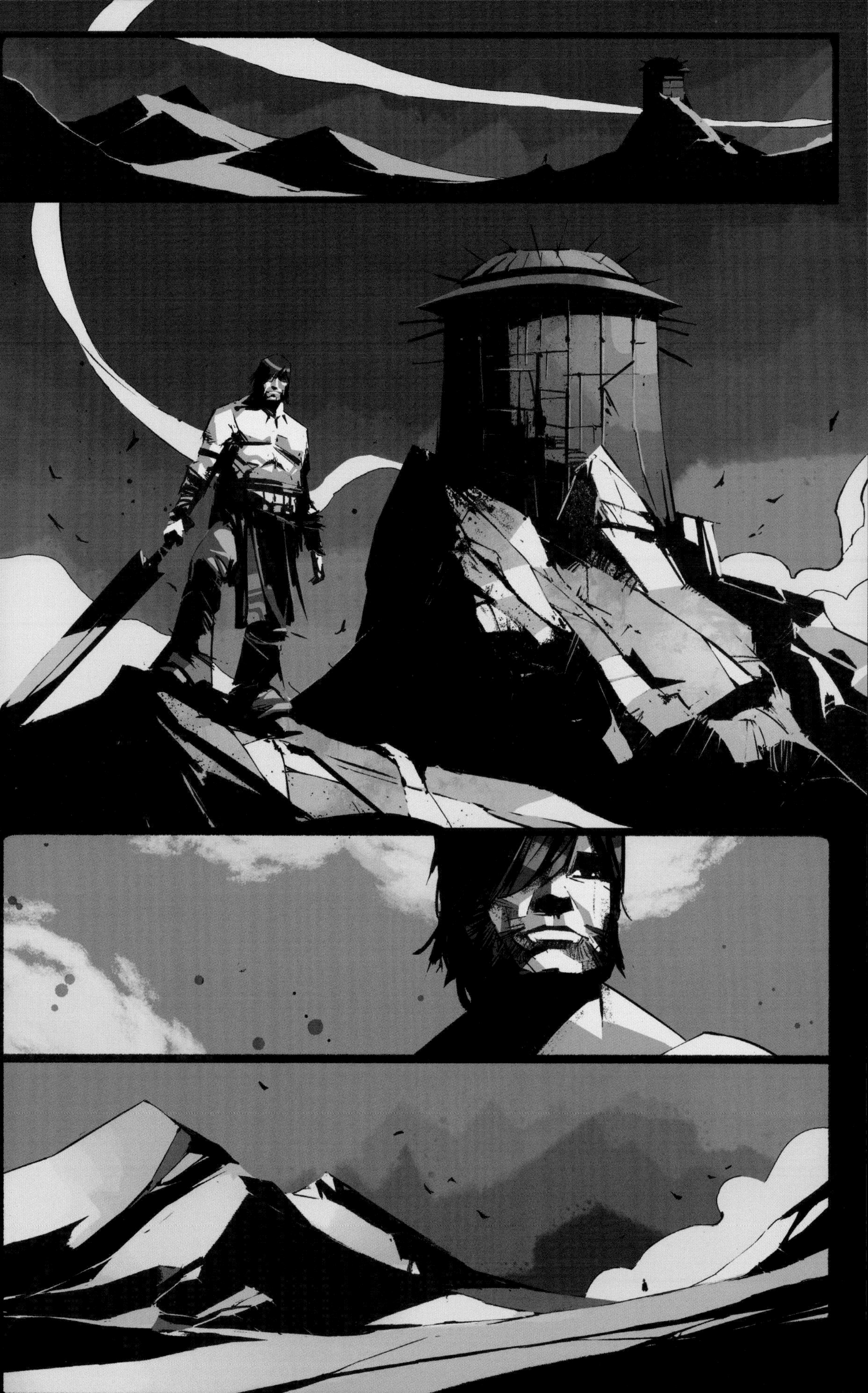

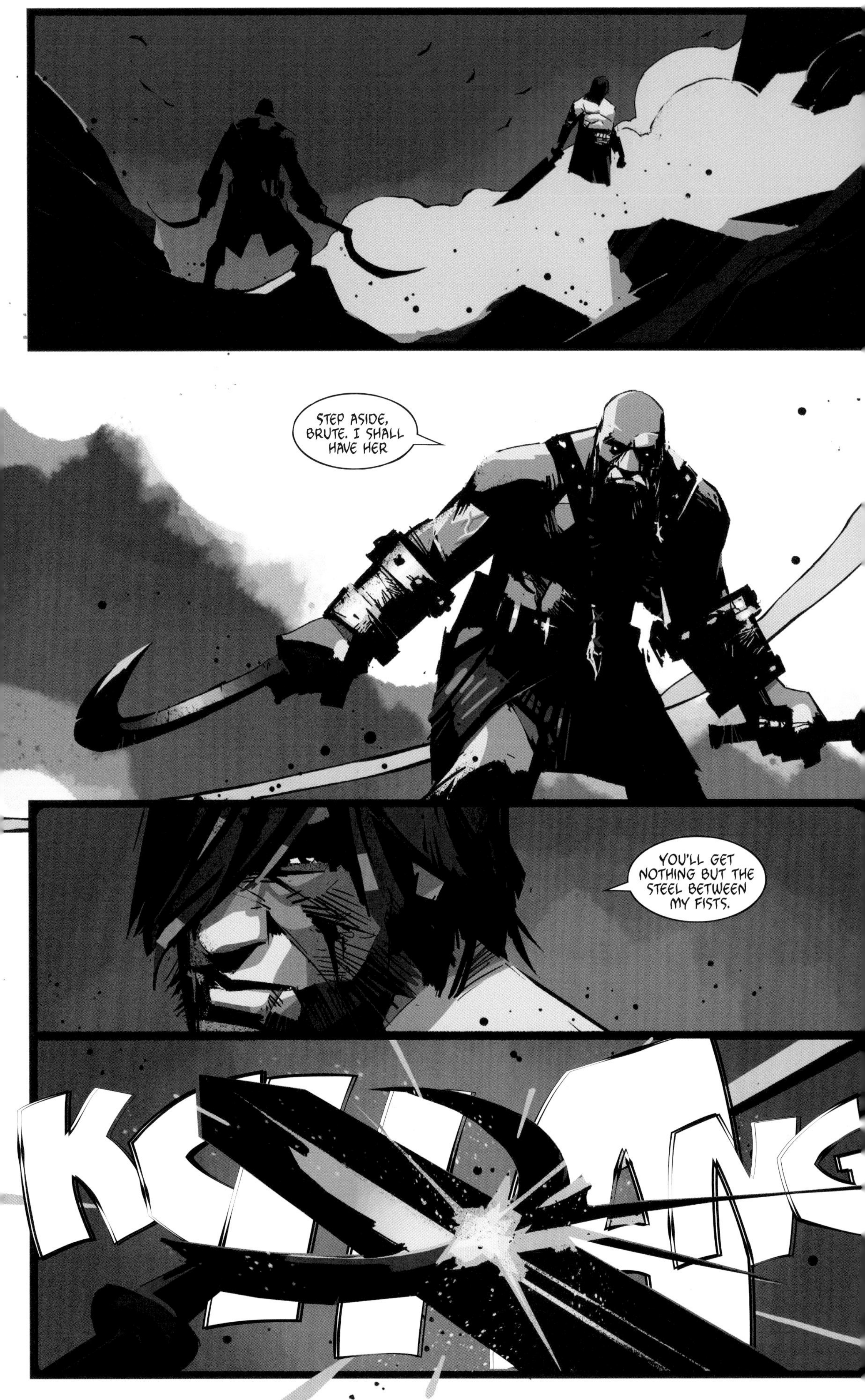
STEP ASIDE, BRUTE. I SHALL HAVE HER
YOU'LL GET NOTHING BUT THE STEEL BETWEEN MY FISTS.

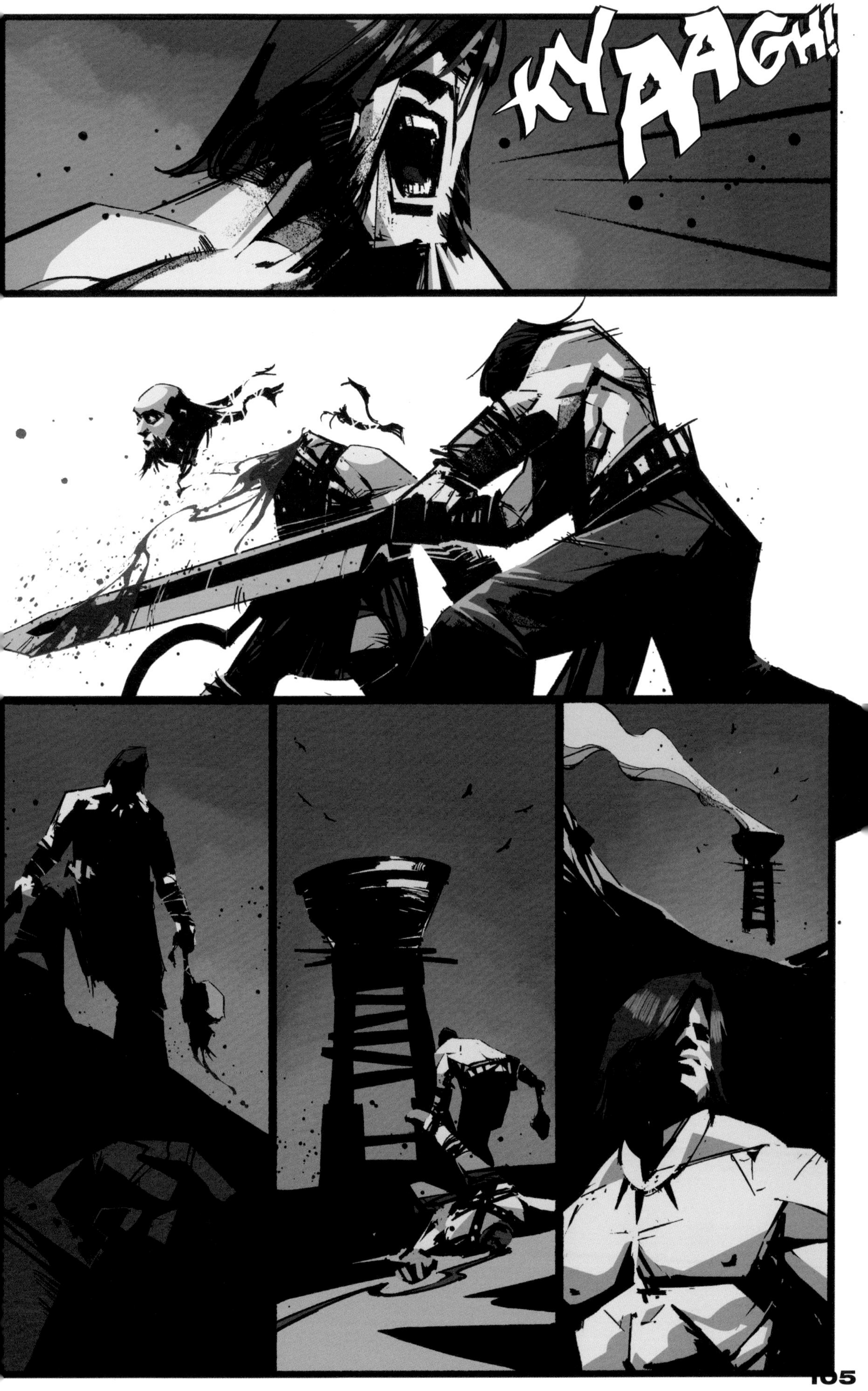
KYAAGH!

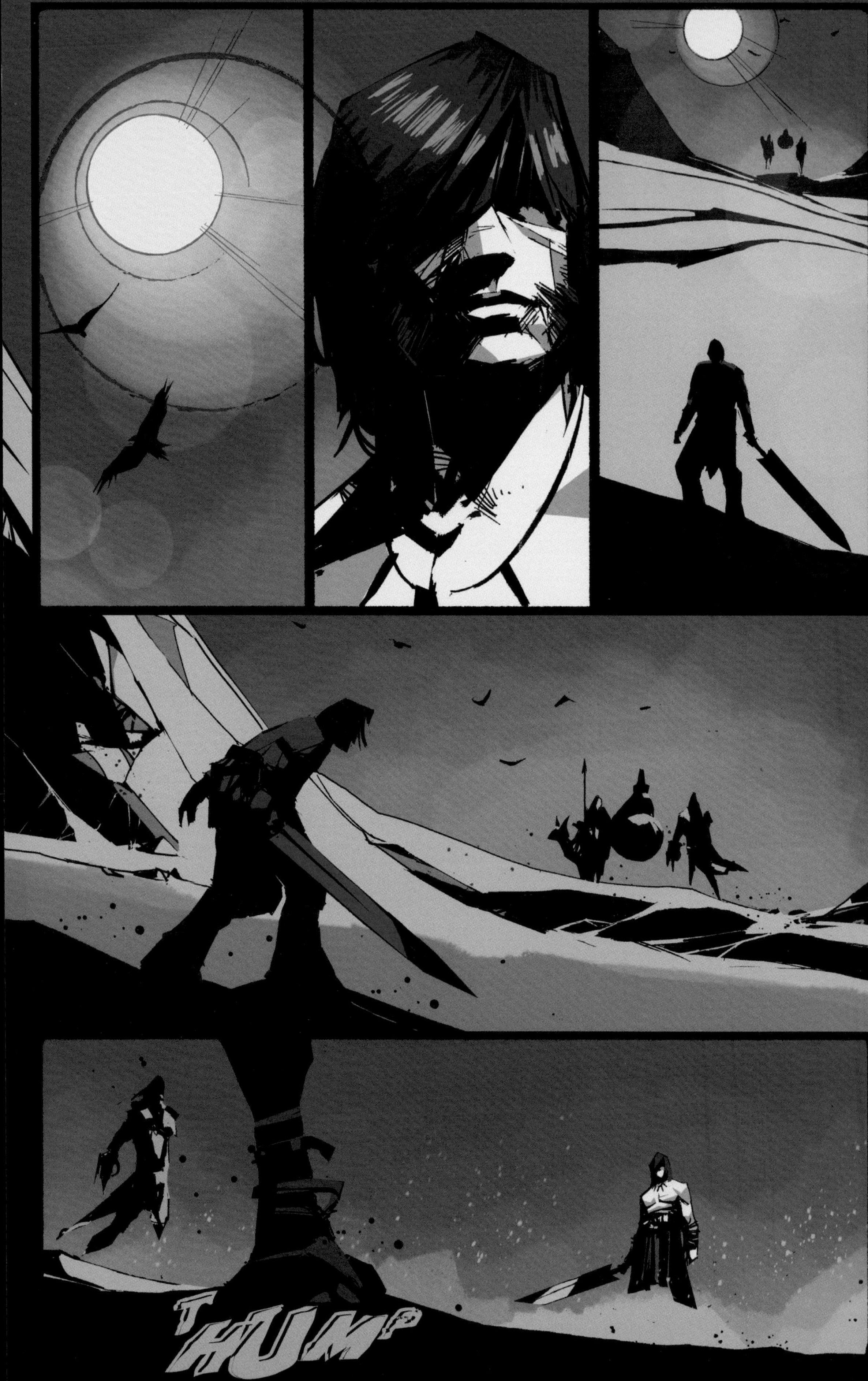
THUMP

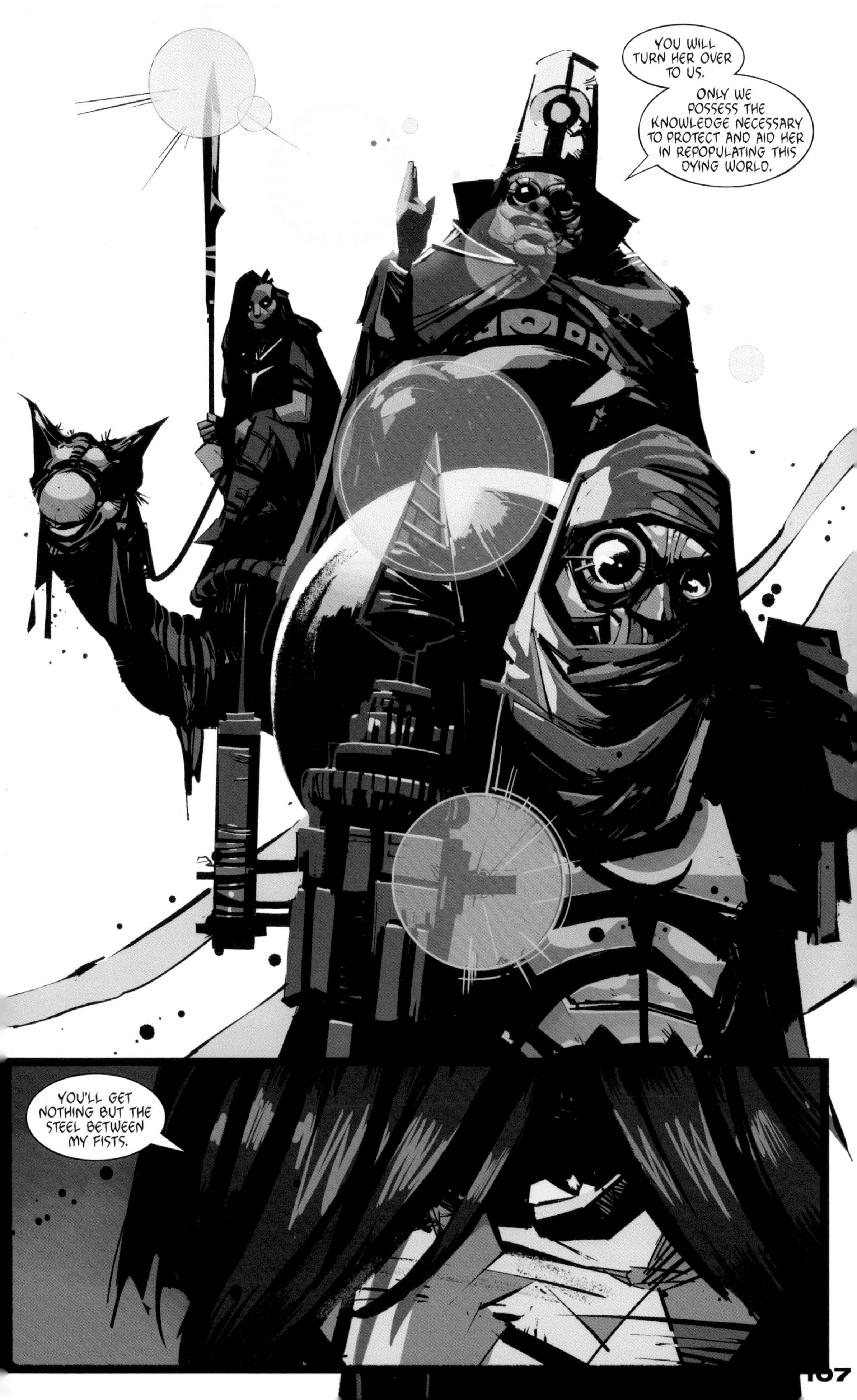
YOU WILL TURN HER OVER TO US.
ONLY WE POSSESS THE KNOWLEDGE NECESSARY TO PROTECT AND AID HER IN REPOPULATING THIS DYING WORLD.
YOU'LL GET NOTHING BUT THE STEEL BETWEEN MY FISTS.

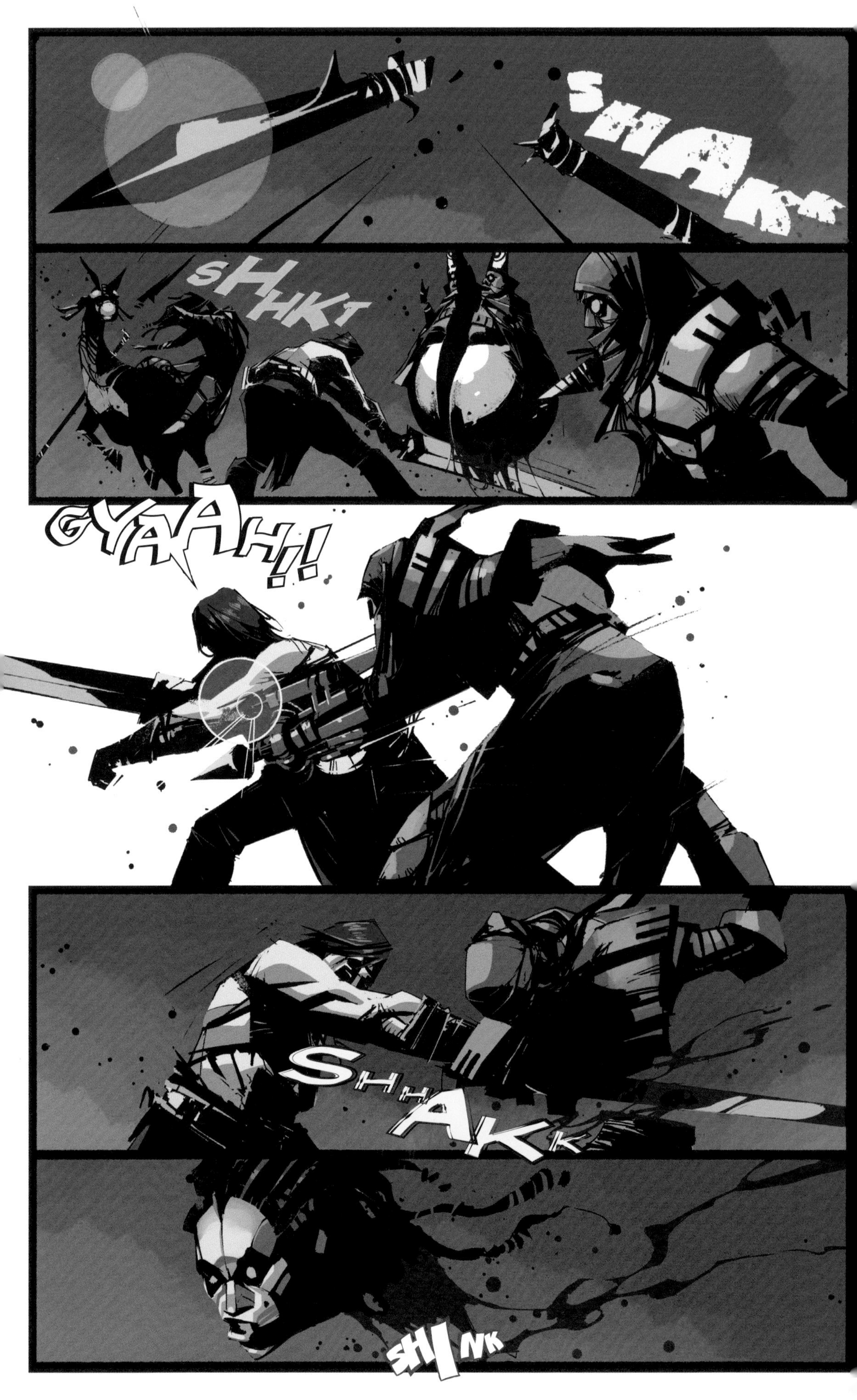
SHAKK
SHHKT
GYAAH!!
SHHAKK
SHINK

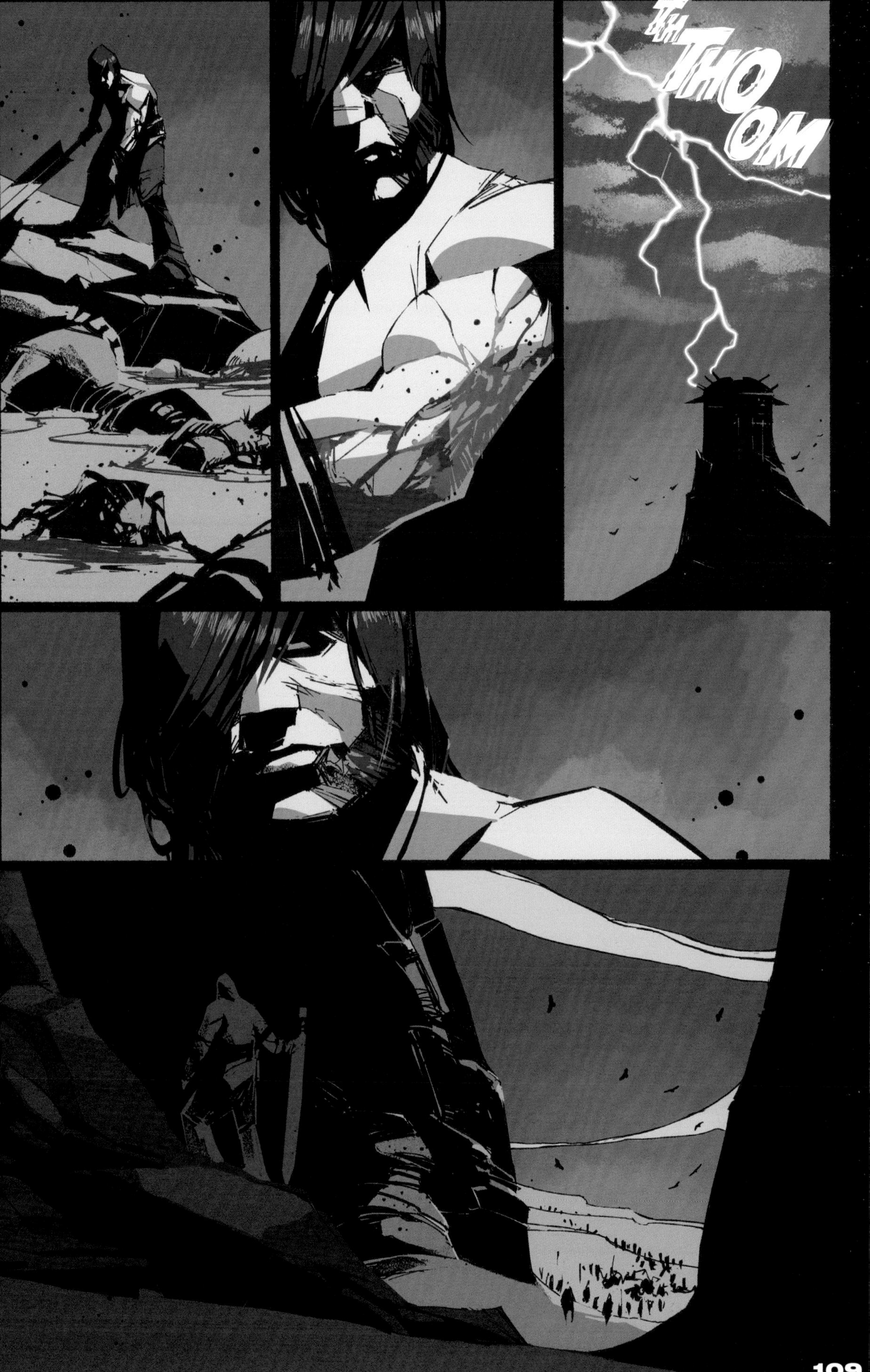
THOOM

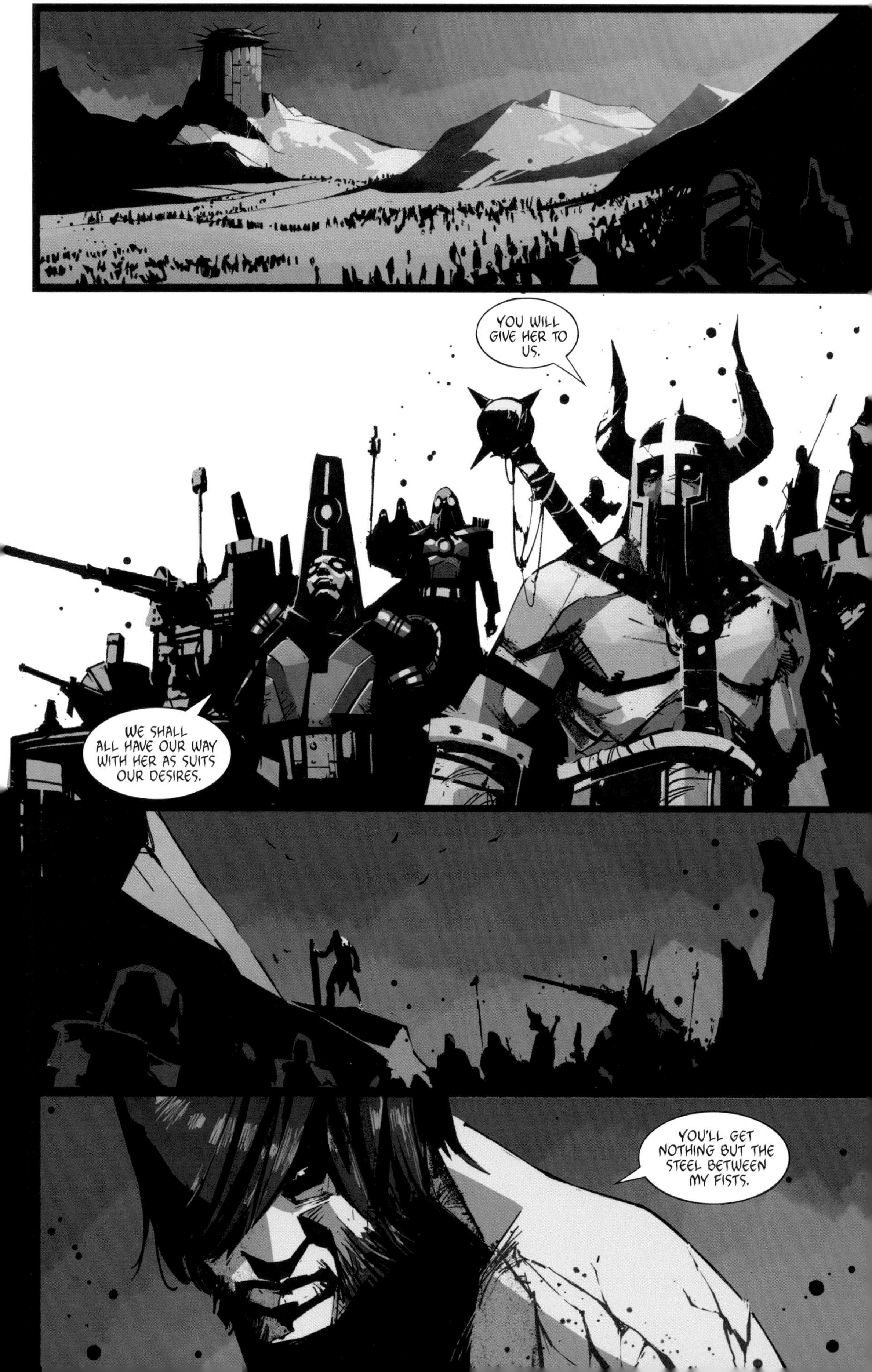
YOU WILL GIVE HER TO US.
WE SHALL ALL HAVE OUR WAY WITH HER AS SUITS OUR DESIRES.
YOU'LL GET NOTHING BUT THE STEEL BETWEEN MY FISTS.

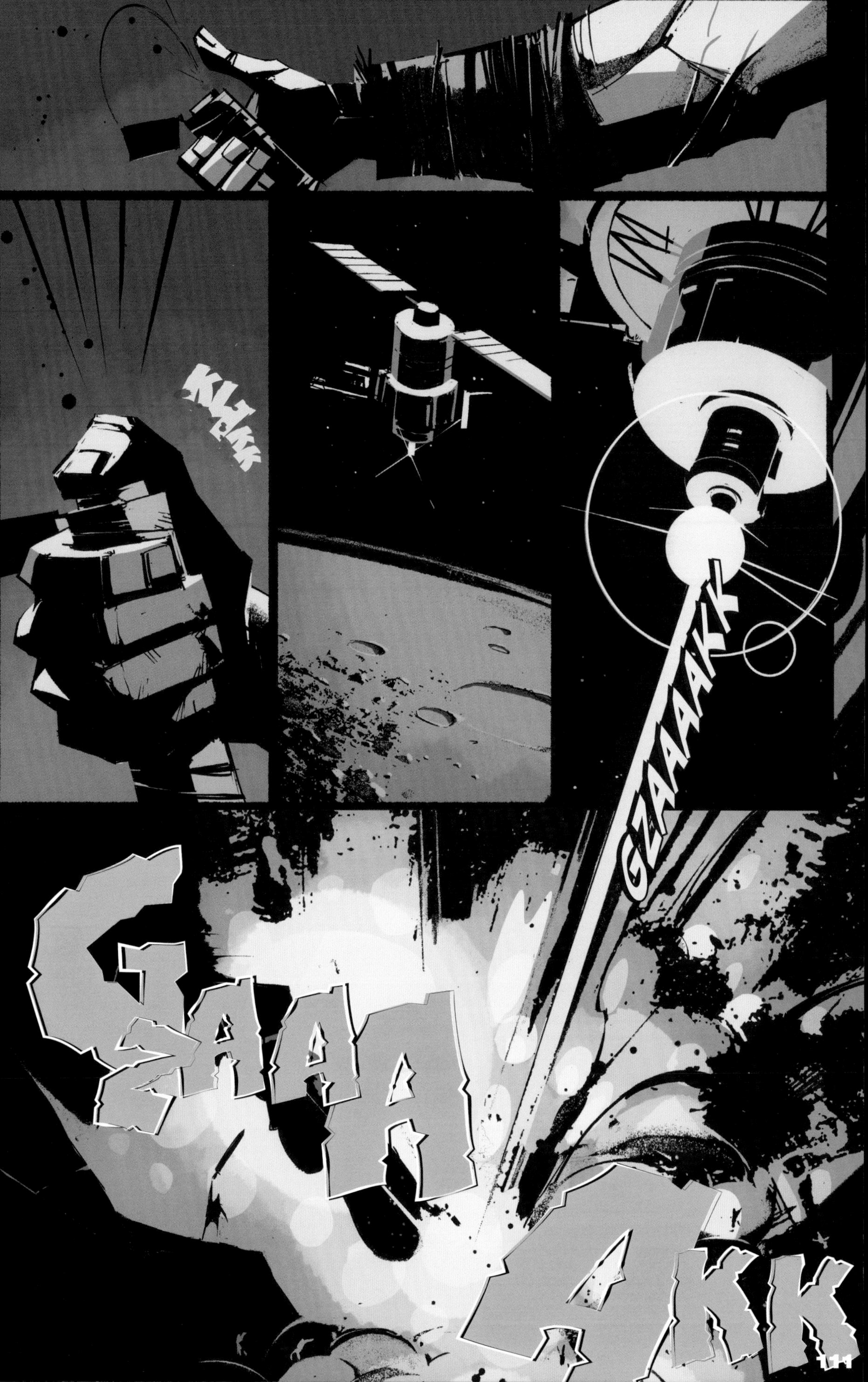
KLIKK
GZAAAKK
GZAAAAKK

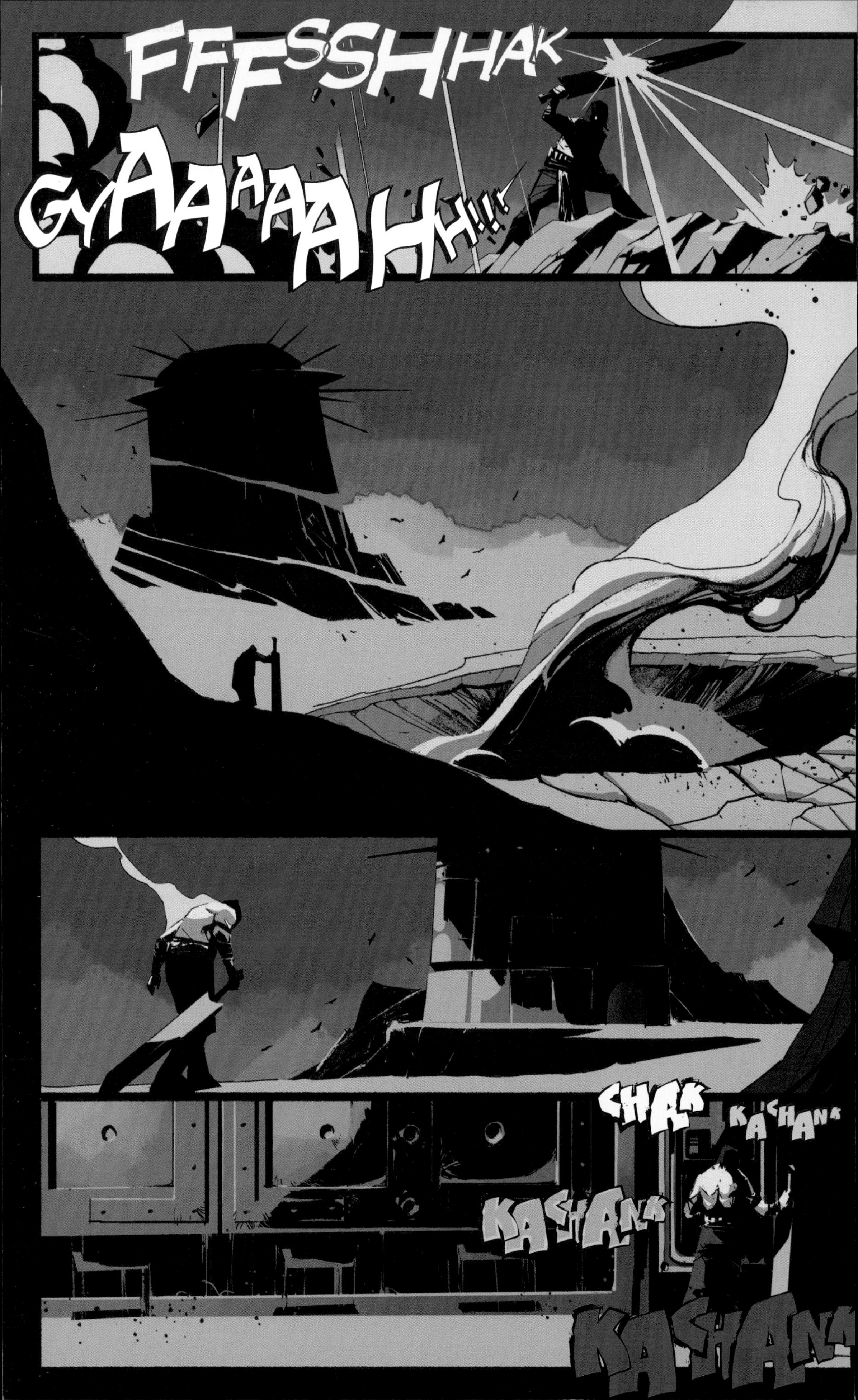
FFFSSHHAK
GYAAAAAHHH!!!
CHAK
KACHANK
KACHANK
KACHANK

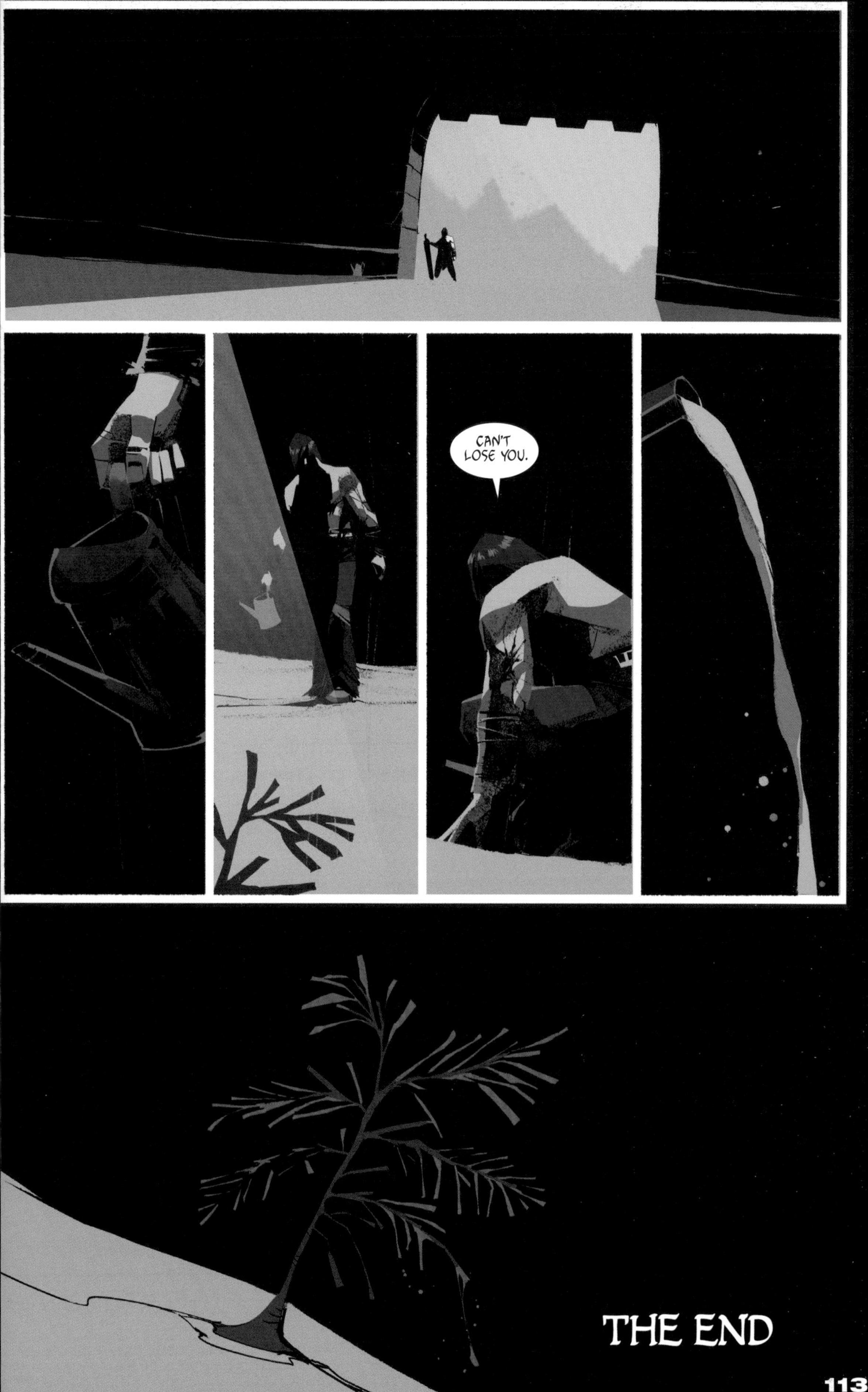
CAN'T
LOSE YOU.
THE END

SUSPENDED IN DUSK

WRITER: RYAN J. DOWNEY
ARTIST: ADAM MARKIEWICZ
COLORIST: FRANCESCA CAROTENUTO
LETTERER: BUDDY BEAUDOIN

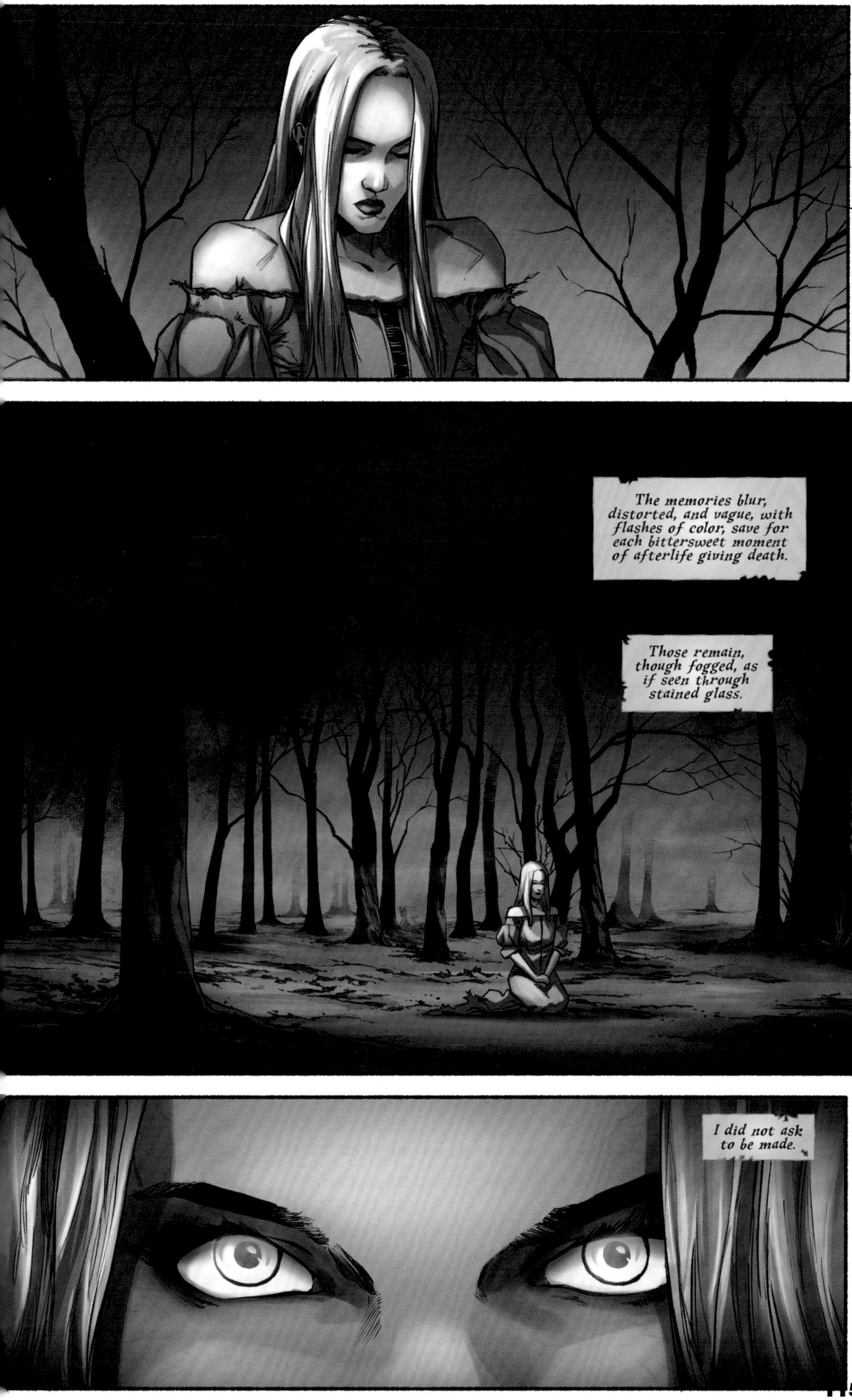
The memories blur, distorted, and vague, with flashes of color, save for each bittersweet moment of afterlife giving death.
Those remain, though fogged, as if seen through stained glass.
I did not ask to be made.

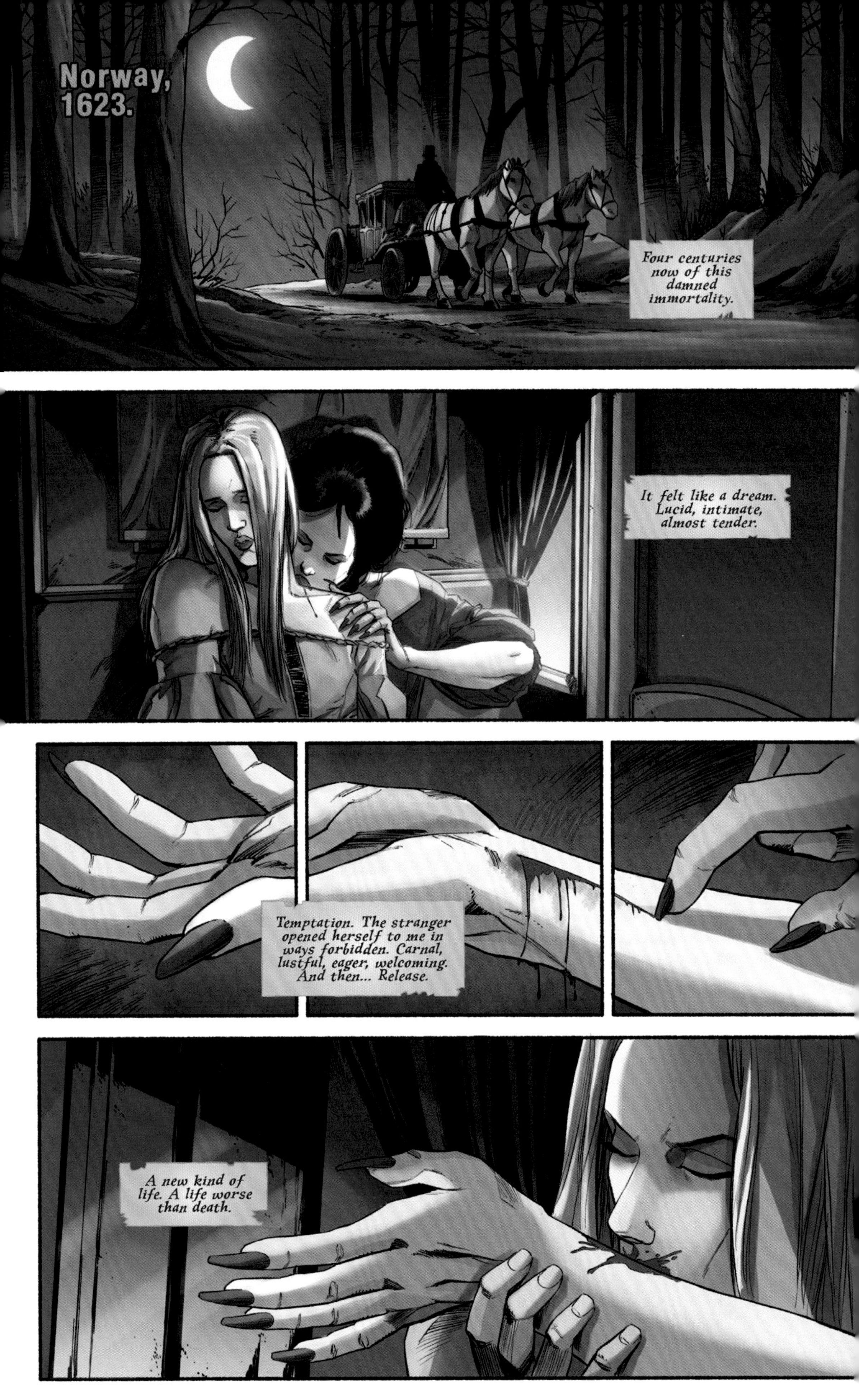
Norway, 1623.
Four centuries now of this damned immortality.
It felt like a dream. Lucid, intimate, almost tender.
Temptation. The stranger opened herself to me in ways forbidden. Carnal, lustful, eager, welcoming. And then... Release.
A new kind of life. A life worse than death.

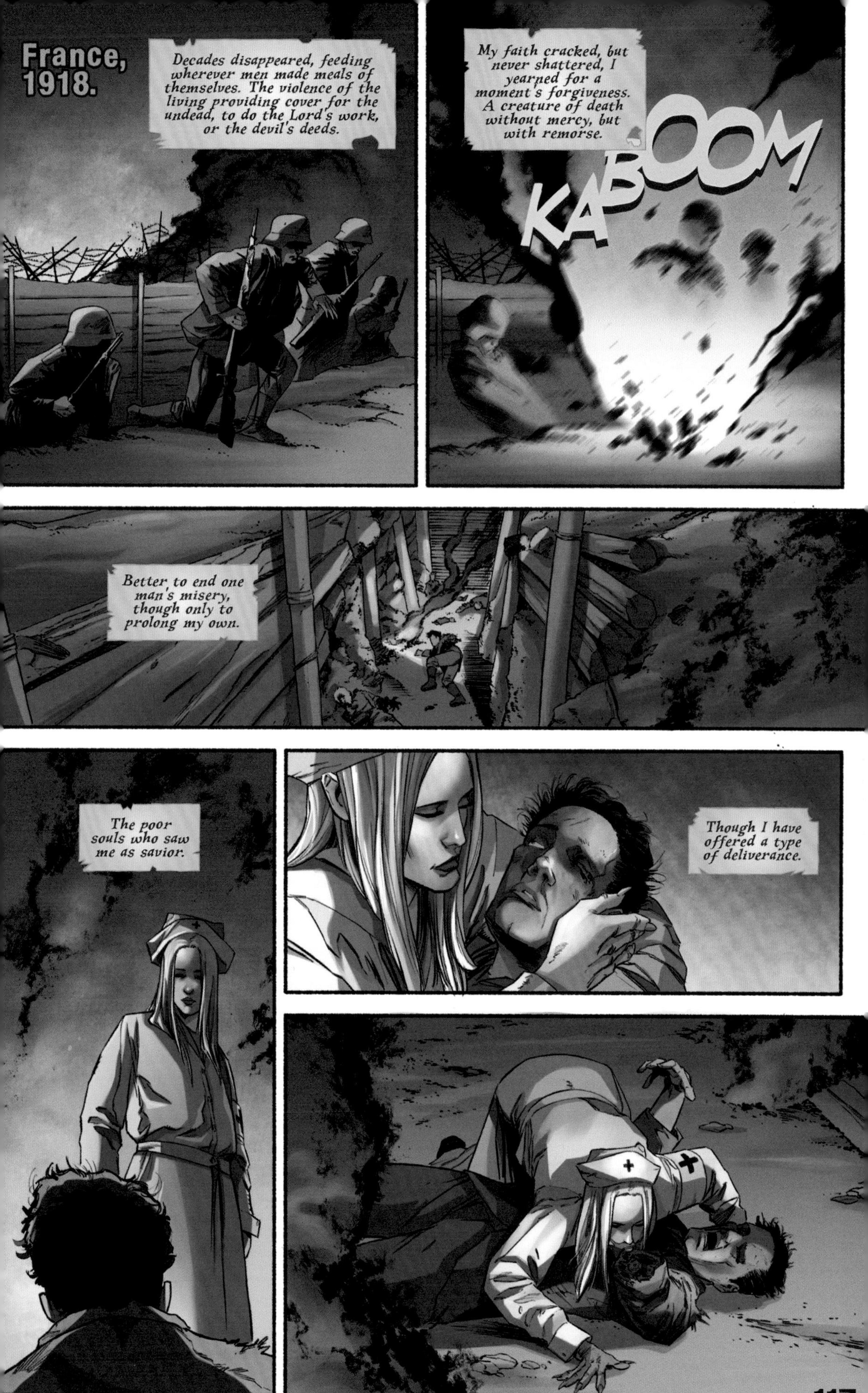

France, 1918.
Decades disappeared, feeding wherever men made meals of themselves. The violence of the living providing cover for the undead, to do the Lord's work, or the devil's deeds.
My faith cracked, but never shattered, I yearned for a moment's forgiveness. A creature of death without mercy, but with remorse.
KABOOOM
Better to end one man's misery, though only to prolong my own.
The poor souls who saw me as savior.
Though I have offered a type of deliverance.

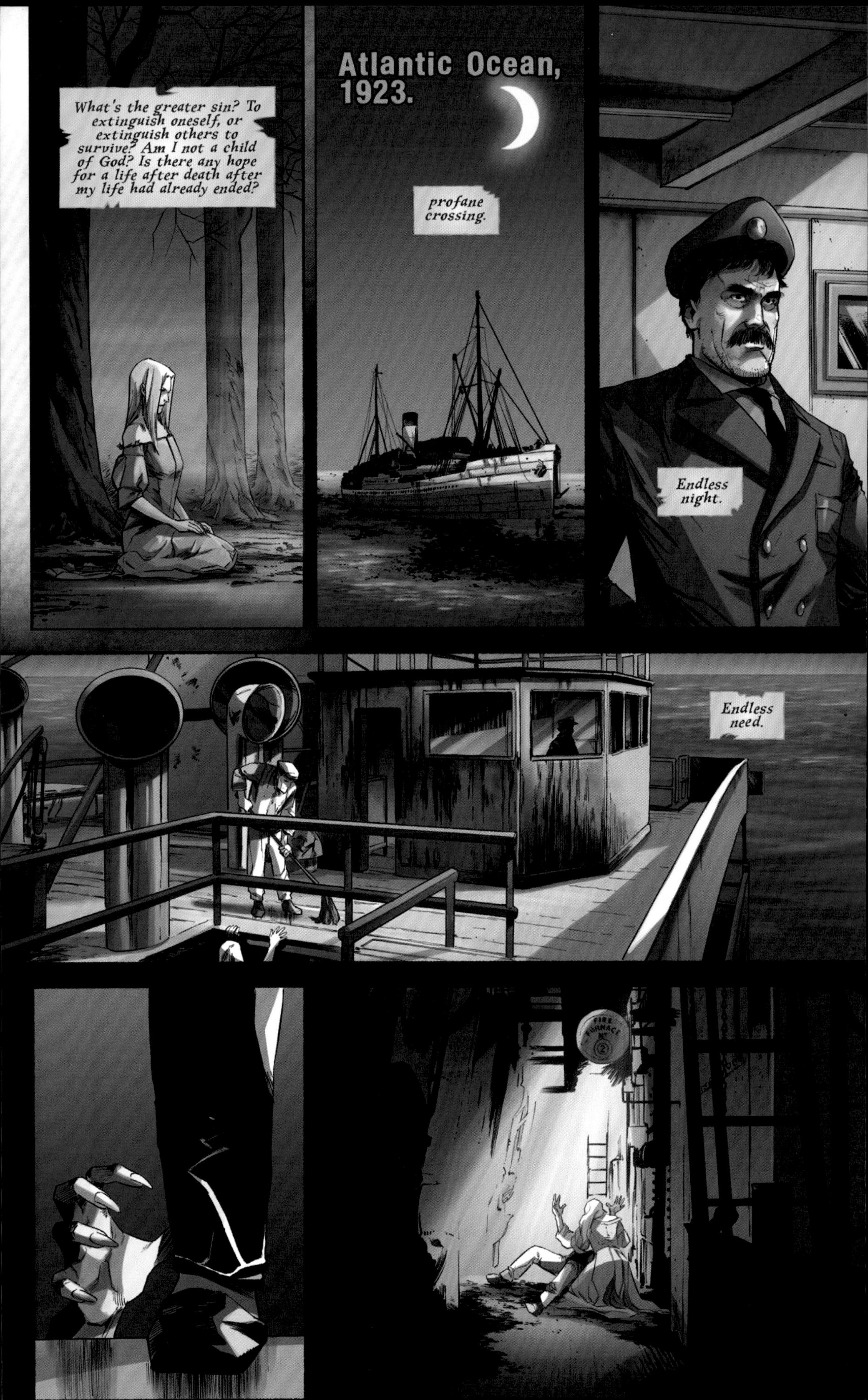
What's the greater sin? To extinguish oneself, or extinguish others to survive? Am I not a child of God? Is there any hope for a life after death after my life had already ended?
Atlantic Ocean, 1923.
profane crossing.
Endless night.
Endless need.
FIRE FURNACE Nº 2

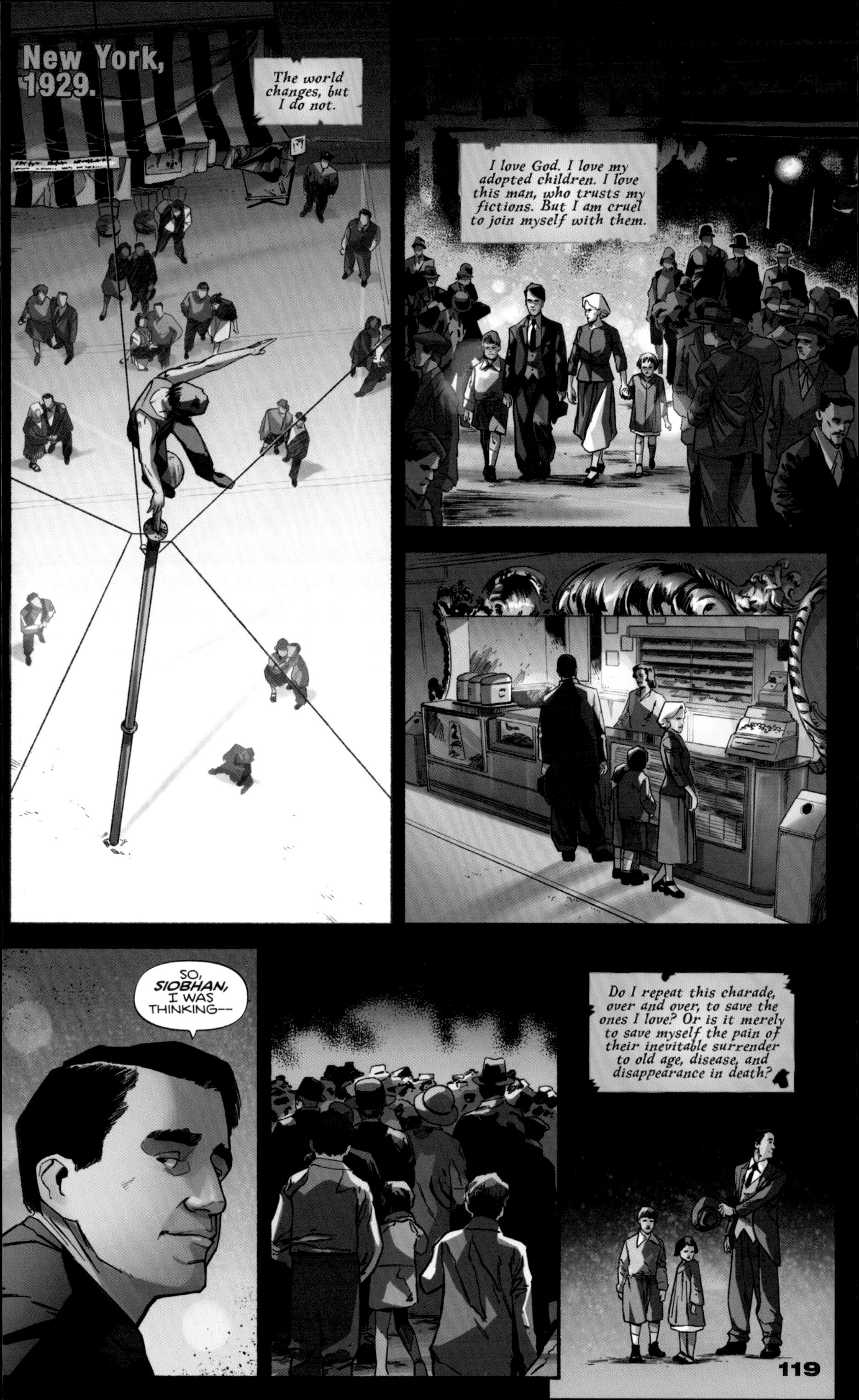
New York, 1929.
The world changes, but I do not.
I love God. I love my adopted children. I love this man, who trusts my fictions. But I am cruel to join myself with them.
SO, SIOBHAN, I WAS THINKING--
Do I repeat this charade, over and over, to save the ones I love? Or is it merely to save myself the pain of their inevitable surrender to old age, disease, and disappearance in death?

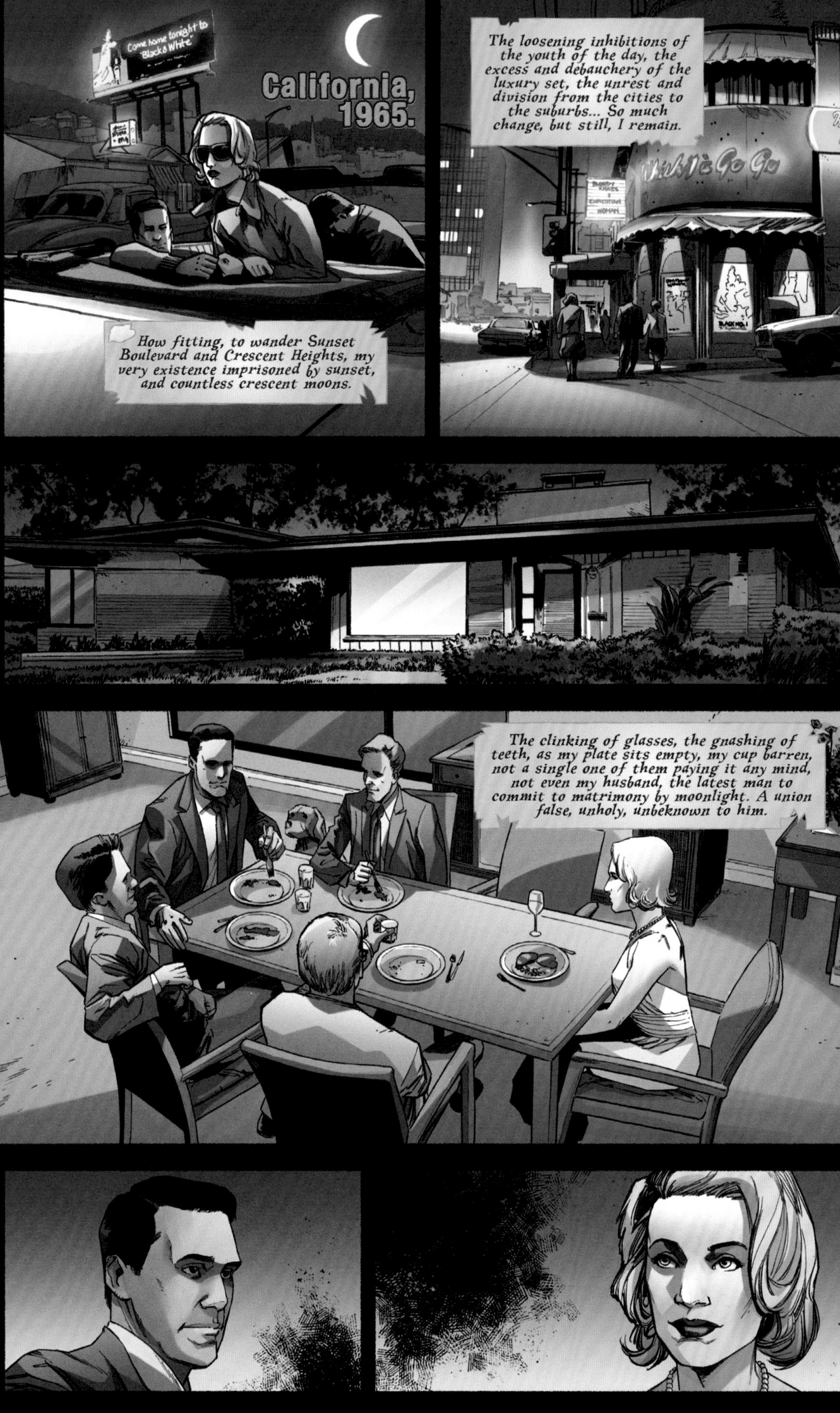
Come home tonight to "Black & White"
California, 1965.
How fitting, to wander Sunset Boulevard and Crescent Heights, my very existence imprisoned by sunset, and countless crescent moons.
The loosening inhibitions of the youth of the day, the excess and debauchery of the luxury set, the unrest and division from the cities to the suburbs... So much change, but still, I remain.
The clinking of glasses, the gnashing of teeth, as my plate sits empty, my cup barren, not a single one of them paying it any mind, not even my husband, the latest man to commit to matrimony by moonlight. A union false, unholy, unbeknown to him.

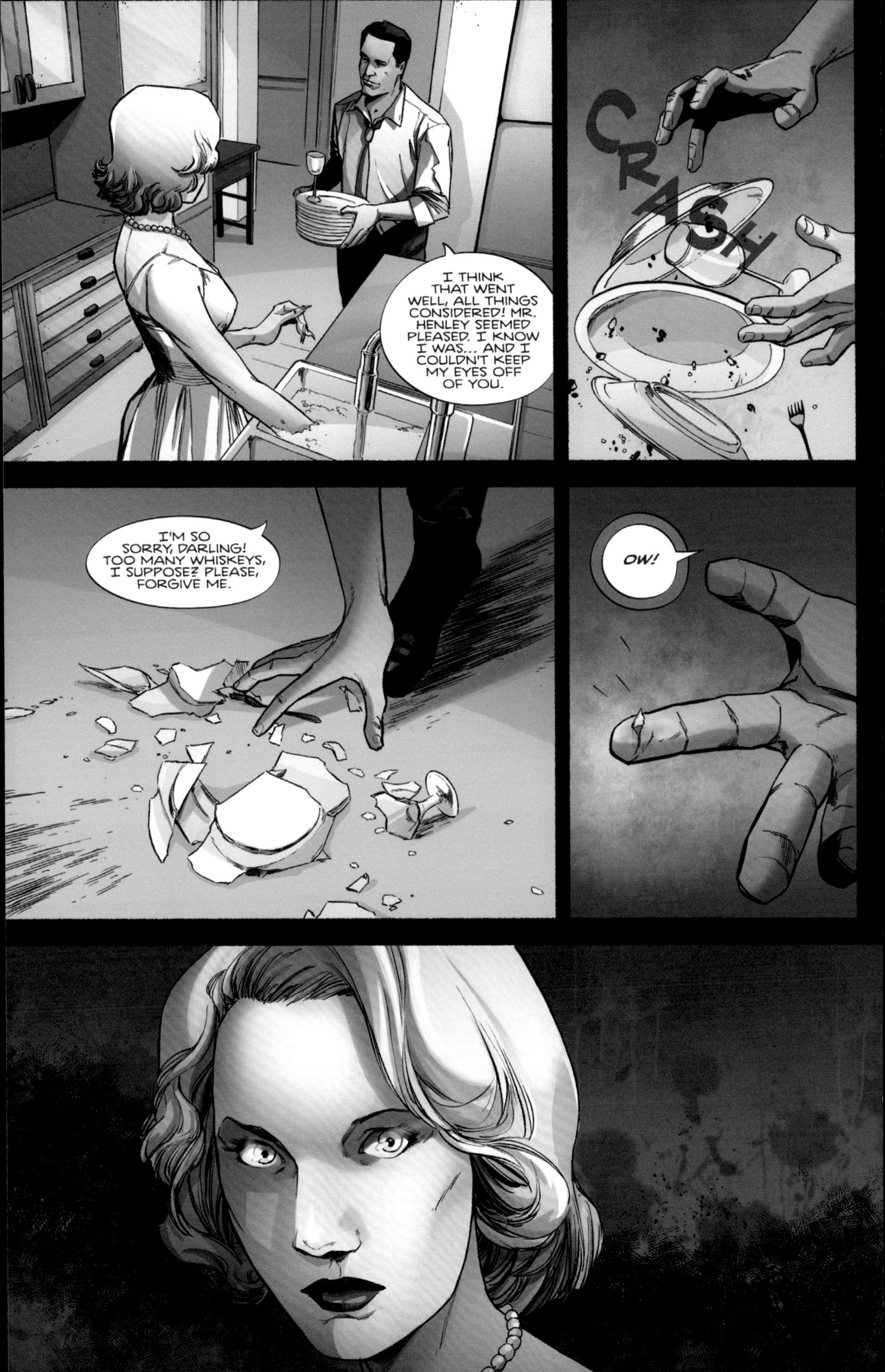
I THINK THAT WENT WELL, ALL THINGS CONSIDERED! MR. HENLEY SEEMED PLEASED. I KNOW I WAS... AND I COULDN'T KEEP MY EYES OFF OF YOU.
CRASH
I'M SO SORRY, DARLING! TOO MANY WHISKEYS, I SUPPOSE? PLEASE, FORGIVE ME.
OW!

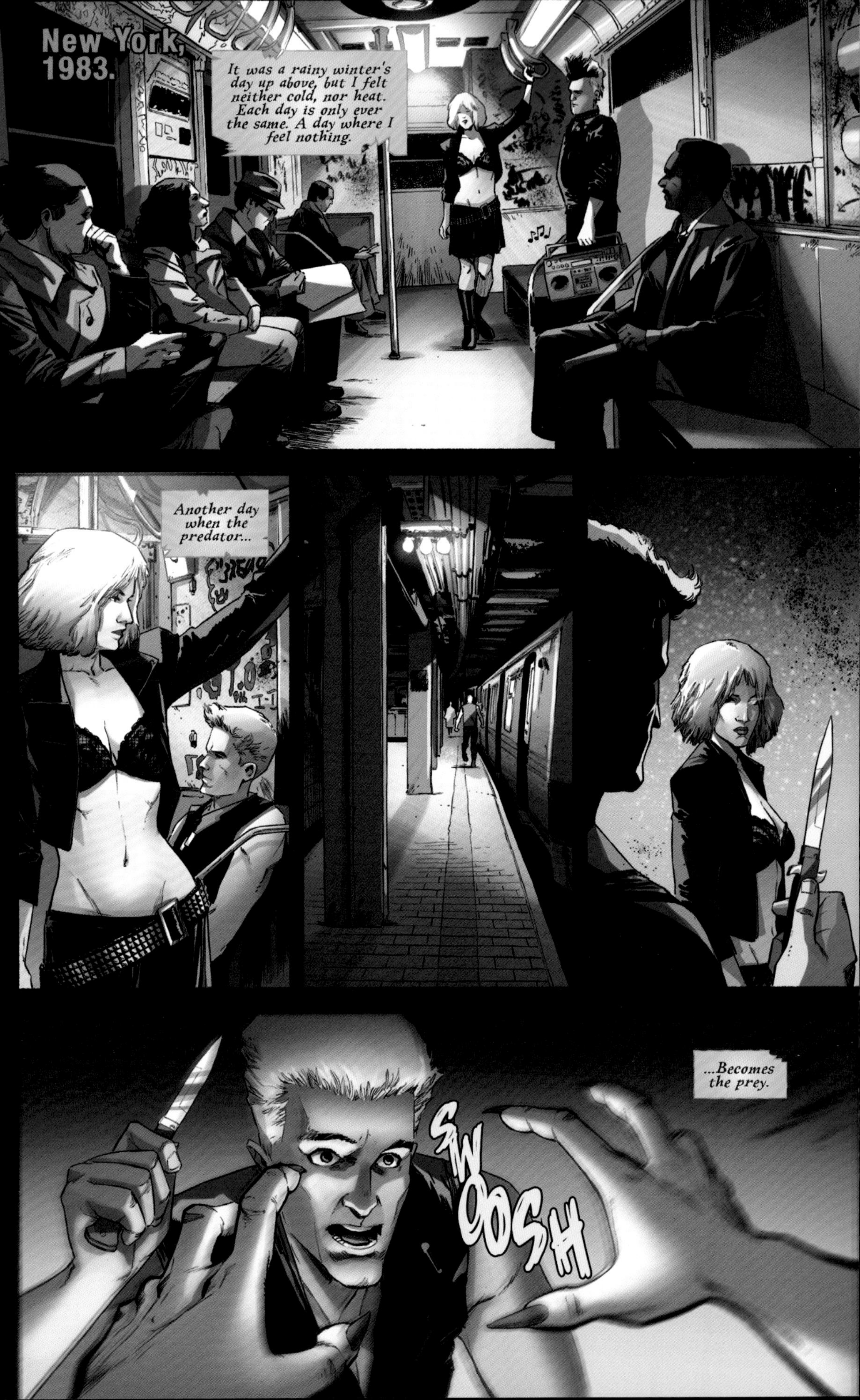
New York, 1983.
It was a rainy winter's day up above, but I felt neither cold, nor heat. Each day is only ever the same. A day where I feel nothing.
Another day when the predator...
...Becomes the prey.
SWOOSH

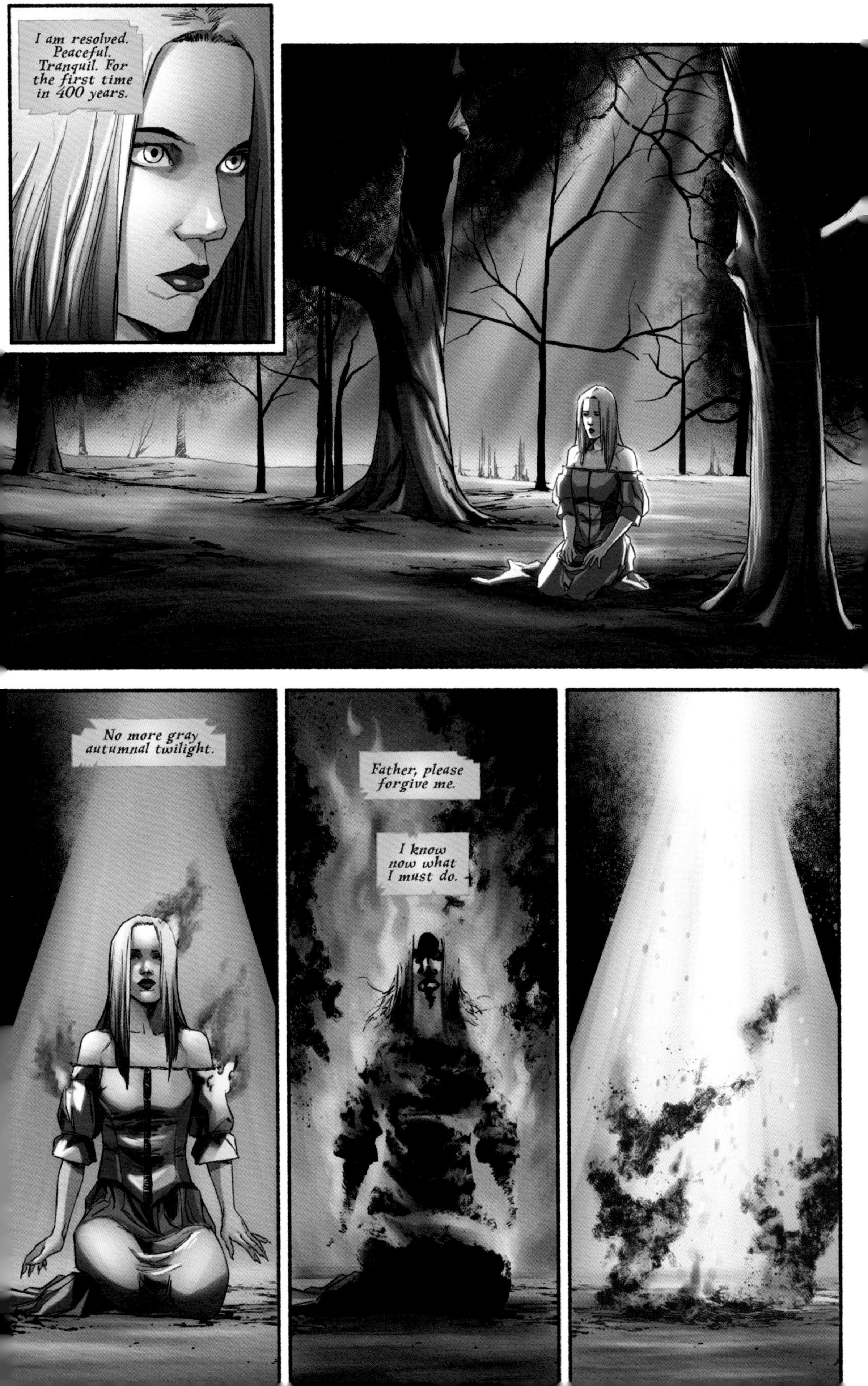
I am resolved. Peaceful. Tranquil. For the first time in 400 years.
No more gray autumnal twilight.
Father, please forgive me.
I know now what I must do.

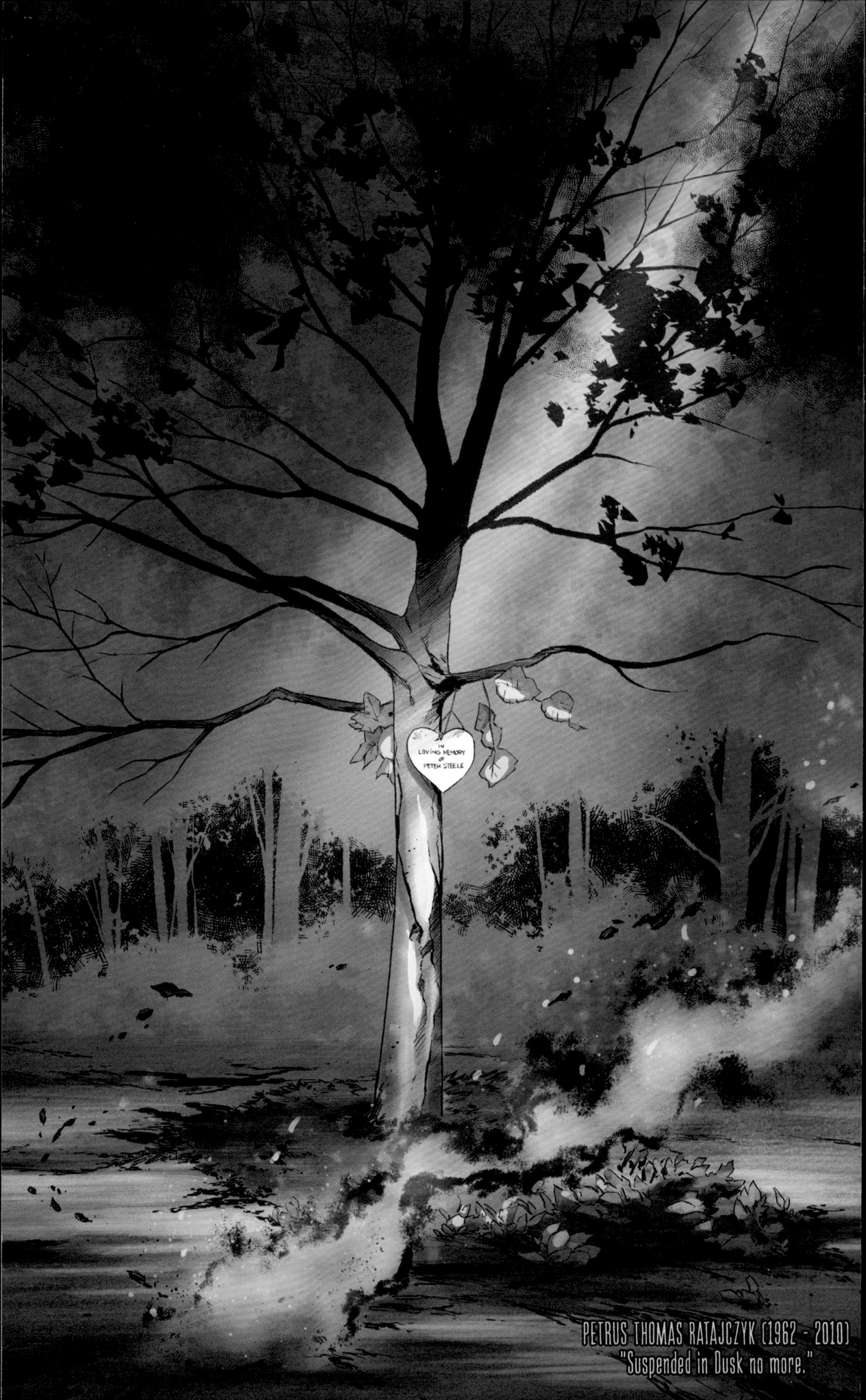
IN LOVING MEMORY OF PETER STEELE
PETRUS THOMAS RATAJCZYK (1962 - 2010)
"Suspended in Dusk no more."

CONTRIBUTORS

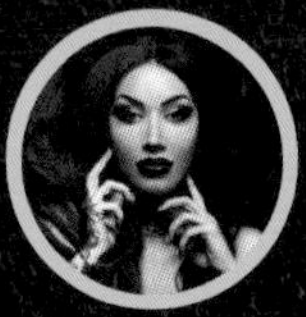

Ash Costello

Ash Costello is best known as the vocalist of the band New Years Day, Ash also elevates the world of dark fashion at https://www.ashcostelloscloset.com/

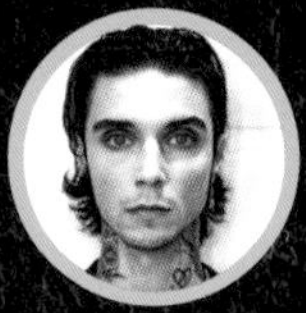

Andy Biersack

Andy Biersack is the singer and co-founder of Black Veil Brides. Andy has a deep passion and love for comics, including his previous graphic novel and album project, The Ghost of Ohio.

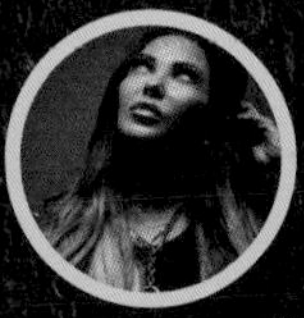

Carla Harvey

Carla Harvey is best known as vocalist for Butcher Babies. She is also a mortician and grief counselor who found her voice in art and comics when she began to use her own experiences of being a woman with a career spanning these industries to create her ample-bosomed antiheroes.

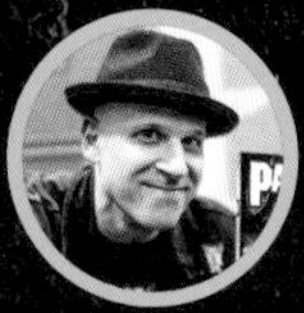

Alan Robert

Alan Robert is an internationally renowned musician (Life of Agony) and illustrator Alan Robert dubbed "The King of Horror Coloring Books" by Revolver for the bestselling series The Beauty of Horror.

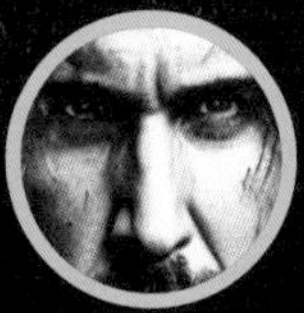

Seth Adams

Seth Adams was raised in California on healthy doses of metal and government cheese. As of this writing he resides in Singapore where he tells stories and raises Chihuahuas with his family.

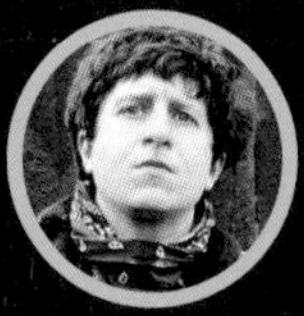

Sean Pryor

Sean Pryor is a New Jersey based artist who has worked with artists and writers such as Alfred Yankovic, Blondie, and Harvey Pekar. He also makes art for the skateboarding company Metal Skateboards.

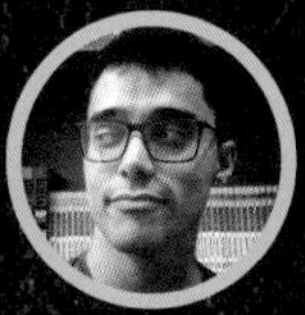

Gustavo

Gustavo Novaes is the co-creator of A Cabana, published in Brazil in 2019. He was also the artist for Bittersweet Vows, and Parting Ways.

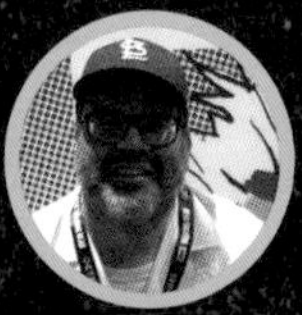

Marco Finnegan

Marco Finnegan is an educator by day and writes and draws comics by night. He lives in Temecula, California with his family.

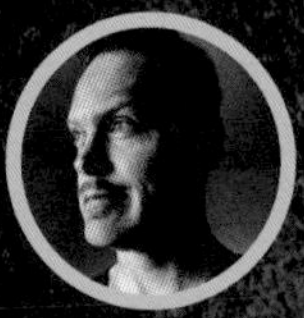

Shane Patrick White

Shane Patrick White is a writer and artist who's worked in comics, commercials, films, and video games for the past 30+ years.

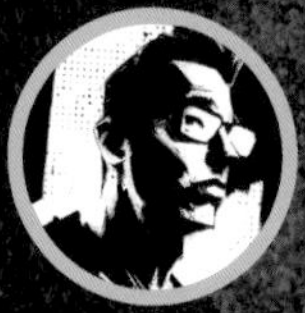

Nick Marinkovich

Nick Marinkovich is a Canadian illustrator and comic artist, best known as co-creator of the critically acclaimed series Dead Romans by Image Comics, Shadowline and the best-selling graphic novel, Kenk – A Graphic Portrait.

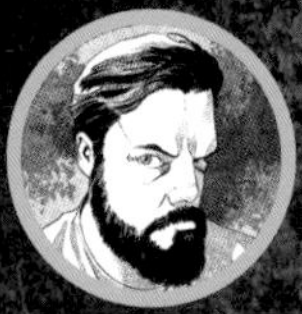

Adam Markiewicz

Adam Markiewicz is a comics illustrator whose works include The Great Divide, Dying Light, Broken Bear and Eat My Flesh, Drink My Blood.

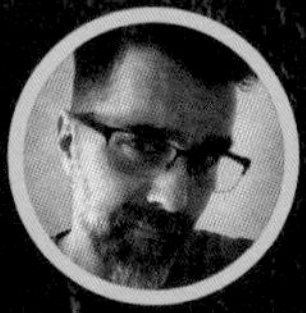

Steve Kurth

Steve Kurth is a comic book artist based in Wisconsin, best known for his comic work on The Avengers, Iron Man, X-Men, Ghostbusters, Hulk, Wolverine, Green Arrow, and more.

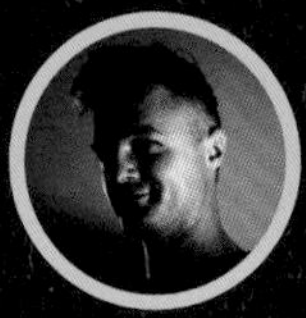

Paolo Armitano

Professionally drawing comics and advertising stuff since the age of 18, Armintano currently is known for drawing the horror comic series Dylan Dog, for the Italian publisher Sergio Bonelli Editore.

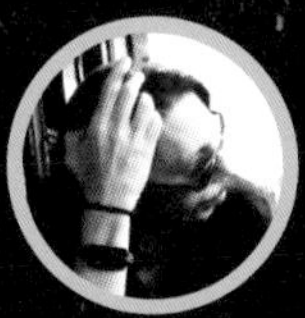

Thomas A. Tenney

Thomas A. Tenney is professional illustrator whose career spans nearly 4 decades. He has worked for Comico, Marvel, DC, Image, the rock band AC/DC, Shudder's Creepshow and more.

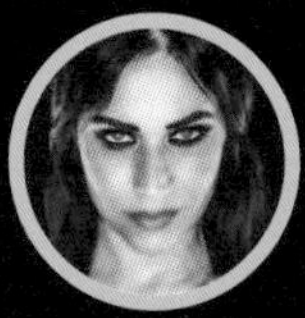

Cristina Scabbia

Cristina Scabbia is the Italian singer of the Italian rock metal band Lacuna Coil. Very active online and supported by a loyal community, she splits her career between touring globally, and being a fierce supporter of the nerd world 360°.

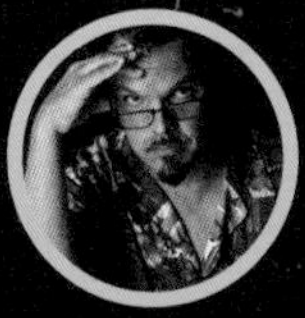

Rantz A. Hoseley

Rantz A. Hoseley is an Eisner & Harvey Award-winner, who started his career on music videos like Aerosmith's Dude Looks Like a Lady. He's been making music-related comics for the last 20 years.

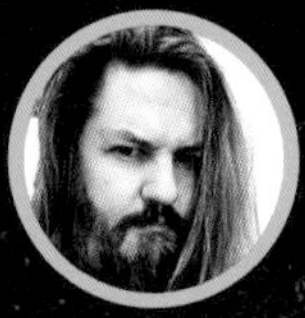

Michael Patrick Sullivan

Michael Patrick Sullivan is an award-winning writer of comics, screenplays, and pulp fiction. His other work has been featured in Image Comics, McSweeney's, and Doctor Who Magazine.

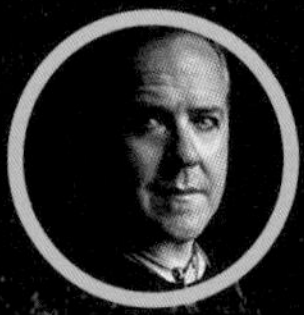

Burton C. Bell

Burton C. Bell is a Grammy nominated musician, most notably as a founding member of Fear Factory. Burton has released his graphic novel, The Industrialist. Go to burtoncbell.com to learn more.

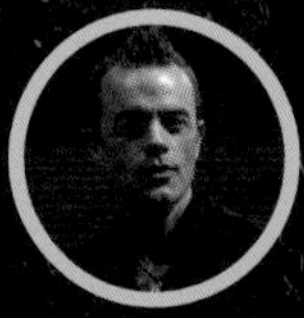

Gavin Hignight

Gavin Hignight is a writer and producer and co-owner of Wandering Planet Toys. His writing credits include Star Wars: Resistance and the graphic novels The Concrete World and Motor City.

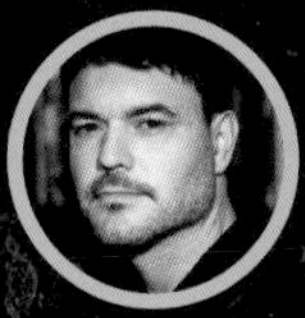

Roy Burdine

Roy Burdine is an Emmy-winning animation director of such series as TMNT and She-Ra and the Princesses of Power. He also writes and draws his own comics featured at https://royburdine.substack.com/

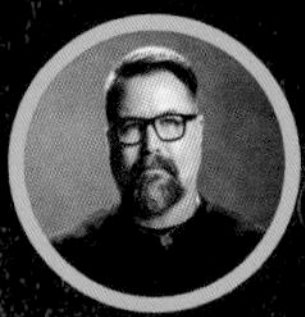

Ryan J. Downey

Ryan J. Downey is a longtime writer and journalist whose credits include They Don't Need to Understand (with Andy Biersack) and Z2's Inked in Blood II (with Spencer Charnas).

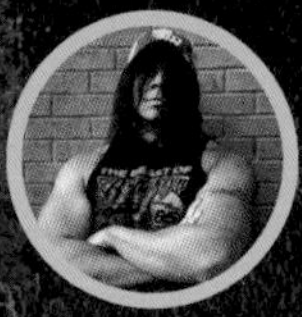

Joey James Hernandez

Joey James Hernandez is a Brooklyn born Illustrator who has done merchandise designs for O Negative, Duff's Brooklyn, Catfight Coffee, Biohazard, Death Angel, Steel Panther, Alice Cooper, Butcher Babies, Tommy Vext, Doyle, Otep and Sevendust.

GALLERY

ARTISTS
ALAN ROBERT
CHARLIE BENANTE

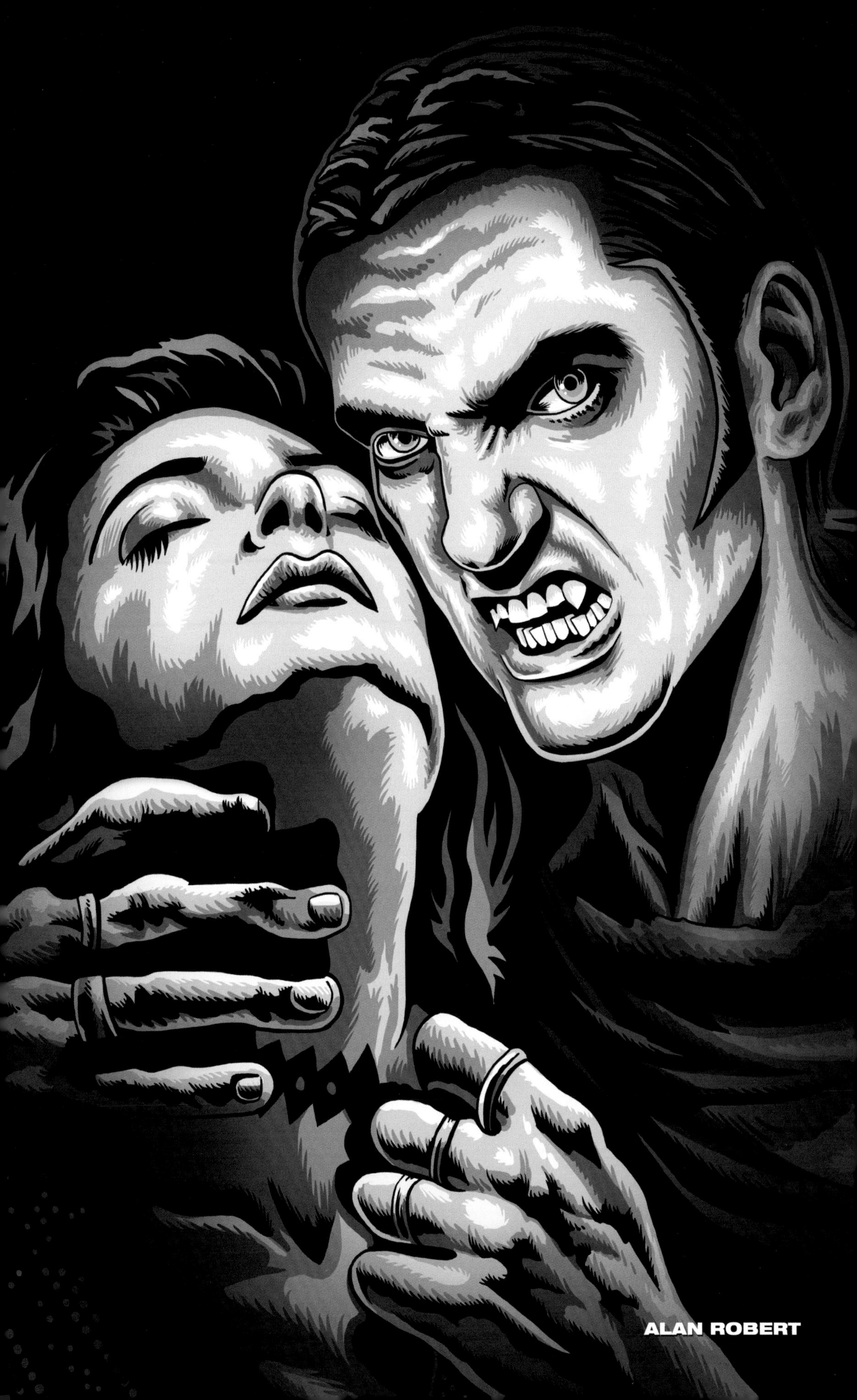
ALAN ROBERT

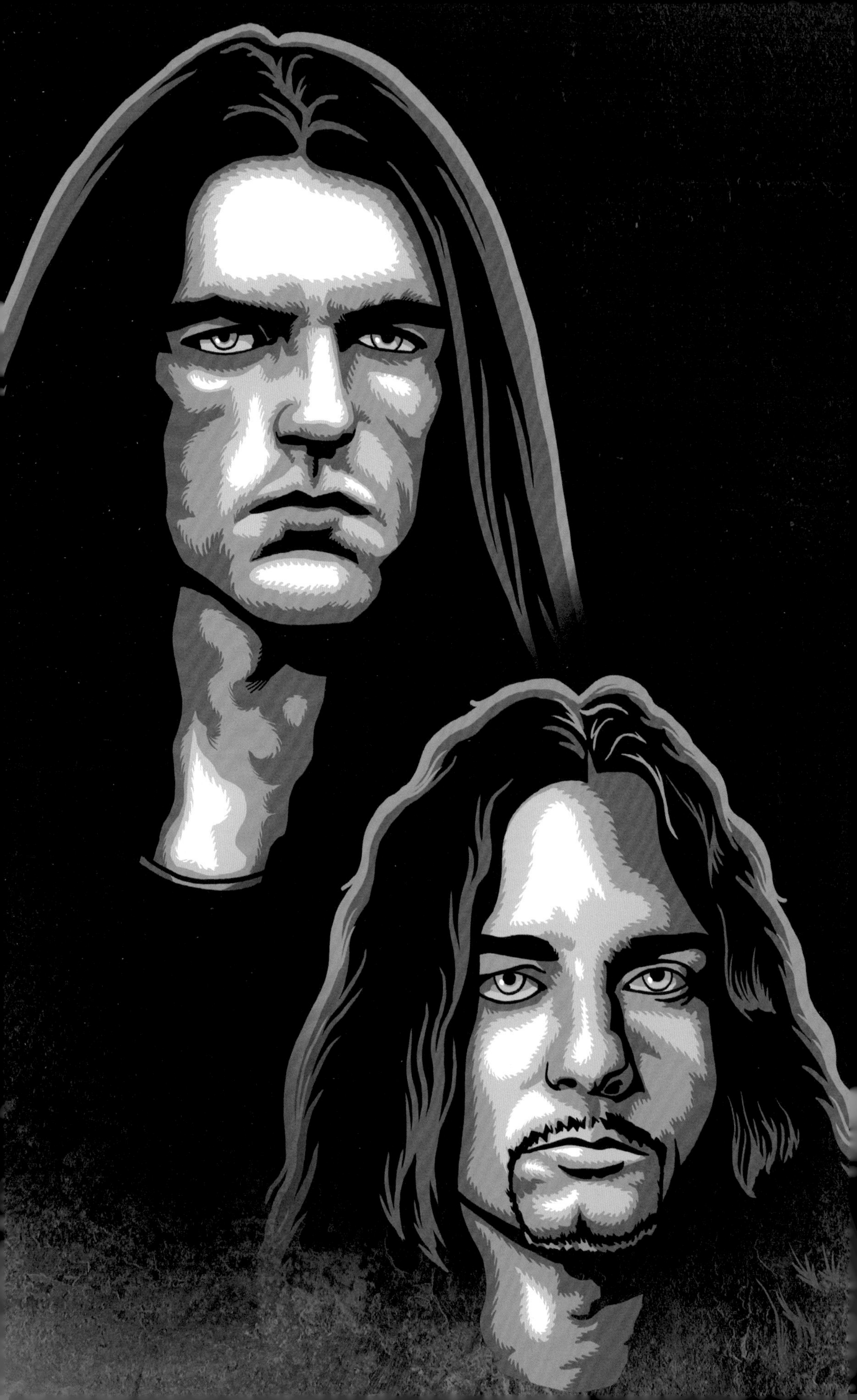

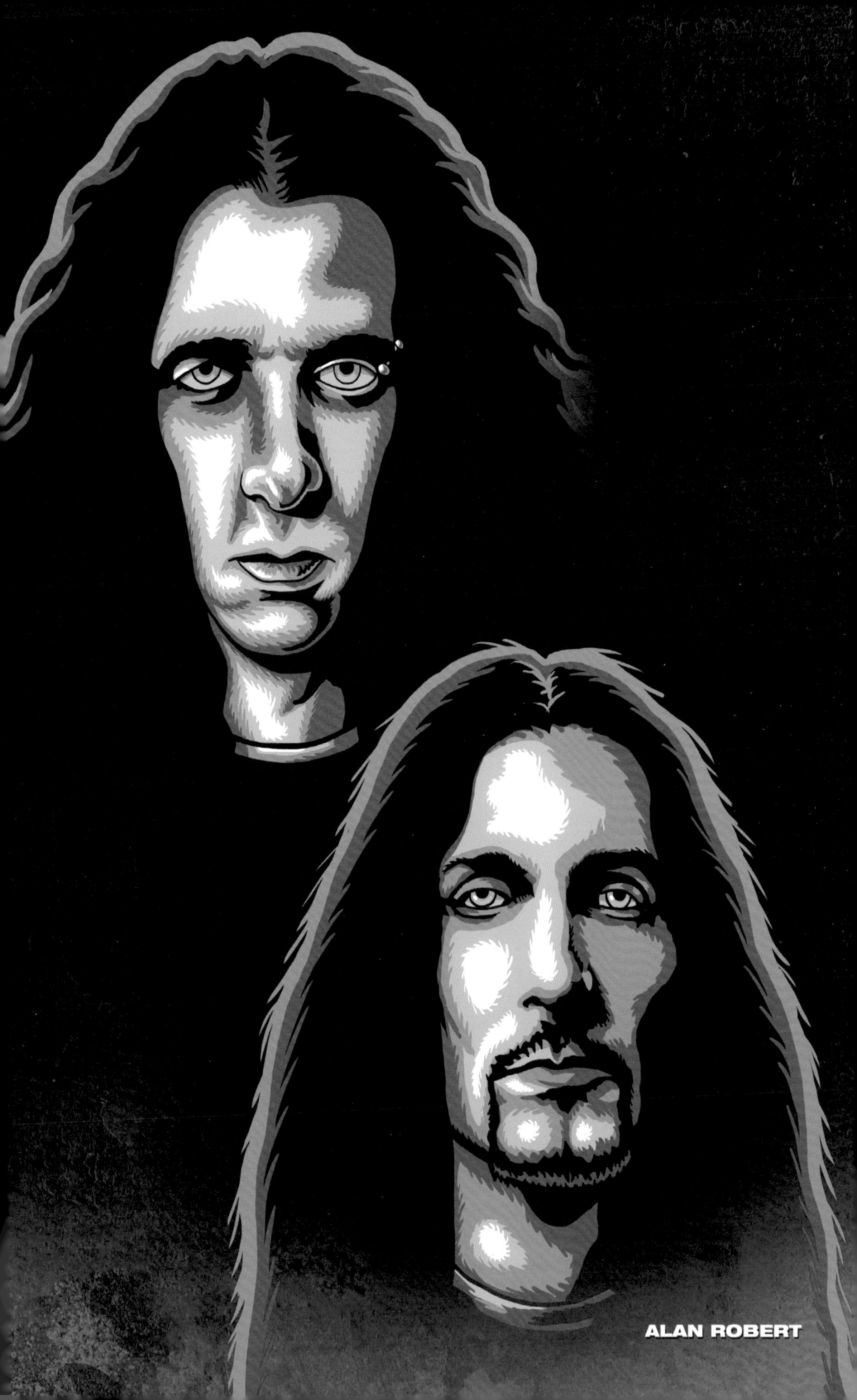
ALAN ROBERT

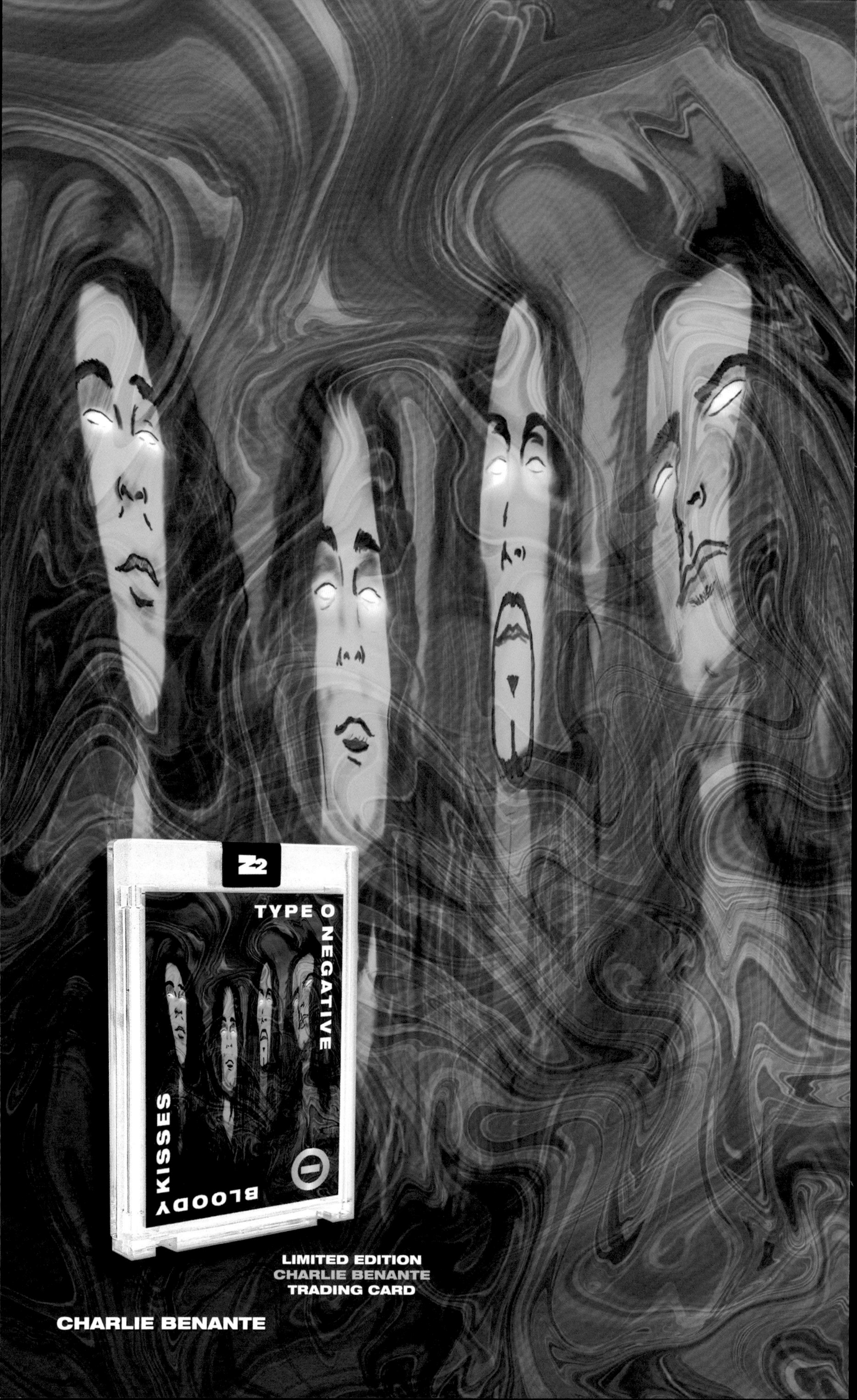
TYPE O NEGATIVE
BLOODY KISSES
LIMITED EDITION
CHARLIE BENANTE
TRADING CARD
CHARLIE BENANTE

THE HISTORY OF THE
REPULSION
"NONE MORE NEGATIVE" CASSETTES

THE NINE COPIES OF THE *"REPULSION"* artifact edition of this commemorative graphic novel included the legendary *"Repulsion"* demo cassette, which had been discovered in an attic in Brooklyn.

These cassettes stem back to the era before the band went by the Type O Negative moniker.

Two years after the band Carnivore went on an indefinite hiatus, Peter Steele recruited long-time friend, Sal Abruscato into his new music project. Shortly afterwards, Josh Silver was convinced to join, with fellow childhood friend Kenny Hickey following suit.

Initially the group went by the names "Repulsion" and "Subzero", but after an extensive search they realized "Subzero" had already been taken.

Having been attached to the "Subzero" name, members of the band had already gotten tattoos of the "O" negative tattoos, to represent subzero, which carried forward onto the branding of the *"Repulsion"* demo cassettes.

Despite using the name on the demos, the members abandoned *"Repulsion"* because they didn't really like the name, and another established band was already using it.

Since the "O Negative" symbol has been

> ## "Despite using the name on the demos, the members abandoned Repulsion because they didn't really like the name"

firmly established with the band members, and on the demo cassette, they decided to carry it forward by choosing Type O Negative as the final name of the band.

These *"Repulsion"* cassettes were sent out as a demo, containing tracks that would become the album "Slow, Deep and Hard"

REPULSION

NONE MORE NEGATIVE.

SIDE BLOOD:
...ssfully coping with the natural beauty of infidelity
...vitational constant: G=6.67X10⁻⁸cm⁻¹·gm⁻¹·sec⁻²
...pretation of silence and its disasterous consequences
SIDE FIRE:
...ony • der untermensch • xero tolerance
... Unauthorized duplication is a violation of applicable la...

"REPULSION" 6-SONG
DEMO CASSETTE,
RELEASED IN 1990.

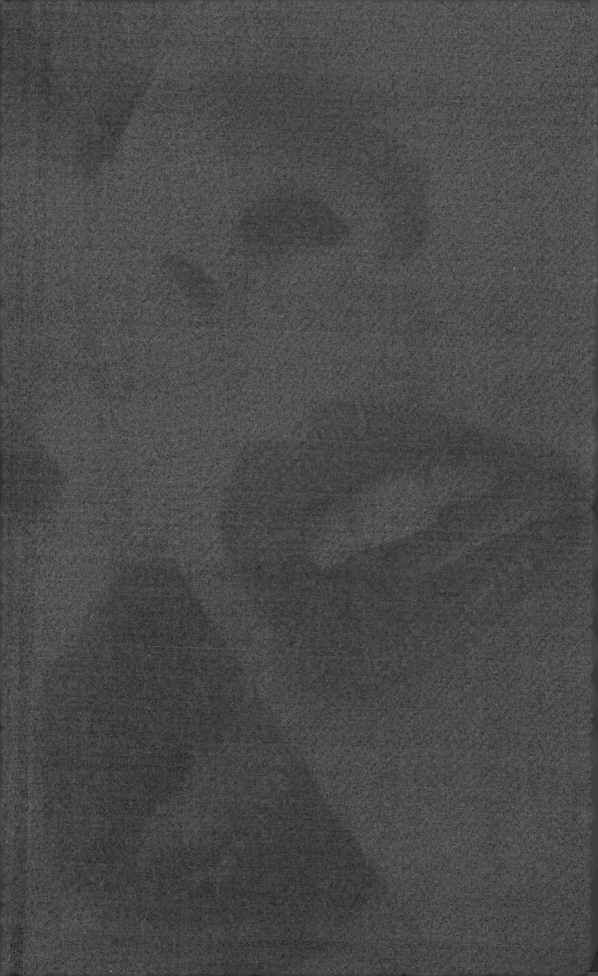